POSTCARD HISTORY SERIES

Around Little Rock

A Postcard History

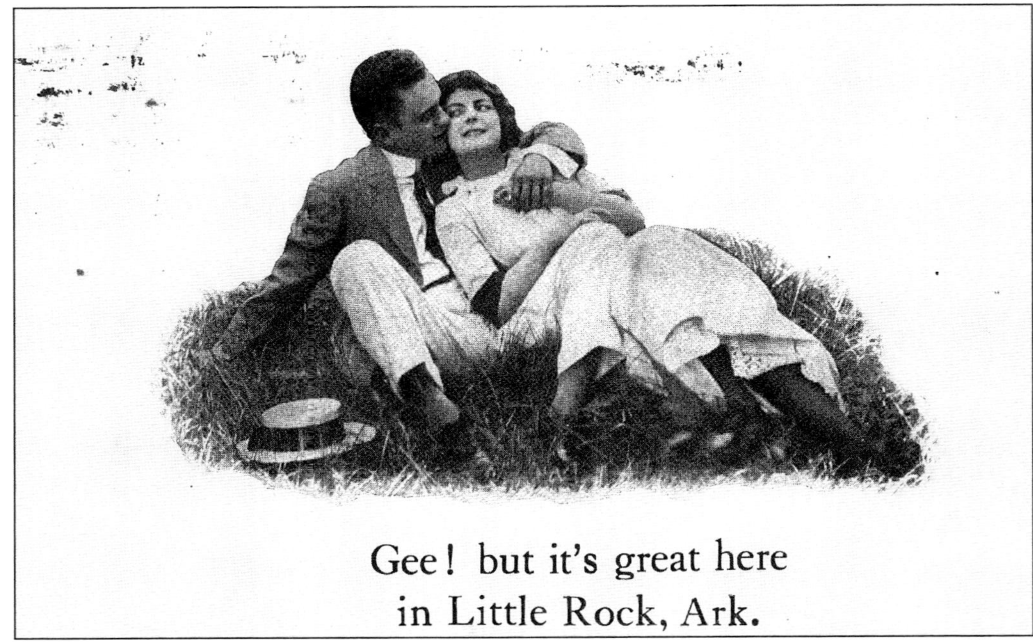

"Am having a grand time...wish you was here" were the words of a woman named Ethel, as penned to Mr. W.H. Adams of Fordyce in 1913. The imprinted message, "Gee! but it's great here in Little Rock, Ark.," was printed on a stock card that could have been used in a number of cities around the nation. The printer would insert the name of the city desired by the merchant purchasing the cards.

POSTCARD HISTORY SERIES

Around Little Rock

A Postcard History

Steven G. and Ray Hanley

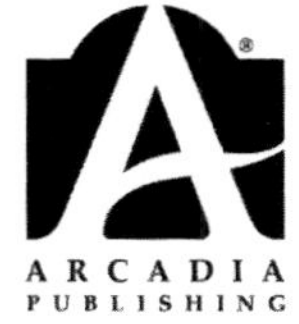

ISBN 978-0-7385-6867-6

Published by Arcadia Publishing
Charleston, South Carolina

Printed in the United States of America

Library of Congress Catalog Card Number: 98-85861

For all general information contact Arcadia Publishing at:
Telephone 843-853-2070
Fax 843-853-0044
E-mail sales@arcadiapublishing com
For customer service and orders:
Toll-Free 1-888-313-2665

Visit us on the Internet at www.arcadiapublishing.com

To our friend
Laura Alice Henson (1919–1996)
a lifelong resident of Little Rock.

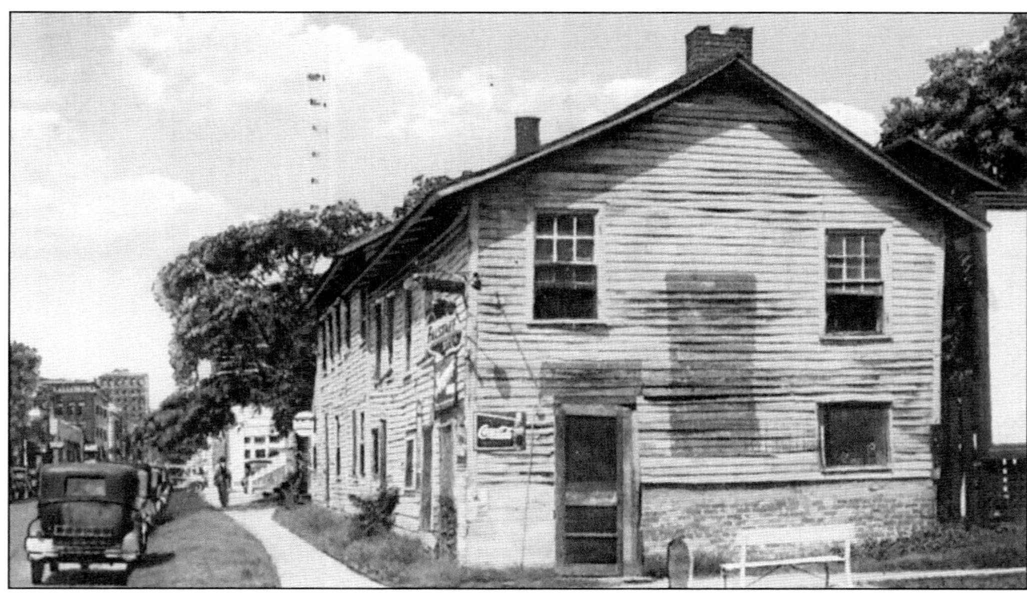

In 1936, the centennial year of Arkansas's statehood, one of its important territorial era buildings stood grossly neglected. This building at Third and Cumberland Streets, with Coca-Cola and Falstaff Beer signs nailed to its warped siding, was erected in 1828 by the family of Jesse Hinderliter to serve both as their home and as a tavern. The historic building was saved by Mrs. J.H. Loughborough, wife of a prominent local attorney, who persuaded the Arkansas Legislature to purchase the property for restoration. Today the restored building is a part of the Arkansas Territorial Restoration. Despite the card's wording about serving as "the Territorial Capitol," no evidence has been found to support such a claim.

Contents

Introduction 7

Acknowledgments 11

1. 1900 to 1919:
A Time of Growth and Change 13

2. 1920 to 1939:
Decades of Growth and Depression 87

3. 1940 to 1960:
Recovery, War, and Social Change 97

4. Argenta and North Little Rock:
The Capital City's Across-the-Bridge Neighbor 115

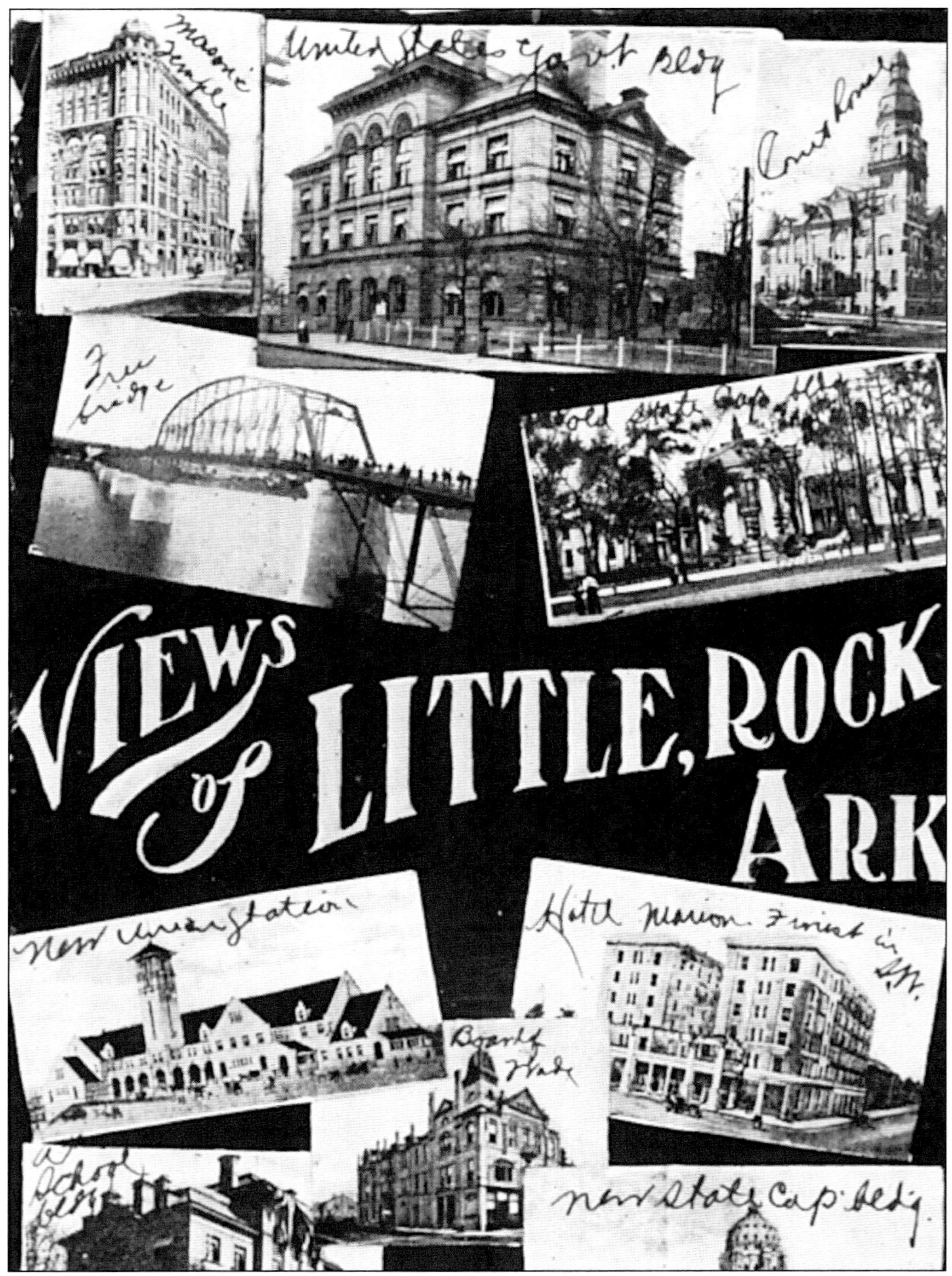

Miss Irene Jackson of Belchertown, Massachusetts, received this card from Little Rock in 1907, before the law changed to allow additional messages to accompany a name and address on the backs of postcards. The card pictured here was a collage of reduced-size postcard views of the city's best-known landmarks, and the sender penned in identifying information for Miss Jackson. Among the sights on the card are the Free Bridge, the new capitol building under construction, the Pulaski County courthouse, and Union Station.

Introduction

French explorer Bernard de LaHarpe journeyed up the Arkansas River in May 1722, in search of what Native Americans described as a "giant green rock." LaHarpe hoped it might turn out to be a huge emerald. He found no precious stones, but he did find a large rock outcropping on the north side of the river and a smaller one on the south bank. The smaller formation was christened "La Petite Roche"—The Little Rock.

Because it was a convenient fording place, the landmark became an important crossroads in the nation's westward movement. The Southwest Trail, the busiest route between St. Louis and Texas, crossed the Arkansas River there. A rugged frontier settlement grew up at the ford. In March 1820, a post office was established with the official name "Little Rock," and Amos Wheeler was appointed postmaster. The town boasted only 12 to 15 white residents, all male, and one frame building surrounded by three or four log cabins.

Postmaster Wheeler submitted a proposal to the new Arkansas Territorial Legislature to move the capital from the malaria-ridden bottom lands of Arkansas Post in southeastern Arkansas, to the healthier elevated location of Little Rock. Wheeler included an offer to donate land for a public square if the move were made. In October 1821, Little Rock became the territorial capital.

The following summer, the first steamboat to dock at Little Rock, *The Eagle*, arrived after a 17–day passage from New Orleans. Within a decade, at least one boat was arriving each week, despite the snags, sandbars, and low water which made the trek up the Arkansas River a hazardous undertaking.

With the commerce provided by the riverboats, the new capital city began to grow. By 1830, the Territorial Capital had 430 permanent residents; three years later, a special census counted 665. The figure had risen to 726 residents on the eve of Arkansas statehood in 1836. This growth in population spurred an interest in intellectual and cultural pursuits in the capital city. The Little Rock Debating Society had been organized as early as 1822, the year the city was established as territorial capital. In 1834, the Little Rock Thalian Society presented its first play, a comedy entitled *The Soldier's Daughter.*

Religion also served as a civilizing element in the lives of the early settlers. In 1824, Rev. Silas T. Toncray, a Baptist minister, established the community's first church. One early worshipper asserted, "The whole thing would be more interesting if all dogs and children were kept home during service." The church building, known as the "Baptist Meeting House," provided space for political as well as religious gatherings. The Territorial Legislature, the Territorial Supreme Court, and the Constitutional Convention of 1836 all made use of the building at various times.

Arkansas was admitted to the Union on June 15, 1836, as the 25th state. The following September, the state legislature met in the new State House on Markham Street. During this first session, the lawmakers authorized the purchase of 36 acres within the city for construction of a federal arsenal. Forty-four years later, in 1880, World War II hero Gen. Douglas MacArthur was born on this post. Today the site is a city park named in his honor.

Throughout the 1850s, Little Rock dreamed of being on the transcontinental railroad. Boosters envisioned a rail line starting at the Mississippi River and running through Arkansas, across Oklahoma and New Mexico territories, and into the new state of California. Early surveys found this route to be eminently feasible. Numerous meetings were held in Little Rock to promote the possibility, but it was not to be. With opposition to slavery mounting, the U.S. Congress was determined that the railway would bypass any state which sanctioned the practice.

The slavery issue was indeed tearing the nation apart. In November 1860, with war looming, the Little Rock Arsenal was reinforced by a 60-man artillery unit. A special convention met at the State House in March of the following year, to consider Arkansas's secession from the Union. Delegates first voted against it, but two months later—after Fort Sumter in South Carolina had been fired upon—a majority voted to join the Confederacy. A substantial minority, however, especially in the northwest section of the state, remained loyal to the Union. In the aftermath of the decision to secede, Capt. James Totten, commander of the Little Rock Arsenal, chose to avoid bloodshed; he evacuated the facility without a shot being fired.

In July 1863, after the fall of Vicksburg, Gen. Ulysses S. Grant appointed Gen. Fredrick Steele to organize an assault on Little Rock. With Union forces approaching, Gov. Harris Flanagin fled to Arkadelphia. A few weeks later, the capital was moved to the town of Washington in southwest Arkansas, where it would remain for the duration of the conflict. Little Rock fell on September 10, 1863, with only token resistance offered. By the end of the war, Arkansas, like the rest of the South, had lost a significant portion of its male population, its resources, and its economic vitality.

The period of reconstruction from 1866 to 1874 was one of travail and bitterness in the city of Little Rock and across the South. Despite its hardships, the capital city continued to grow. In 1870, street addresses were numbered for the first time. By 1875, four different rail systems linked the city to New Orleans, Memphis, and St. Louis. Freed from its isolation, the community became a center of education and culture. As early as 1880, the U.S. commissioner of education predicted the city's schools would "draw a high class of people to Little Rock."

By 1900, Little Rock's population had grown to 38,307 residents, most of whom lived in houses built since the Civil War; the city was poised for a period of great economic growth. Its thriving business district boasted a seven-story commercial building, the tallest in the state, and ground was being broken on the far western edge of the city for a new state capital building. Indeed, Little Rock was on the brink of a period of tremendous growth, and postcard history would be there to capture the images of the early century that had dawned so brightly.

As Little Rock entered the twentieth century, with all its promise, the phenomenon that was the picture postcard was soon to make its presence known. The picture postcard made its debut in the United States at the 1893 World Colombian Exposition in Chicago. The format was originally copyrighted in 1861 as a quick means of sending a written message, but with the option of pictures being printed on the reverse side, the cards soon became a window of discovery for millions of Americans. By the turn of the century, the fad was catching on in sufficient volume to inspire the commercial production of picture cards in the eastern United States. By 1905, the production of picture postcards had spread and become a means to share views of such places as Arkansas and Little Rock with the rest of the nation.

Initially, picture postcards could carry on the back only an address, but with an act of Congress in 1907 it became permissible to use part of the reverse side for brief written messages. Thus, travelers disembarking from the many trains arriving at the two Little Rock depots could send both a photo and their written impressions of the city, or perhaps tales of family, business success, illness, or even the state of their love lives. Many of these cards utilized photos taken in Arkansas, which were then printed in Germany by the world's finest lithographers and then shipped back to be sold in the drugstores along Main Street. By 1910, it was increasingly common for local photographers themselves to print their photos onto postcard stock, a process that provided later generations with sharp, clearly detailed images of everyday life in early-twentieth-century Arkansas.

Passion for collecting postcards caught on rapidly in Arkansas and across the nation. An article in *American Magazine* in 1906 offered this commentary on the postcard fad:

> By far the worst development of the prevailing pests is postal carditis, which affects the heart, paralyzes the reasoning faculties, and abnormally increases the nerve. It had its origin in Germany 20 years ago, but did not assume dangerous proportions until 1897. Sporadic cases of it were observed in the United States and the year 1900 saw the malady rapidly spread from one center of infection to another. . . . From small beginnings the pasteboard souvenir industry has fattened upon epistolary sloth and collecting manias. . . . Bookstores which formerly did a thriving trade in literature are now devoted almost entirely to their sale.

The article, obviously very much tongue-in-cheek, made its point—postcard collecting had arrived.

Thanks to the "malady," citizens of the late twentieth century have a much better visualization of cities like Little Rock, seeing it pass from the age of the horse and buggy to a modern world that bears little resemblance to the postcard images—little resemblance, except, perhaps, in the penned words of hope, misery, workaday burdens, and the message to loved ones, "Wish you were here."

The postcards that illustrate this book come from a collection of some 6,000 Arkansas views collected by the authors over a period of 25 years. Many have illustrated the daily newspaper column, "Arkansas Postcard Past," which has appeared since 1986, first in the *Arkansas Gazette,* and currently in the *Arkansas Democrat-Gazette.* The popularity of the column created considerable interest in postcard collecting and led to the publication in 1997 of our first book, *Wish You Were Here,* which focused on the entire state in the first 25 years of this century.

In the history of postcard production in the United States, the most numerous and varied cards were produced in the period from 1905 to 1920. The fad waned after World War I and the quality of the cards declined, as did the variety of subjects depicted. The selections of postcards presented in this book reflect these trends; however, sufficient cards have been included to document many of the changes that have occurred in Little Rock over a period of more than half a century. The authors hope the reader will learn more of the city's heritage, not only from the images on the front of the cards but also from the penned messages occasionally quoted from the backs of the cards. While the pictures reflect a greatly changed community, the words—often written by persons long since departed this earth—will show that in many ways we are still very much the same.

While the people may have changed little, the landscape itself has undergone profound changes. From the progress of Main Street, the rise and fall of passenger railroads, travel by river, and the building of churches and homes, no where are these changes more evident than in the comparison of what we see and do in our soon to be twenty-first-century lives with the postcard images found in this book—images that trace a 60-year evolution in American life.

A look at the rise of Little Rock's Main Street in the first half of this century and its decline in the century's latter half is reflective of what has happened in many cities of our nation. History has been lost in creeping urban sprawl and "modernization" in a scenario that has been repeated in city after city. Too late, in many cases, have we come to understand that Main Street is at the heart of much of our American, and Arkansas, heritage.

From the 1860s, when the use of photography became widespread, film images have depicted Main Street and its inhabitants. Preserved are the images of generations of Americans who passed its way, first on horses, then in streetcars, and later in the automobiles, which, due to the onset of "suburban flight," led to the eventual decline of the street's commercial success. Picture postcards captured this transition unlike any other medium of the time. With the dawn of the twentieth century, thousands of Main Street photos found their way onto postcards that forever preserved its everyday life and commerce.

In each of the three sections of this book are postcards of Main Street and adjoining commercial avenues, enabling the reader to follow the progressive changes in buildings, transportation, local customs, and business names. Images preserve buildings now long gone, some having been replaced by parking lots, some consumed by fire, and others so altered as to be unrecognizable. Only a pleasant few have adapted while retaining their original character. A goal of this book is to help present-day Arkansans to learn about and appreciate this part of their heritage.

Today the Arkansas River flows beneath the bridges in Little Rock that carry thousands of vehicles a day over modern interstate highways, its currents tamed by locks and dams. During the early years of the twentieth century, the river was treacherous, and often filled with snags and sandbars; it would not be truly tamed until the creation of a system of locks and dams in the 1960s. The bridges that began to span the river at the turn of the century and the crafts that plied the currents were often the subjects of early postcards.

Among the most historically captivating postcard history subjects in Arkansas is passenger rail travel. By the close of the 19th century, railroads in Arkansas had penetrated all but the most remote hamlets of the Ozark Mountains. Seventy-five percent of some 3,000 miles of track were owned by five companies, all controlled by Northern industrialists such as Jay Gould. Pulaski County, with its location in the center of the state, was the hub of much of this railroad traffic, with grand depots and huge switching and maintenance stations. In the first two decades of the twentieth century, railroads dominated transportation in Arkansas and brought great vitality to once backward, out-of-the-way cities like Little Rock. Travel time to Little Rock from distant points in the nation was reduced from weeks to days, and travelers spent only a matter of hours to get to the capital city from any of the state's borders. Thousands of jobs were created and great numbers of people from around the globe passed through Pulaski County, some drawn to stay and invest their futures in the growing capital city area.

Readers of this book will take notice of many handsome public buildings, including schools, that rose as a symbol of the first-class city Little Rock became as the century advanced. The people who contributed to the rise of these buildings, with their tax money and the toil of their labor, built many homes—some magnificent, others modest. These homes were captured on postcards that record a bygone era of front porches and a slower pace of life. The pace of that life, when time allowed for recreation, led to numerous public and private parks that developed along with the city. These images, too, are preserved in postcard history.

As Little Rock's population began to grow at the end of the 19th century, so did its houses of worship. They increased both in number and in grandeur, with over 50 churches and one synagogue spanning the breadth of the city by 1900. Designs for these buildings were often taken from the architecture of the great medieval churches of Europe. The view from any tall structure in the city would show, from any direction, steeples rising toward the sky. Many of these turn-of-the-century churches are gone today, having fallen victim to fire, urban renewal, freeways, and the shift of congregations to new housing areas in the expanding western reaches of the city. Fortunately, almost all these early churches were recorded on postcards that survive now, long after the last bell chimed and the last hymn was sung.

Illnesses, some long eradicated, were serious burdens in early-20th-century Little Rock. As health care facilities developed, the buildings often became postcard subjects. Today Little Rock and North Little Rock are the medical hub not only for Arkansas, but in many cases for the region and beyond. Institutions such as Arkansas Children's Hospital and the University of Arkansas for Medical Sciences draw patients from across the nation and around the world for life-saving and reconstructive procedures. These modern healthcare centers stand in stark contrast to the early-20th-century hospitals preserved on postcards.

Little Rock is rich in history, and we are indeed fortunate that so much of it was recorded on postcards like the ones to be found in this book.

Acknowledgments

Special thanks to Audrey Burtrum-Stanley, Curtis Sykes, and John Cook,
for special input on North Little Rock.
Appreciation is given to Peg Smith, Jim Pfeifer,
Jim Eison, and Tom Mertens of Little Rock
for loaning their postcards
and for providing us access to their store of knowledge about our community.
Very special appreciation is extended to Diane Hanley,
for endless hours of editing, patience, and invaluable advice.

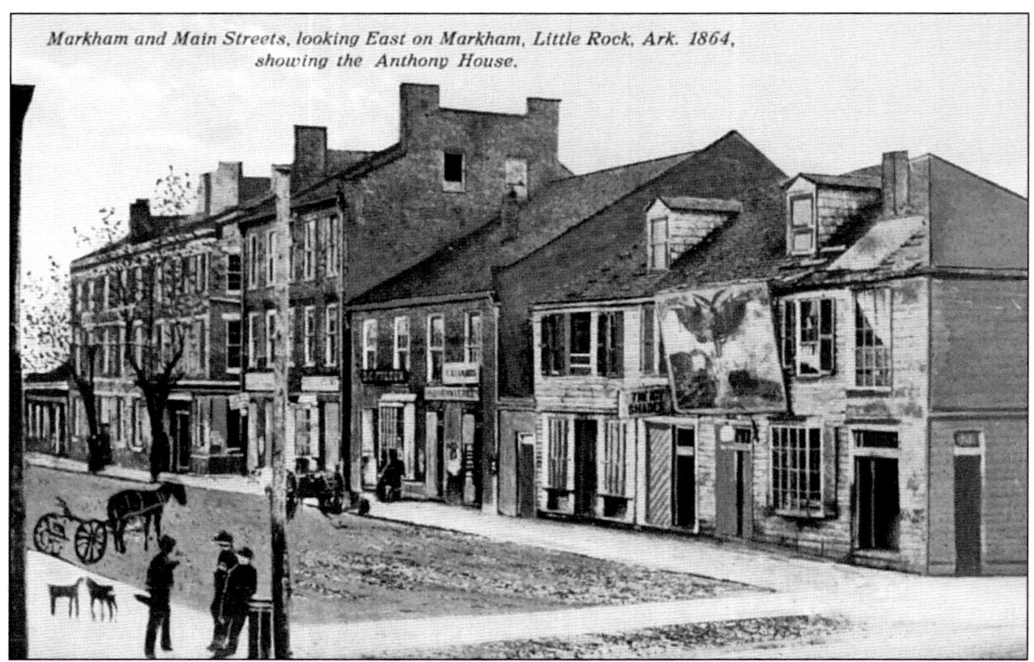

"Little Rock is quite historic. It dates back a century. The *Arkansas Gazette*, with which I did business, is 94 years old." These words were written on a *c.* 1913 postcard of a painting showing an 1864 view of the heart of the capital city, which was then occupied by the Union Army. The three-story building was the Anthony Hotel, built in 1840 and burned in 1875. Today the site is occupied by the Little Rock Convention Center. Little Rock is indeed "quite historic," and as this book is intended to reflect, much of this unique history is recorded on postcards.

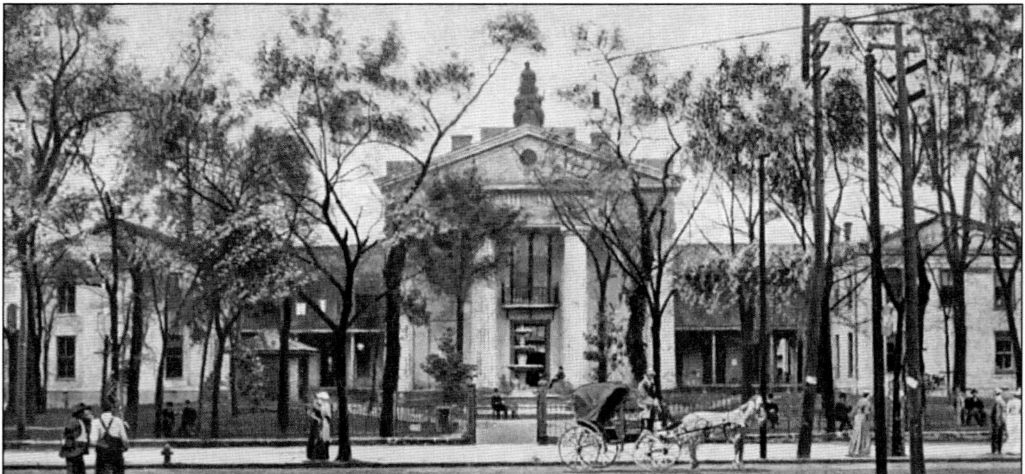

Four years after statehood, Arkansas had its first state capitol, known today as the Old State House. Building began in 1833 and was not declared complete until 1842. The Greek Revival building faced the city's main thoroughfare, Markham Street, with the Arkansas River behind offering a sweeping view of steamboats and the still wild north side of the river. The building was not without its critics; eccentric poet Albert Pike said it was "a great, awkward, clumsy, heavy edifice." When this *c.* 1900 card's view was taken, the cornerstone had been laid for the modern-day capitol, and the future fate of the state house was uncertain. Fortunately, the structure was saved; it has become one of the city's best-known landmarks.

One

1900 TO 1919
A TIME OF GROWTH AND CHANGE

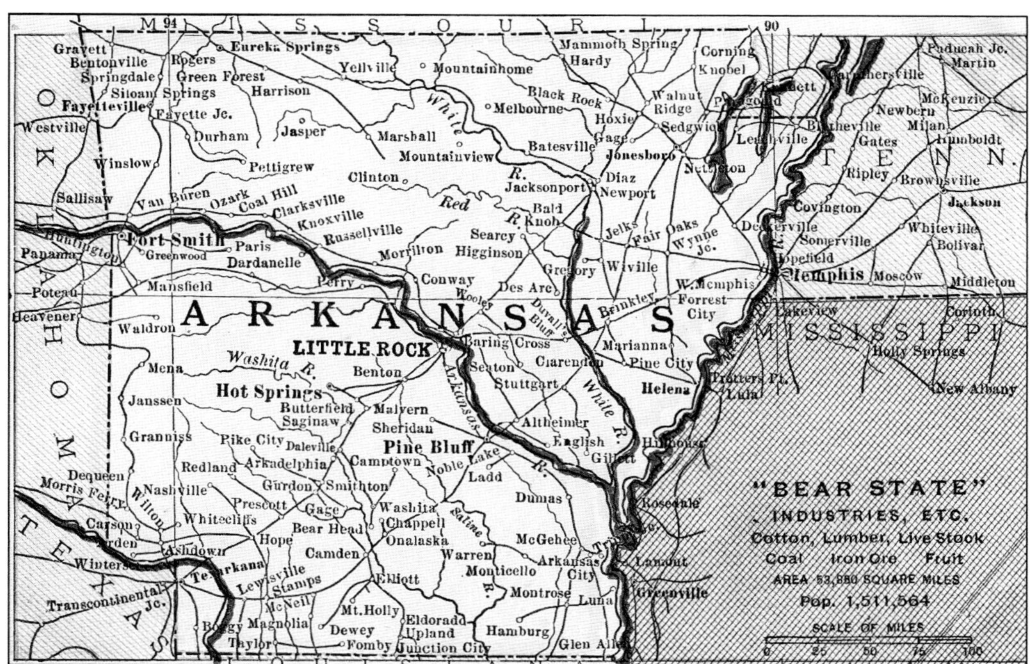

At the turn of the century, Arkansas had a population of 1.5 million people, most of whom lived on farms or in small towns. Little Rock, the state's largest city with almost 40,000 people, was in many ways still a small town. There were few paved roads, and horseless carriages had yet to appear. Commerce traveled by the burgeoning spider web of rail lines and on the three rivers reflected on this *c.* 1900 postcard map.

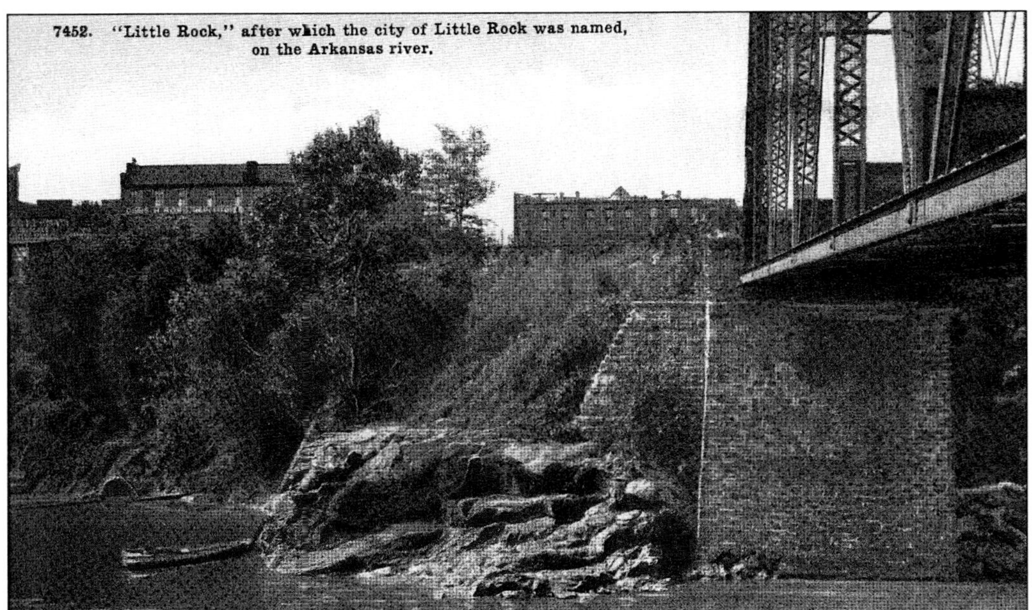

The capital city's namesake "little rock," discovered by French explorer Bernard de LaHarpe in 1722, became the subject of a popular postcard. The landmark was partially destroyed early in the century, during the construction of the railroad bridge shown on this 1905 card. For much of the 20th century the rock was obscured by weeds and neglect. It was cleaned up and marked as a part of the city's riverfront redevelopment in the 1980s.

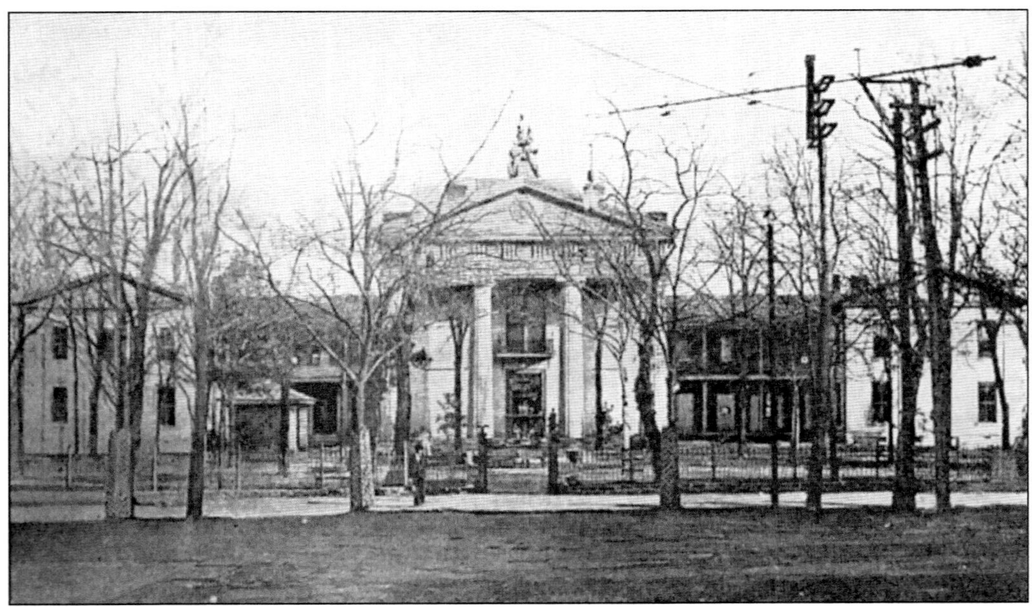

Designed by noted Kentucky architect Gideon Shyrock, the Old State House was opened in 1836, the year Arkansas was admitted to the Union. The state's first governor was inaugurated here, and the Arkansas General Assembly met here until moving to the present capitol building in 1911. Today, the Old State House is a museum devoted to Arkansas history, and is known to the nation as the backdrop before which Bill Clinton declared victory in both of his elections to the presidency. (*c.* 1905.)

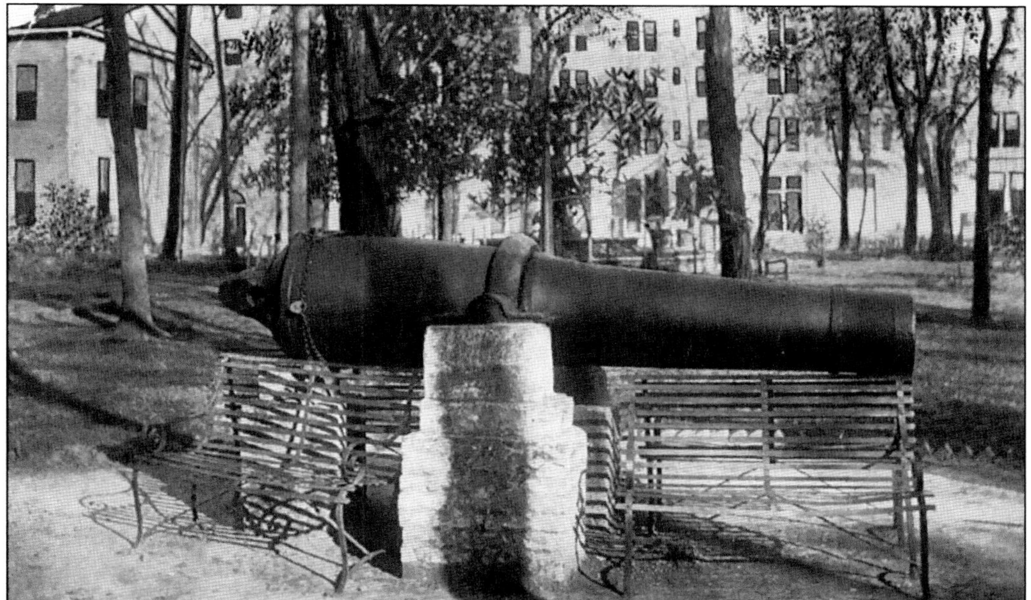

Known as "Lady Baxter," this cannon in front of the Old State House was fired only once: to celebrate the end of the so-called Brooks-Baxter War. The war ended in 1874 after a month-long armed struggle between two factions of Reconstruction Republicans. The conflict involved two men—Joseph Brooks and Elisha Baxter—both of whom claimed to be the rightful occupant of the governor's office. Eventually, Pres. Ulysses S. Grant declared Baxter to be the state's chief executive. (*c.* 1905.)

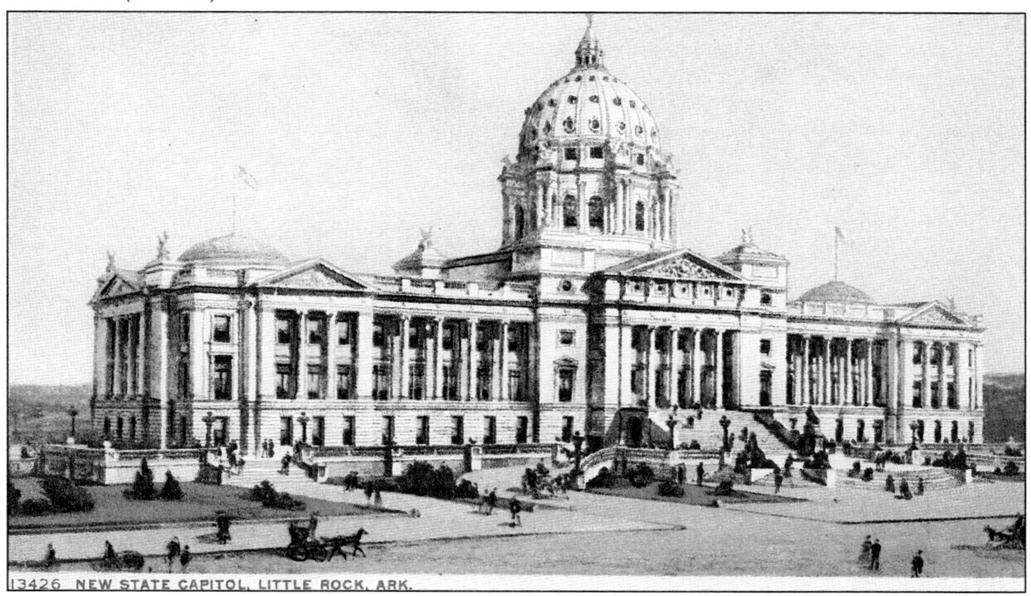

After years of legislative bickering, the need to build a new state capitol became evident in 1899, when a portion of the ceiling in the Old State House collapsed, injuring several lawmakers. The cornerstone for a new capitol building was laid in 1900, on the site of a prison used by Union troops, who occupied Little Rock during the Civil War. This *c.* 1905 card reflected the architect's vision of what the building would look like, though changes were made in the dome design before completion.

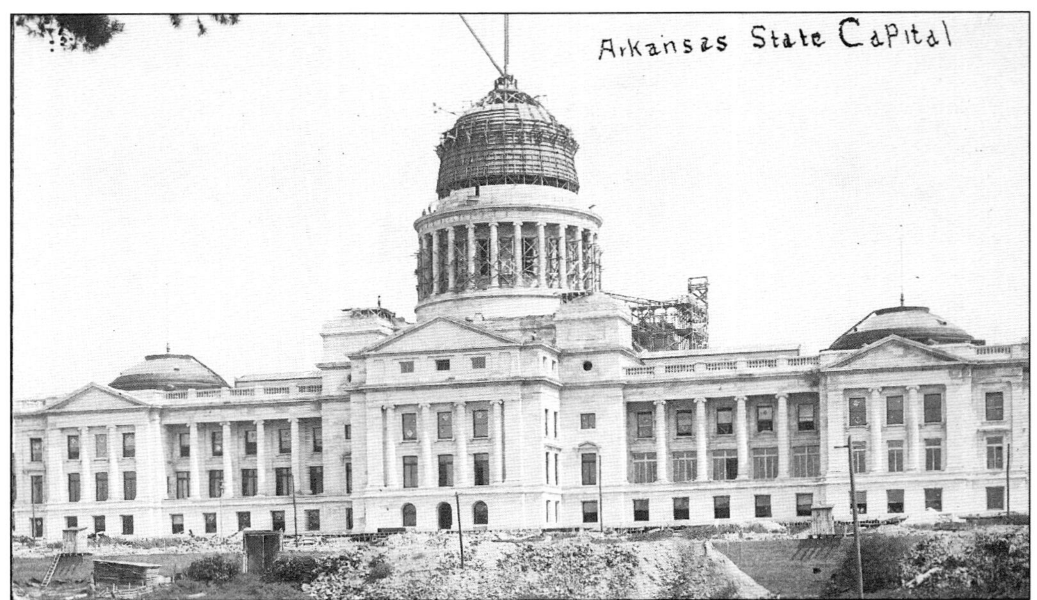

With the erection of its dome, the new state capitol was nearing completion in 1910. The capitol's completion had been delayed for several years by inefficiency and a bribery scandal. The legislature first met in the partially completed building in 1911. The *Arkansas Gazette* summed up the state's pride in the new building declaring, "The Capitol Commission's gift to the state of Arkansas in 1910 will be the magnificent new State Capitol that stands like the Parthenon of old on the eminence of the western extremity of the Fifth Street."

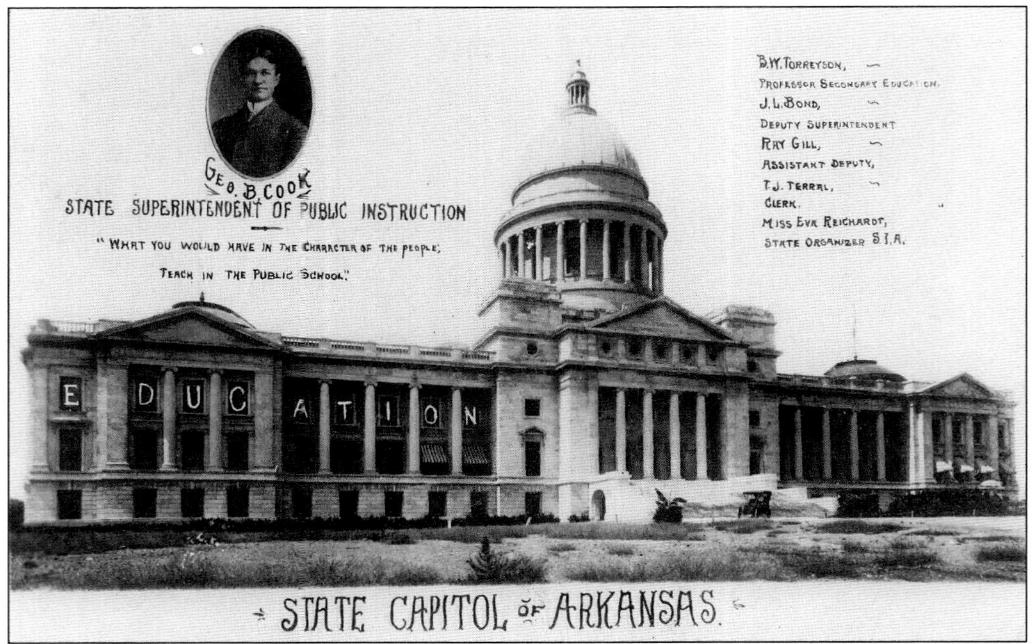

The signs in the windows of the newly completed State Capitol Building were promoting a teachers' meeting held in Little Rock. On this 1911 card, George Cook, state superintendent of public education, urged, "What you would have in the character of the people, teach in the public schools."

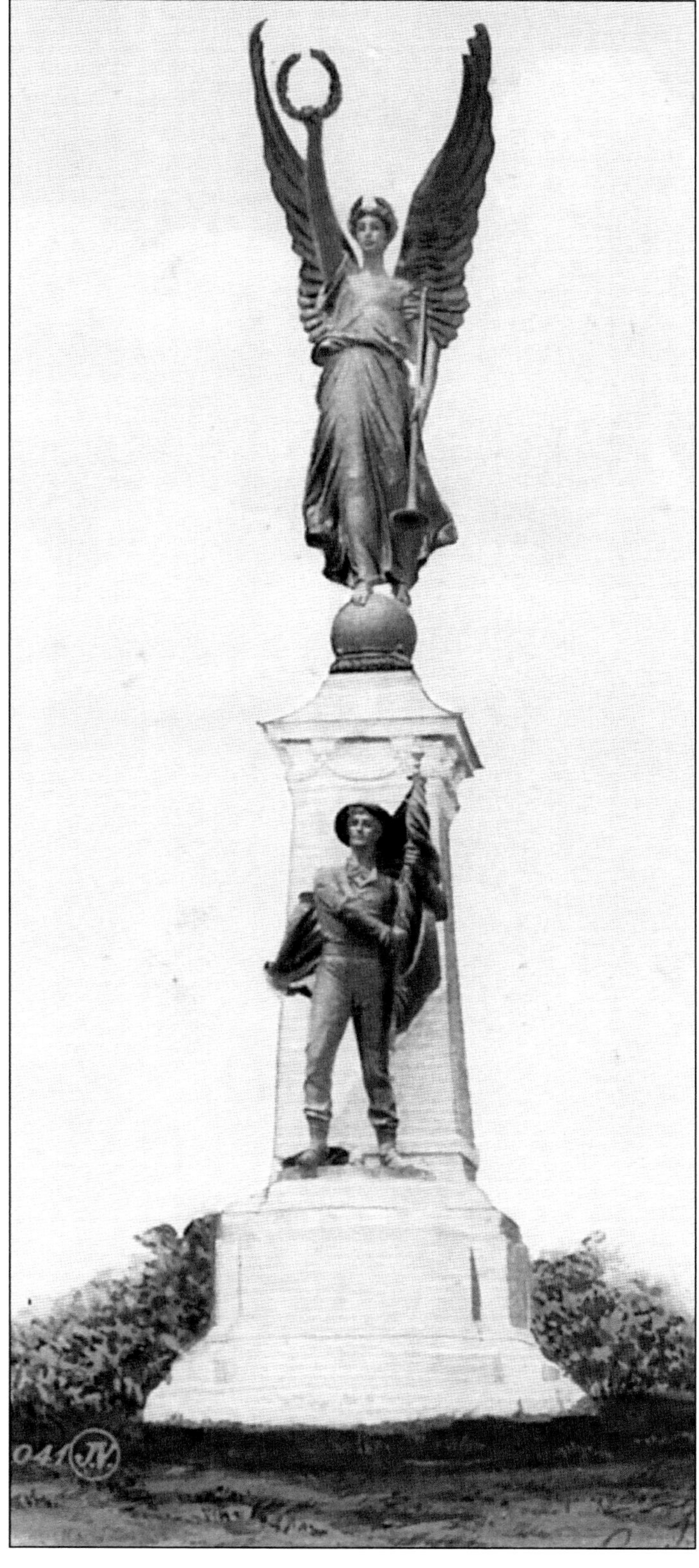

While the new capitol building was still under construction, the state funded the erection of a monument to the men of Arkansas who fought for the Confederacy some 40 years earlier. In May 1911, State Senator George Christian, from Booneville, decided that there should also be a monument to the Arkansas men who had fought for the Union. Christian sought Senate approval only for the ground upon which to place the monument, pledging that private sources would fund it. Christian's timing, however, was terrible, for Little Rock was then hosting the annual reunion of the United Confederate Veterans (UCV). The legislature feared Northern states would send funds to erect a Union monument that would dwarf that of the Confederacy, and voted against granting a spot on the Capitol lawn. Today the Confederate monument still stands; no Union monument was ever built. The angel was intended to be one of a pair for the top of the State Capitol Building, but when one was being placed on the roof it fell to the ground and shattered. The state lacked funds to have a replacement cast and decided to put the remaining angel behind the Confederate soldier.

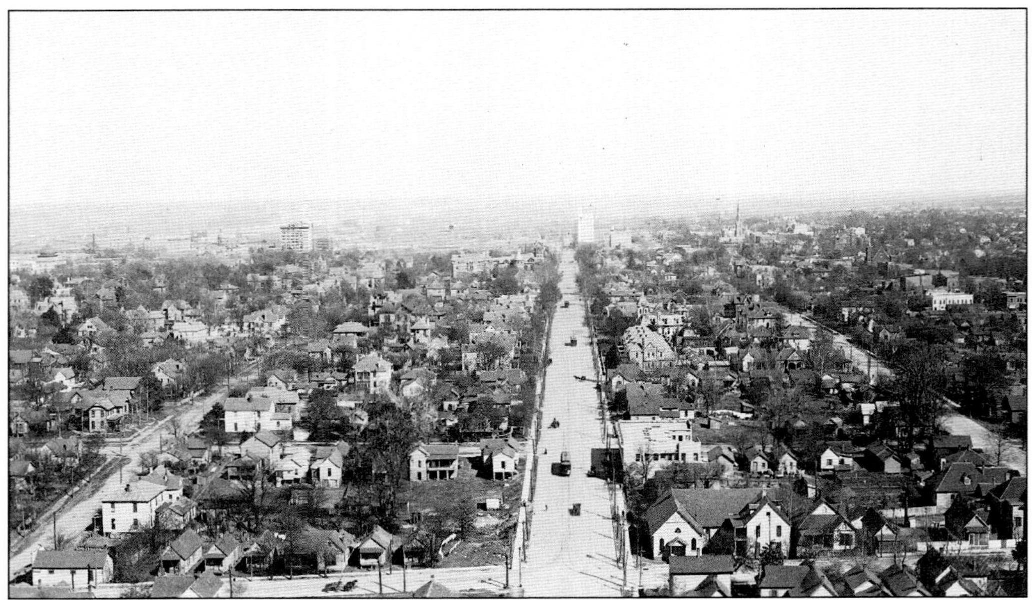

A photographer climbed to the dome of the new capitol building and pointed his camera east down Capitol Avenue toward distant Main Street to capture this *c.* 1910 view. The wide boulevard of Capitol Avenue was being traversed by streetcars and a few wagons that moved past large homes, all of which are gone today.

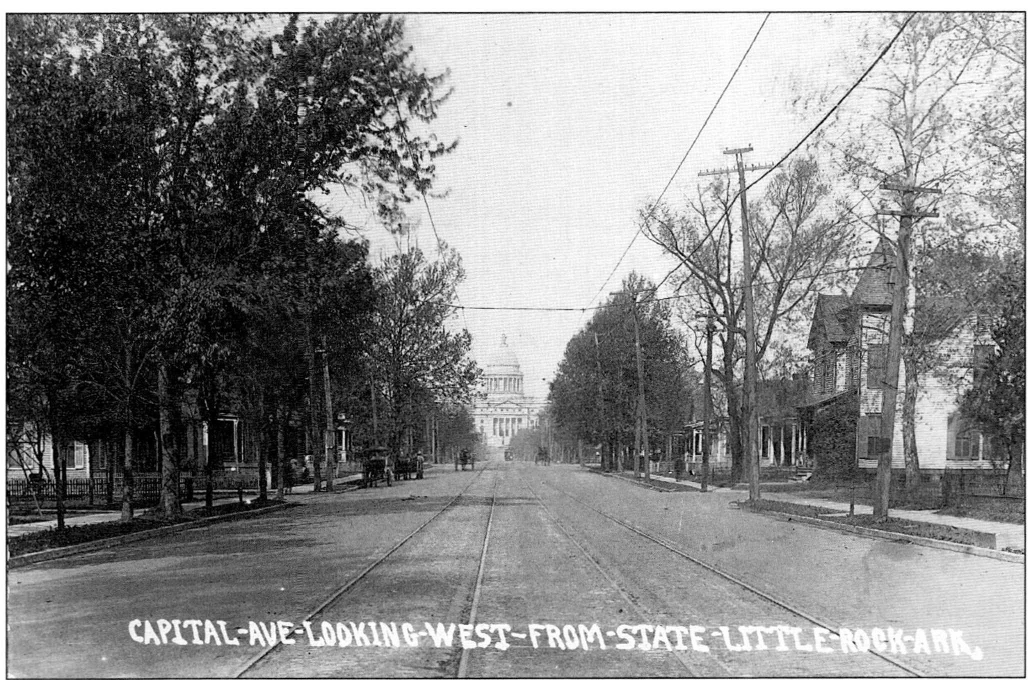

Capitol Avenue took on added significance when the State Capitol Building was built in Little Rock in 1900, on what was then the far western reaches of the city. Twin streetcar tracks, running in each direction, were laid along the stately boulevard that ran between Main Street and the Capitol, shown here in the distance. Today the streetcars are gone and the grand homes have all been replaced by commercial structures. (*c.* 1911.)

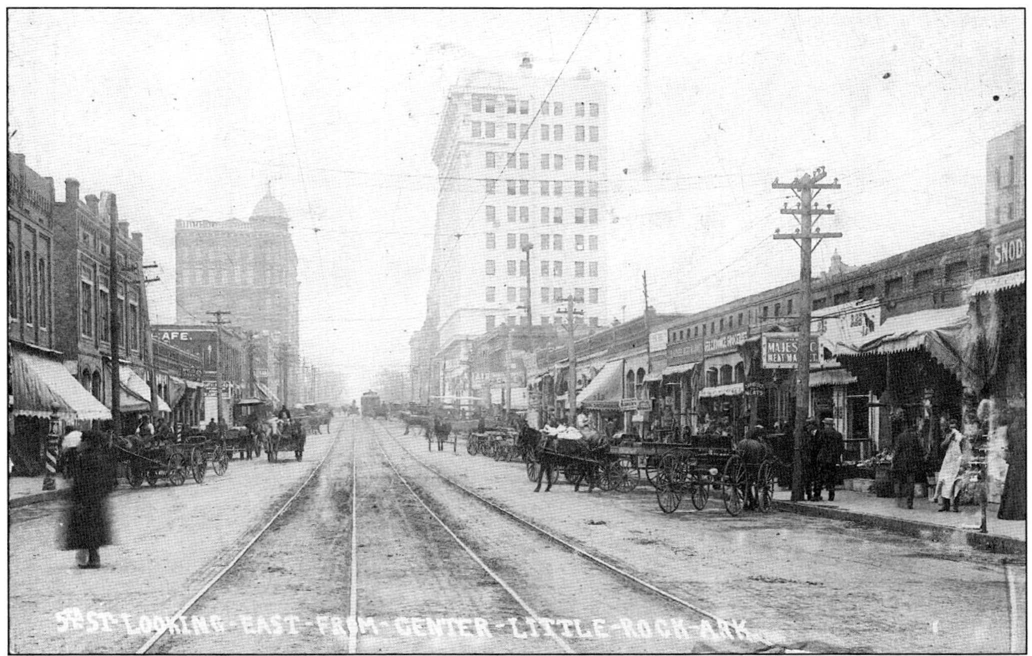

At the far end of Capitol Avenue was its intersection with Main Street at the two tall buildings shown in this 1911 postcard—the Masonic Temple (left) and the 11-story State National Bank (right), which was the tallest structure in the city at the time. The two shops seen on the right are the Majestic Meat Market and a bakery, in front of which wagons were parked. Today all the buildings in the foreground are gone, replaced by modern financial institutions.

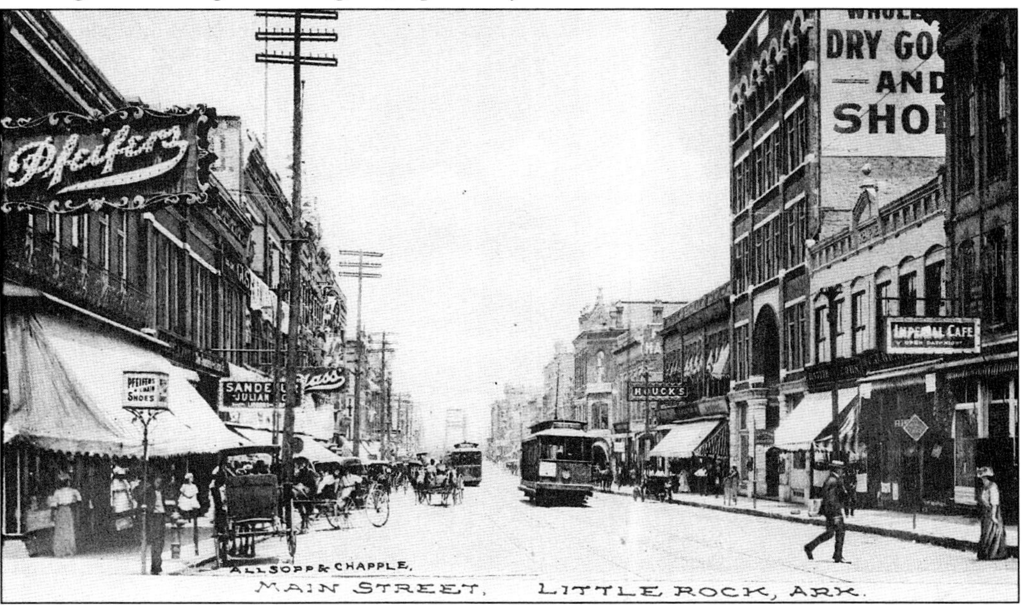

Looking north from the 400 block of Main, the photographer captured the street before automobiles had made an impact. Streetcars, initially pulled by mules, had come to Little Rock in 1877 and would be fixtures until replaced by buses in 1947. Among the businesses seen here are names from retailing history such as Pfeifer's, and the Gus Blass Dry Goods establishment seen on the left. (*c.* 1905.)

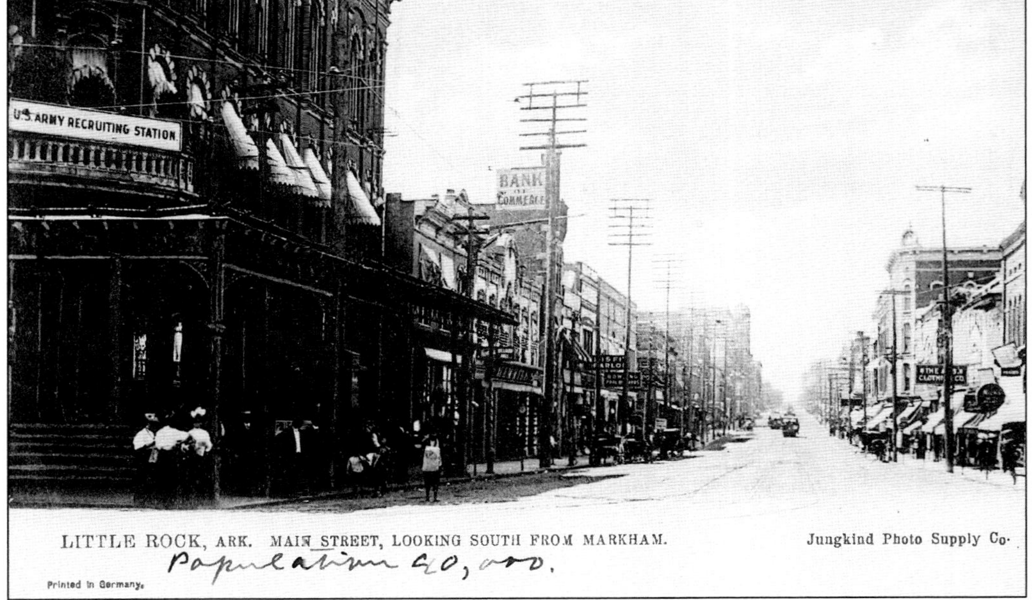

The U.S. Army Recruiting Station occupied the building to the left, at the southeastern corner of Main and Markham Streets. This *c.* 1905 view, looking south on Main Street, contains none of the taller buildings that would be erected in the decade to follow. Today virtually all the buildings seen here are gone. The commander-in-chief of recruits who enlisted when this card was printed would have been Theodore Roosevelt.

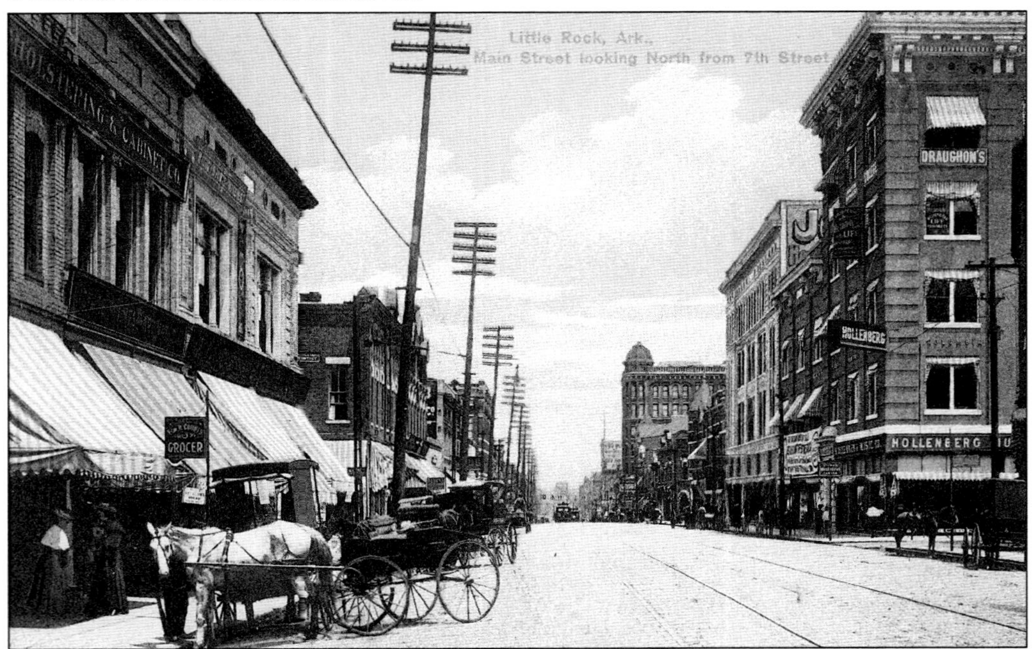

This *c.* 1908 view shows Main Street, looking north from Seventh Street. The wagon, with its horse seeming to stare at the photographer, was parked in front of Count's Grocery store. Today this site is a parking lot. On the right is the Waldon Building, erected in 1906 by George Donaghey, an area contractor who helped promote the new state capitol (then under construction). Donaghey was elected governor in 1908.

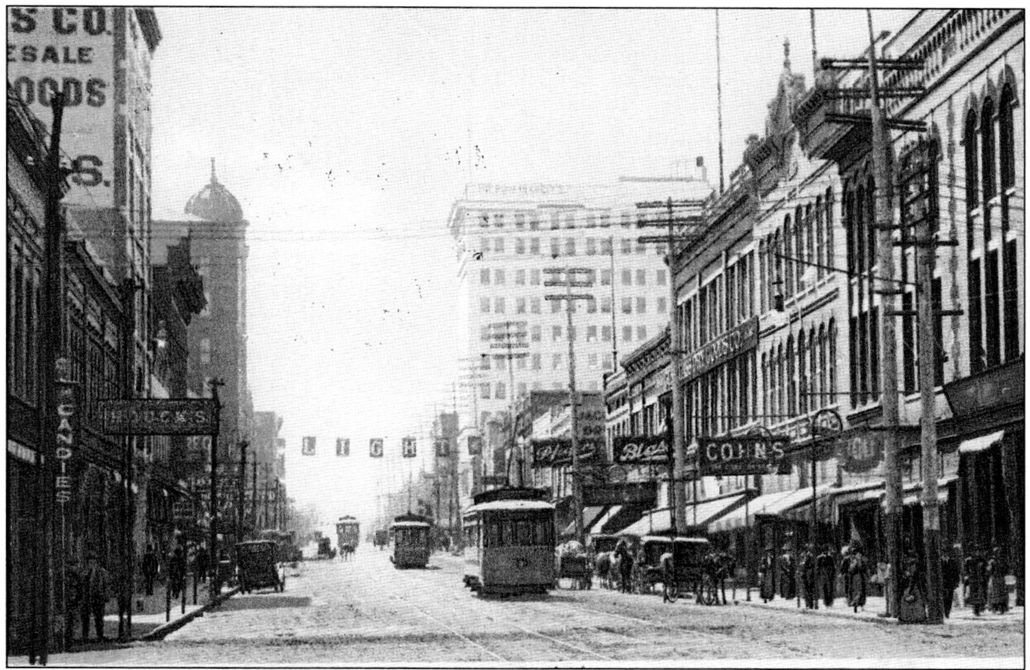

This 1910 view of Main Street (postmarked 1914), looking south from the 400 block, captured the tallest buildings in the city at Fifth and Main Streets—the Masonic Temple with its domed top and the State National Bank (distant right). The buildings to the lower right were home to M.M. Cohn's, an upper-end retailer which is now only found in suburban shopping malls.

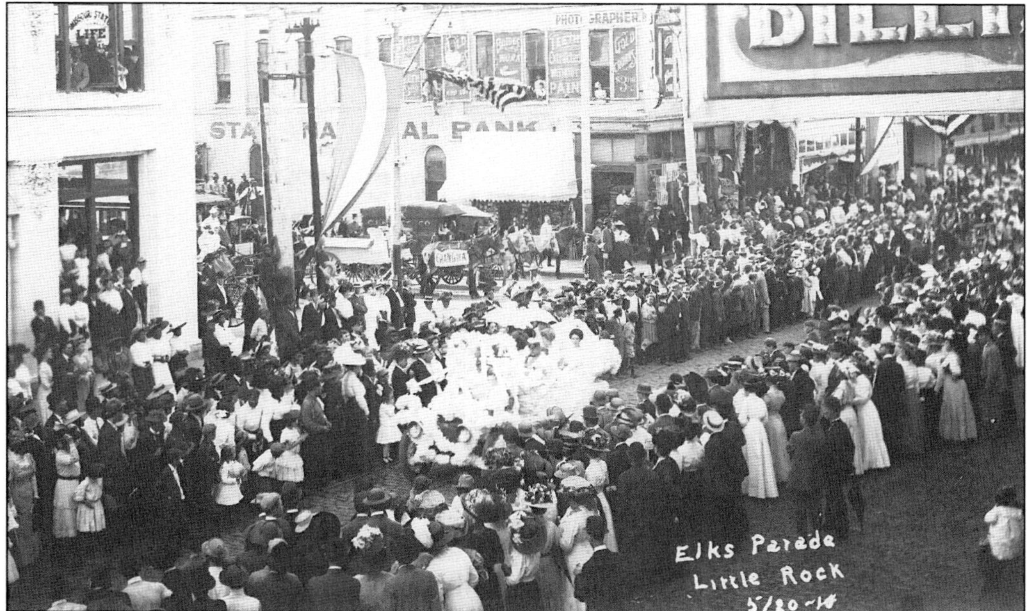

This 1911 photo was taken at the crossroads of Arkansas, Fifth, and Main Streets, on a day when the Elks' Parade was drawing a large crowd. Spectators lean out of the windows of the Boyle Building (left) and from the State National Bank (right). The bank building also housed Union Dentists, who promised on their signs, "Teeth Extracted Without Pain" and "Gold Crowns $3."

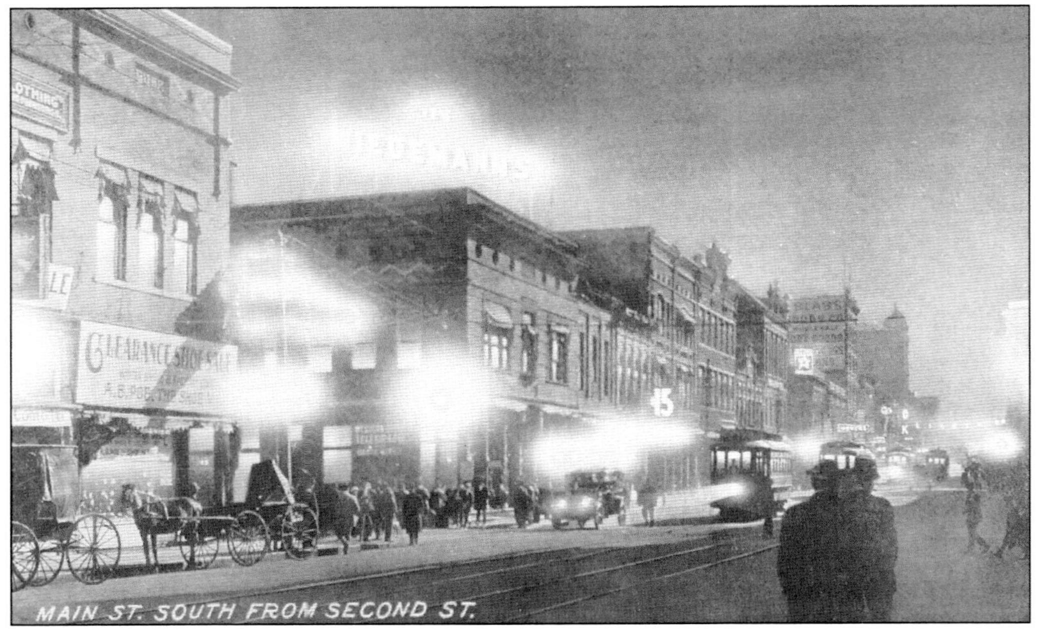

The new electric streetlights were on in this unusual nighttime postcard. Made in 1910, this card is a view looking south down the east side of Main Street. Such technological improvements were signs of the first-class city Little Rock was emerging to become in the young century.

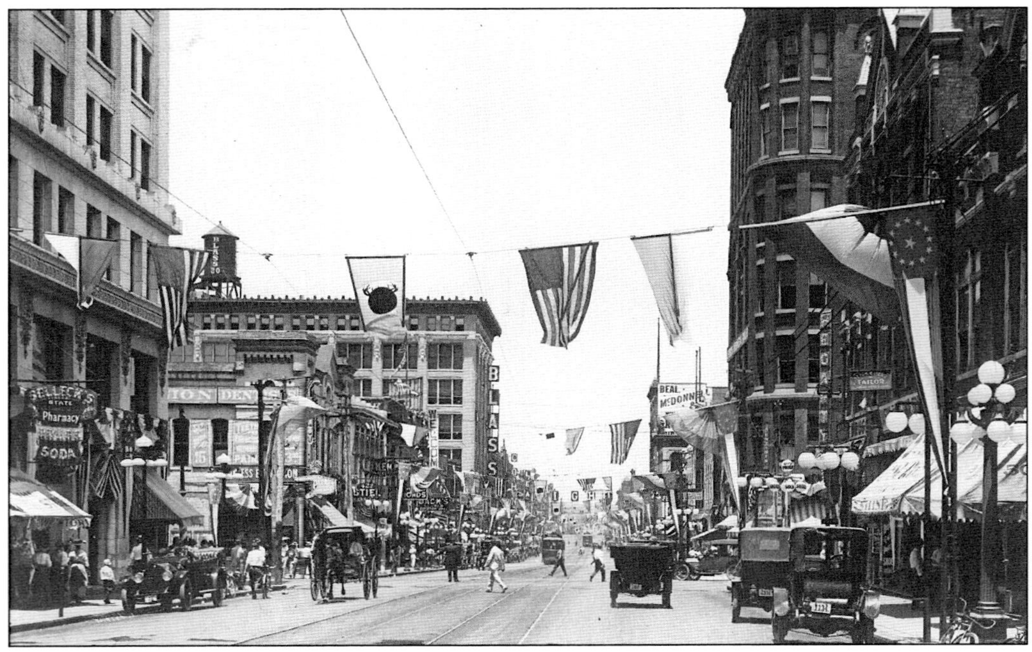

Looking toward Fifth and Main Streets on this 1918 postcard, it is apparent that the age of the automobile is approaching. The large building on the right is the Masonic Temple. In the background is Blass Department Store, its seven floors topped by a water tower also bearing the Blass logo. The water tower was necessary to help maintain water pressure in the tall building.

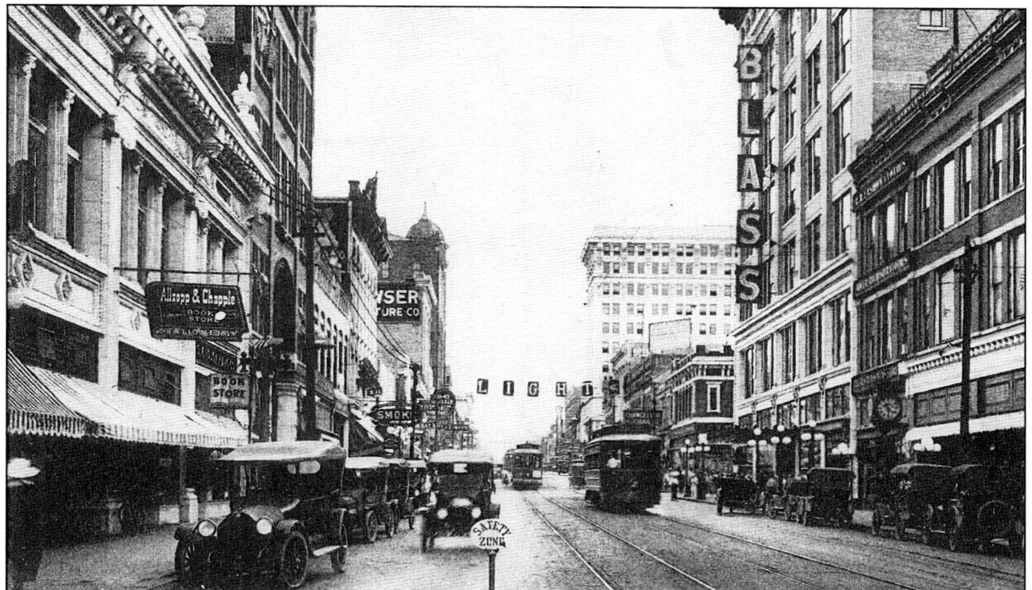

This 1918 card, with a view looking south from the 400 block of Main, was sent by a soldier stationed at nearby Camp Pike, to his mother. In training to fight the Germans in France, the young man wrote, "Just a card to let you know I am still alive but very busy. To be out here and not go anywhere is like being out on a farm." Of particular note is the "safety zone" sign in the foreground, apparently intended to keep people out of the path of the busy streetcars.

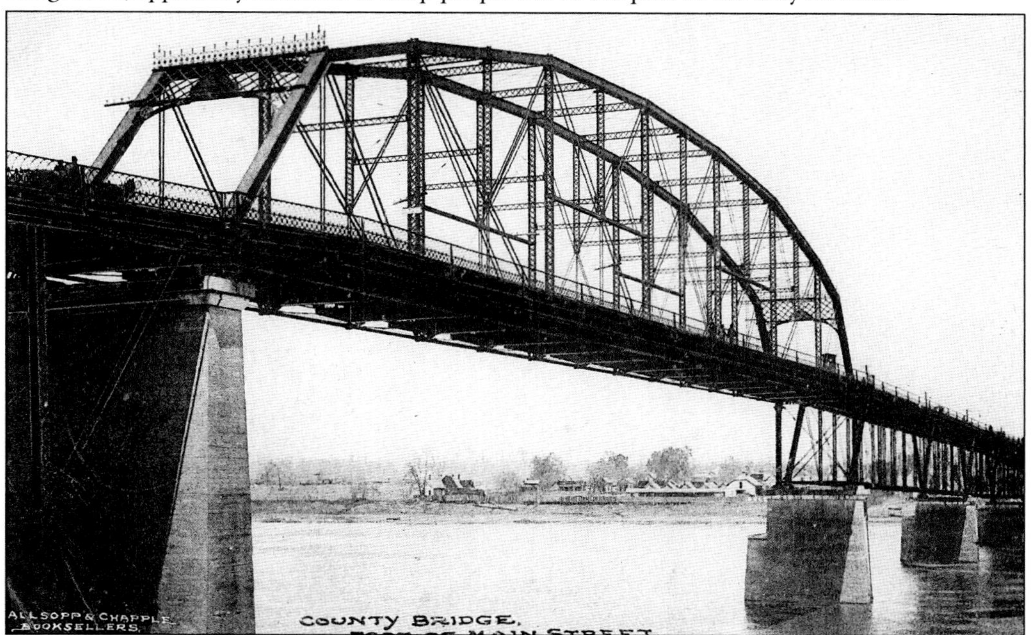

The "Free Bridge" was built in 1897 by the Pulaski County government and was the area's first true non-railway bridge. It was designated as free, and no toll was collected, hence the common name applied to the structure. This 1907 card was mailed by a soldier stationed at Fort Roots, who wrote that he "crossed this bridge today, the river is very muddy looking. One way to cross the Arkansas River in [*sic*] route to Little Rock from our post. This is the free bridge, there is another bridge which is a toll bridge but army people don't have to pay."

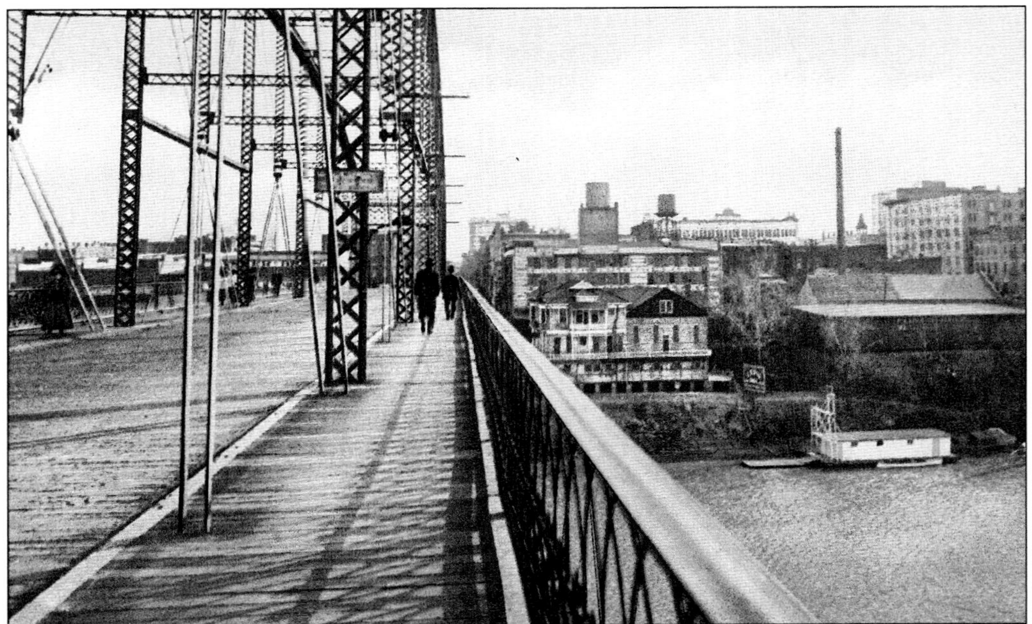

The Free Bridge was designed for foot and wagon traffic when it was erected in 1897. The wide path along the rails provided ample space to separate pedestrians from horses and wagons. The bridge ran from the foot of Main Street in Little Rock to Maple Street on the north side of the river. (*c.* 1905.)

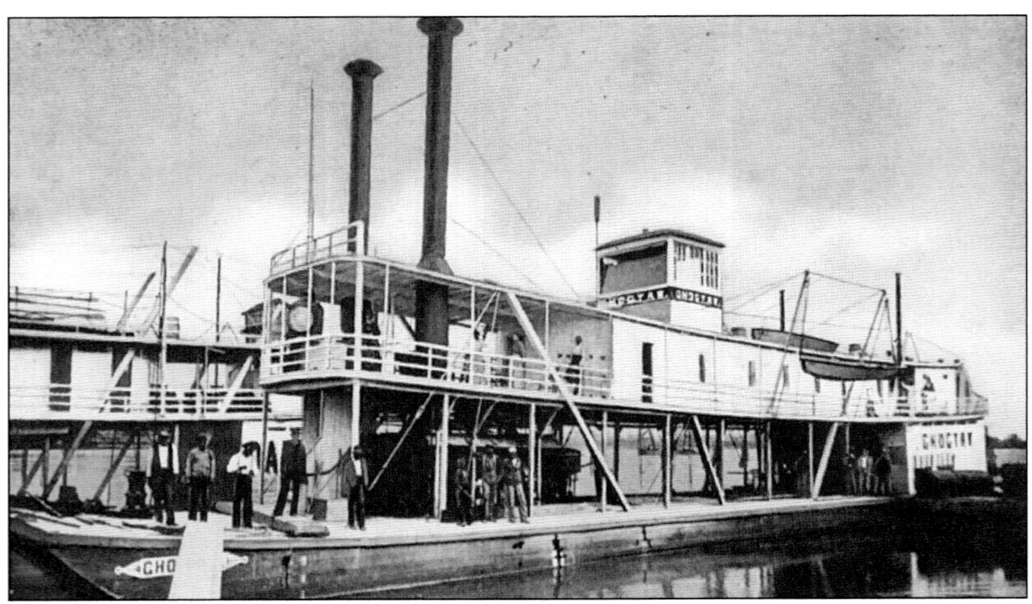

Riverboats of all types and sizes were a vital part of commerce on the often treacherous Arkansas River, in part because of its connection with the mighty Mississippi in the southeastern part of the state. The riverboat *Choctaw* transported cotton, livestock feed, and other goods, while a few passengers and crew could be housed on its second level. The arrival of the more reliable railroads in the late 1800s greatly diminished the importance of the riverboats. (*c.* 1900.)

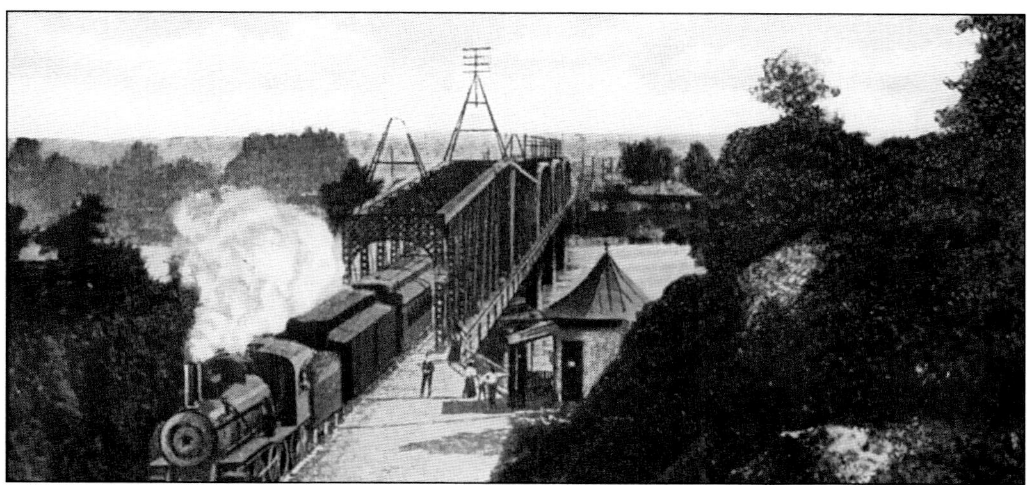

Trains from the north and east entered Little Rock across bridges. Perhaps the most noteworthy of these was the Baring Cross Bridge, shown in this *c.* 1905 view of a train crossing to the Little Rock side of the Arkansas River. The Baring Cross Bridge Company was formed in 1873 to build the bridge and leased it to the Cairo and Fulton Railroad. The name was taken from the Baring Brothers, the company in London which financed the structure. The bridge was washed away in the record flood of 1927.

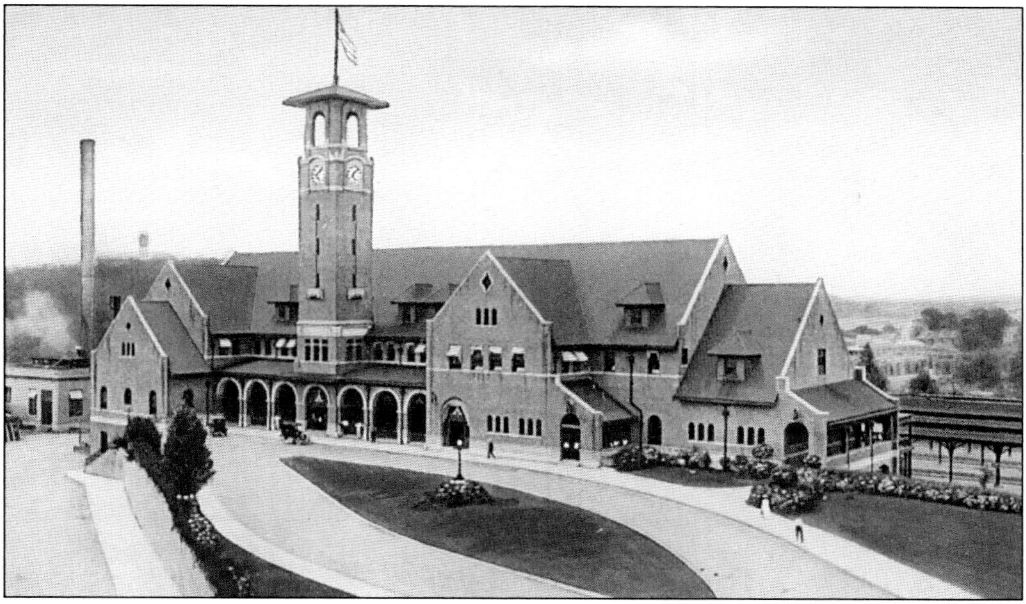

The Missouri Pacific-Iron Mountain Railroad erected this impressive station in 1911 on Victory Street, in prominent view of the new state capitol building. This *c.* 1912 card, published by the railroad, boasts on the back the following: "[This is] one of the handsomest and most conveniently arranged railroad stations in America. No state in the Union surpasses Arkansas in natural resources. In this great state Missouri Pacific-Iron Mountain has a total mileage of almost 2,400 miles or almost ten times the extreme length of the state. Its lines reach out in all directions from Little Rock. Forty-two Missouri Pacific passenger trains arrive at and depart from Little Rock daily. Little Rock is the shortest route between St. Louis, Texas, and Mexico." The number of daily passenger trains mentioned clearly reflects the major role railroads played in Little Rock at the time. The station burned in 1922 but was quickly rebuilt.

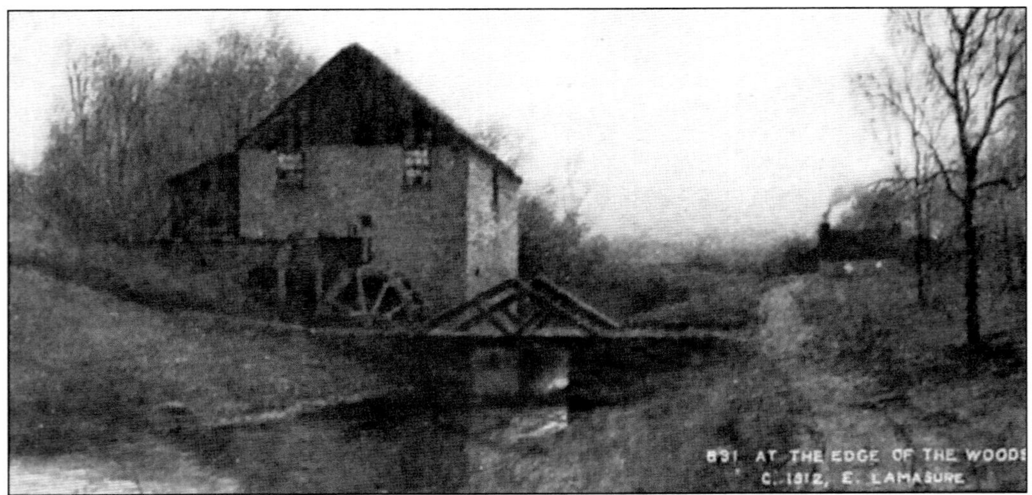

The E.T. Teter and Company attempted to be in a position to greet arriving potential investors, having acquired an office opposite Union Station. With plans to sell 40,000 acres of Arkansas land, the company enticed speculators and investors by charging a down payment of $1.50 to $3 per acre, with the promise of "no hills, rocks, or swamps." On December 23, 1914, Mr. Teter wrote on this card to an agent in St. Louis the following: "Do not like to show land Xmas day but if Mr. L. has two or three men will do so."

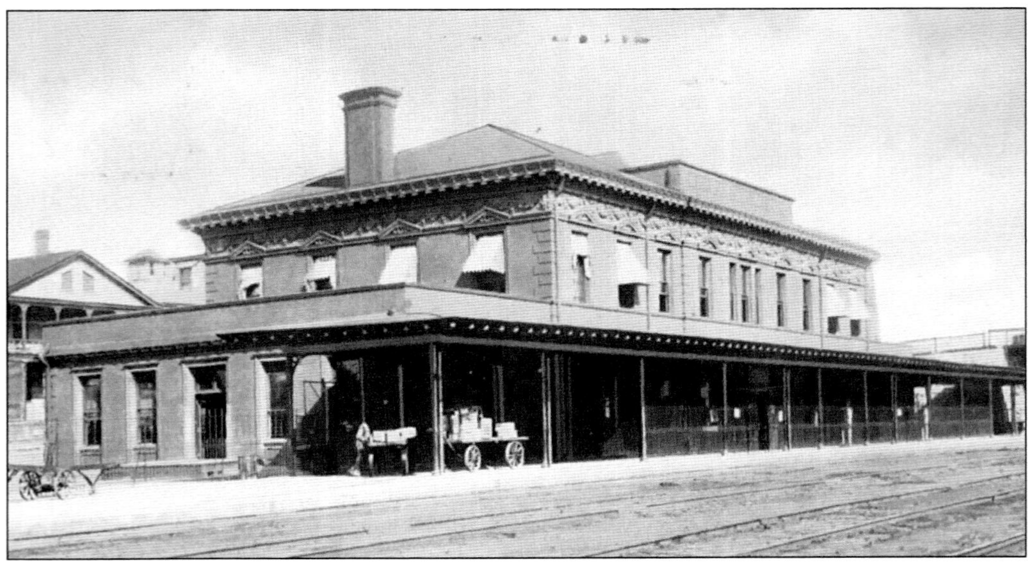

Little Rock was home to two railroad stations. Photographed *c.* 1910, this railroad station located on East Third Street was erected in 1899 and belonged to the Rock Island Line. When built, the station belonged to the Choctaw, Oklahoma, and Gulf Railroads, but was sold to the Rock Island in 1902. The station served passengers until the 1950s. The depot sat idle and decaying for several years before it was restored in the 1980s for use as a restaurant and nightclub.

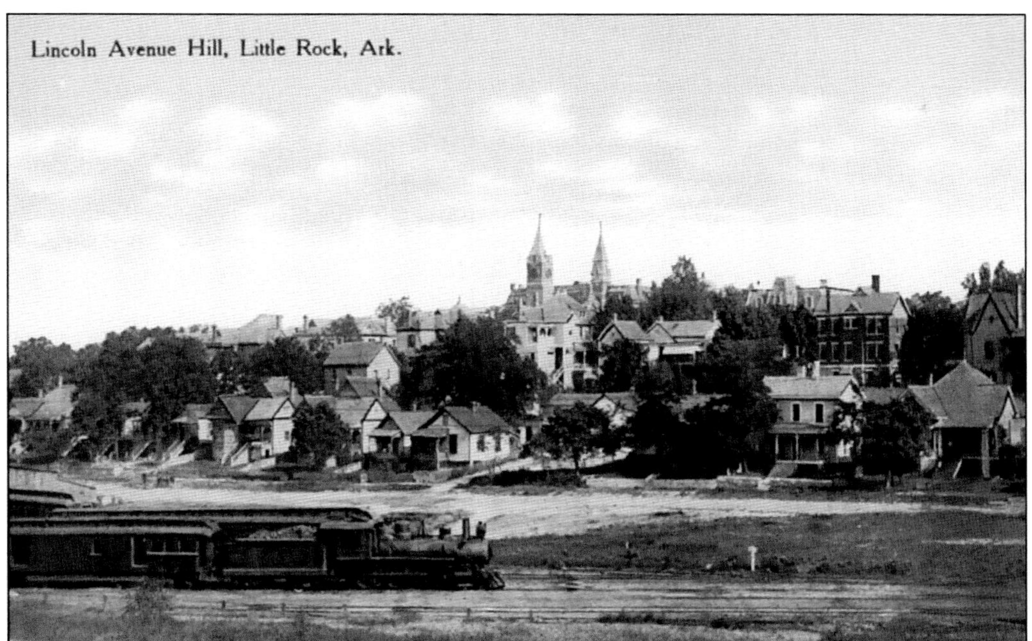

This train steaming south would have been only minutes out of the Union Station, as it passed the area known as Lincoln Avenue Hill, near what is presently called Cantrell Road. The area was also known locally at that time as "Carpetbagger Row," because of the mansions built by wealthy Northerners who came to the city during the Reconstruction period following the Civil War. The twin spires in the background belonged to the Physicians and Surgeons Hospital. (*c.* 1910.)

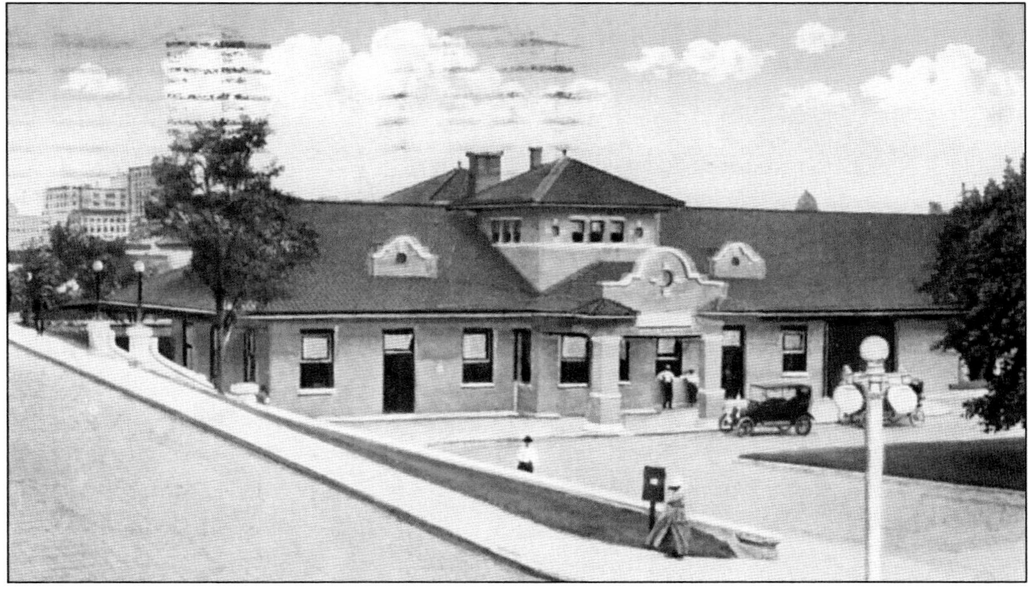

The city of Argenta (now known as North Little Rock) on the north side of the Arkansas River rivaled its larger neighboring city for the attention of the railroads. The Cotton Belt Railroad built this depot in Argenta around 1910 at the foot of the Free Bridge, linking the smaller city with Little Rock. Today both the depot and the railroad are only a memory. (*c.* 1911.)

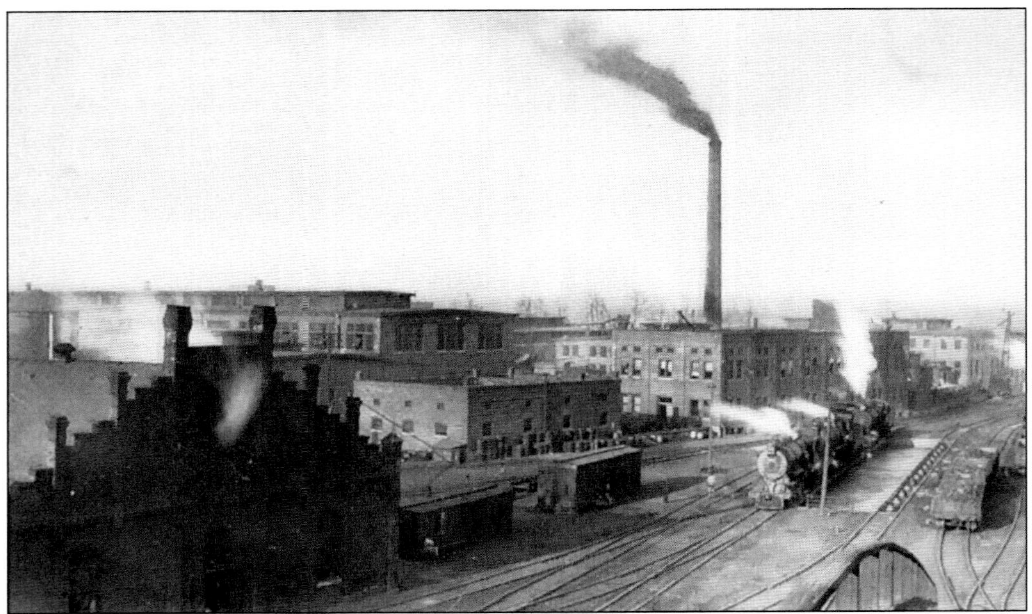

Argenta was destined to become home to the vast maintenance facilities required by the St. Louis, Iron Mountain, and Southern (later the Missouri Pacific) Railroads. In these shops, the engines were repaired and serviced. The railroad created many jobs for skilled men. (*c.* 1905.)

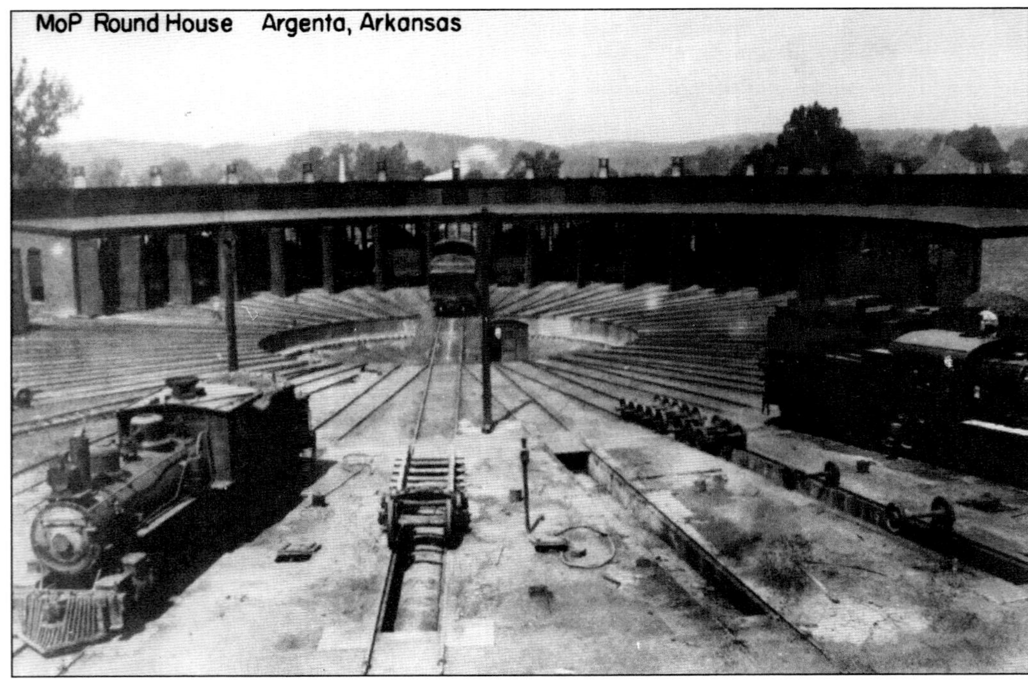

Resembling the spokes on a giant wheel, the "Round House" of the Missouri Pacific railroad reflected how technology and engineering adapted to keep locomotives, which weigh many tons, in service. Multiple engines could be pulled into the roundhouse yard, then swiveled on the track mounted over the oval pit into one of the bay-like workshops. (*c.* 1910.)

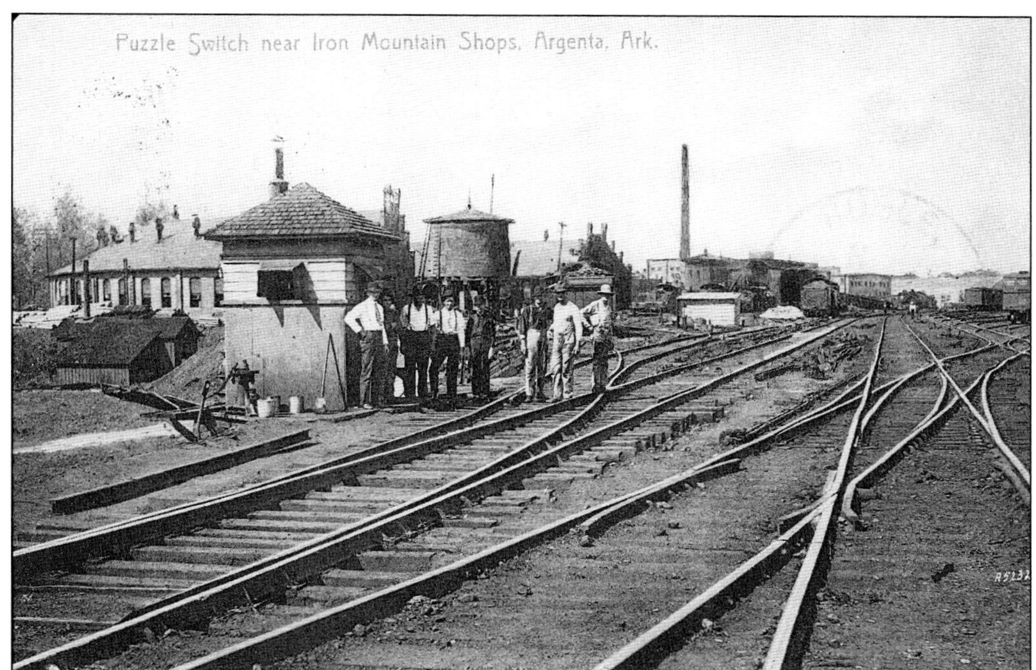

The hazardous nature of employment in the rail yards is vividly documented in the penciled message on the back of the 1910 card of the "puzzle switch" at the Iron Mountain shops. "This is where so many men get killed," presumably when caught among the opening and closing tracks that routed the trains.

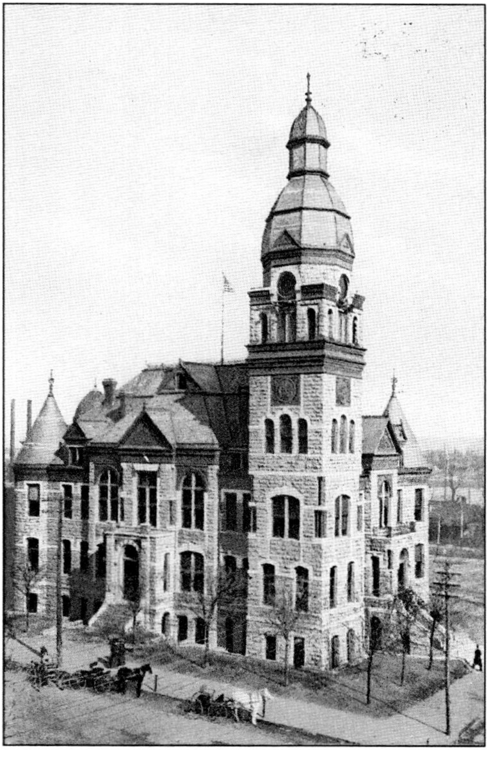

The Pulaski County Courthouse was erected at Second and Spring Streets between 1887 and 1889 at a cost of $100,000. The building was constructed of blue granite taken from the Fourche Mountain Quarry east of Little Rock and was enhanced by terra cotta trim and distinctive gables. The top of the tower was removed in 1961 because of concerns about its structural integrity. The entire building was restored in the 1990s. (*c.* 1900.)

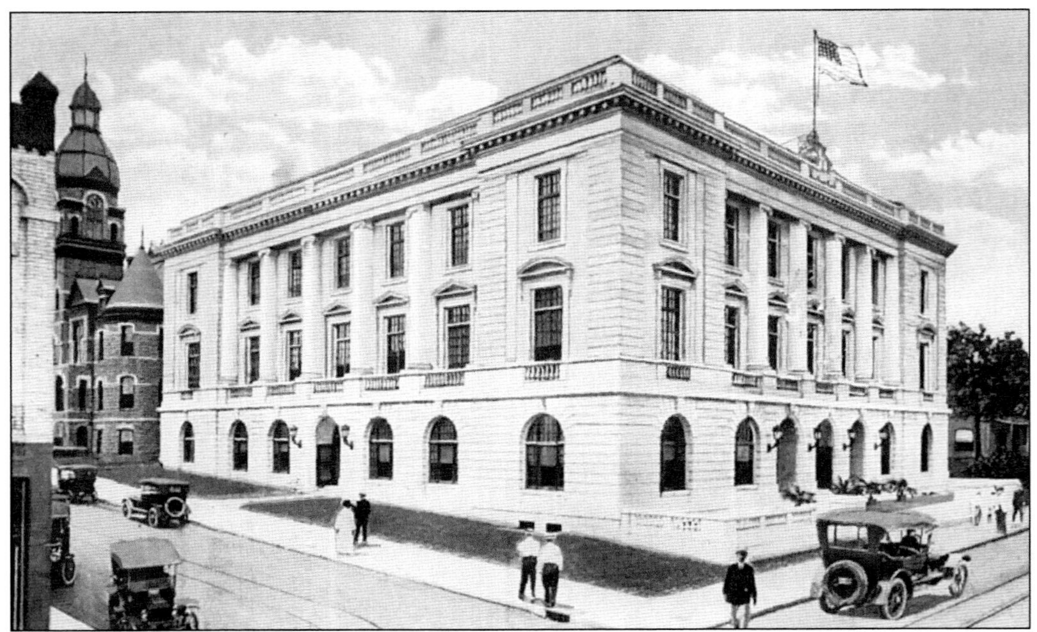

"Fifty cents per hour and time and half for overtime" were the words penciled to "Home Folks" living on Page Avenue in Dallas, about the writer's new-found employment in Arkansas. The front of this 1917 card shows the annex to the Pulaski County Courthouse, which was completed in 1914 from a design by noted architect George Mann, who also designed the new state capitol. The end result was a beautiful building that still serves today.

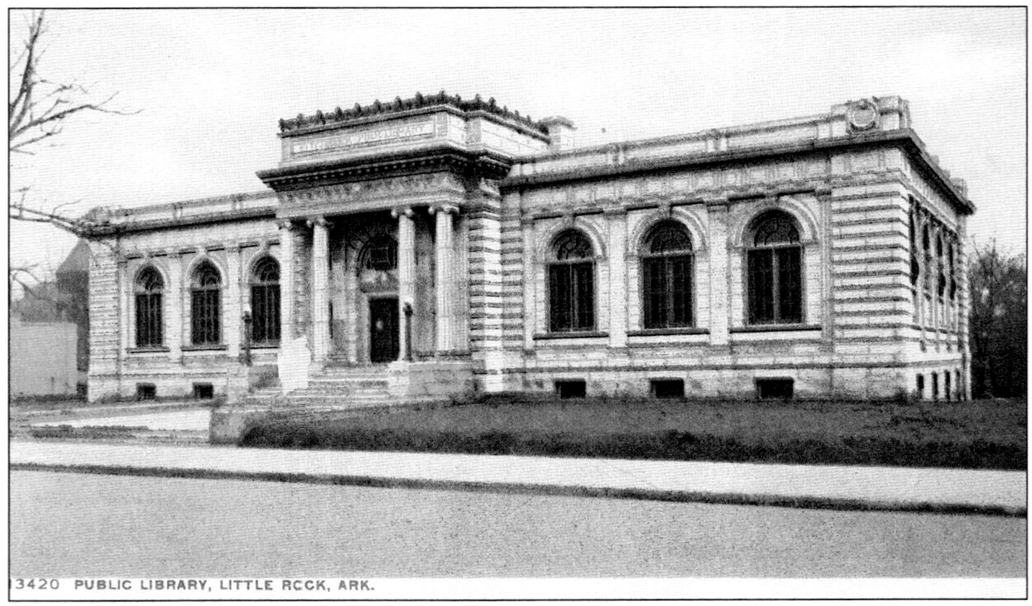

Little Rock's first public library, designed by noted local architect Charles L. Thompson, opened in 1910 at the corner of Seventh and Louisiana Streets. It was funded with the help of Andrew Carnegie, who contributed to the building of many libraries across the nation in the early years of the century. Sadly, the building was torn down in August 1963 to be replaced with a more utilitarian structure at the same location. (*c.* 1910.)

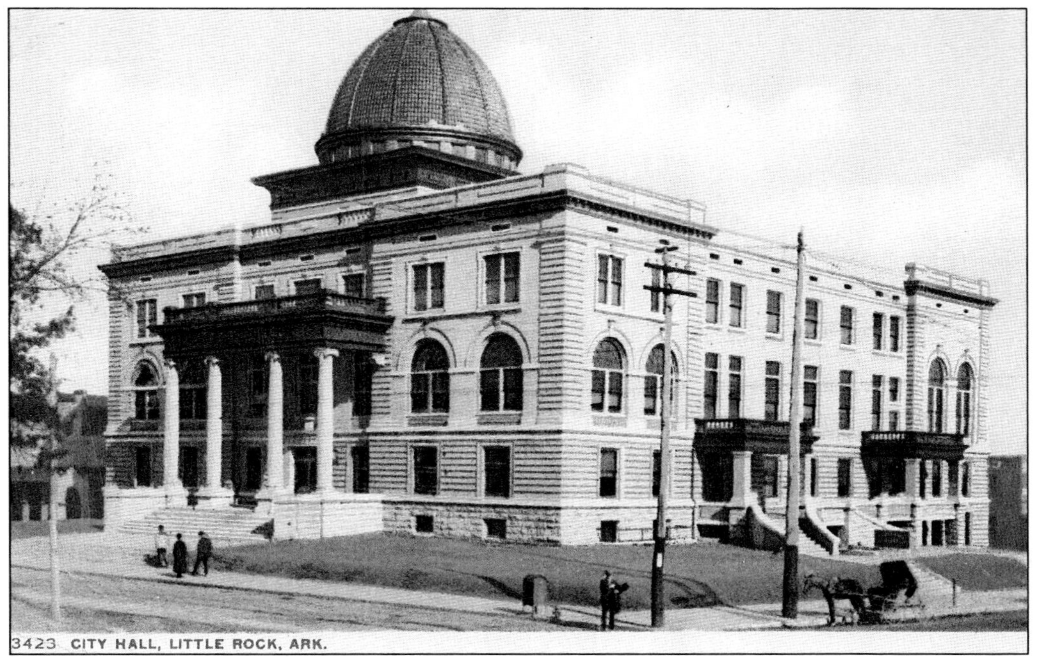

This 1914 card's message reads, "Well, Kate is well, I certainly was surprised to see how big and fat she is, I wouldn't have known her at all. I want to pick cotton while I am here. They have plenty to eat." In 1908 this new city hall building, designed by Charles Thompson, was erected at the corner of Markham and Broadway. In 1956, the city's electorate voted by postcard to remove the dome rather than expend the funds to repair it. Today the building still serves, but it has a flat roof.

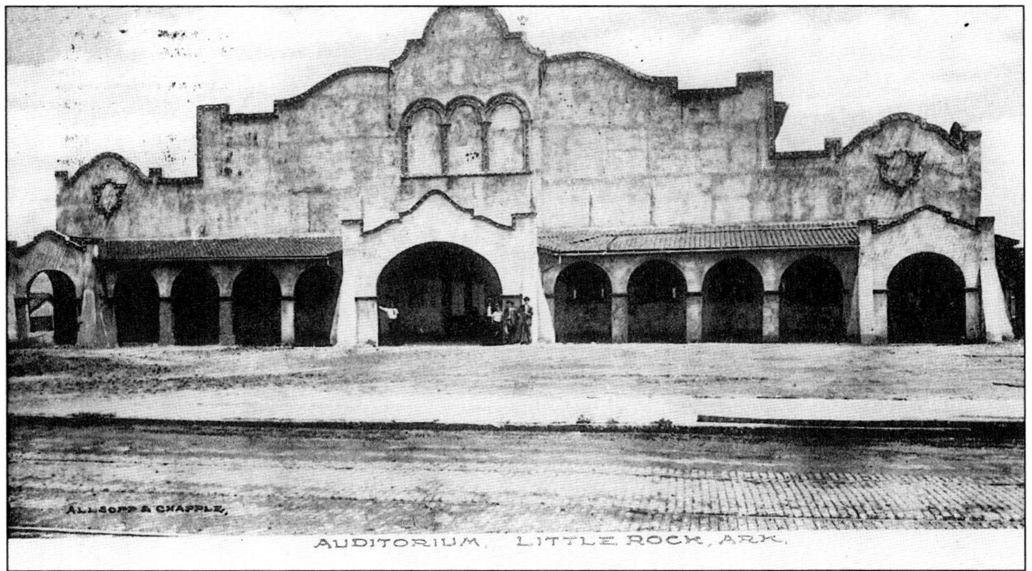

The city auditorium, located near city hall on West Markham Street, was certainly one of the most interestingly designed public buildings in Little Rock. Patterned after the facade of San Antonio's famous Alamo, the building hosted many events, including the Grand Ball in 1911 for the United Confederate Veterans (UCV) Reunion. The structure was torn down in the 1920s. (*c.* 1911.)

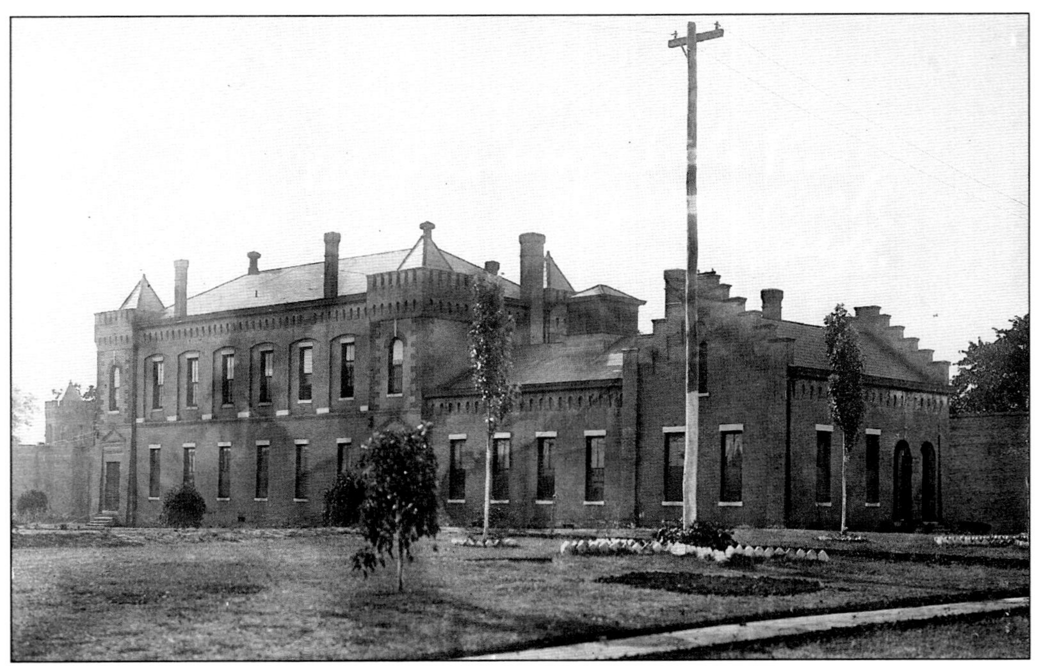

"The Walls" was the locally used term to refer to the state prison, located near what is presently the intersection of Roosevelt and Wright Avenues. Arkansas underwent decades of controversy about its prison system, ranging from graft in prison labor contracts to mistreatment of inmates. (*c.* 1905.)

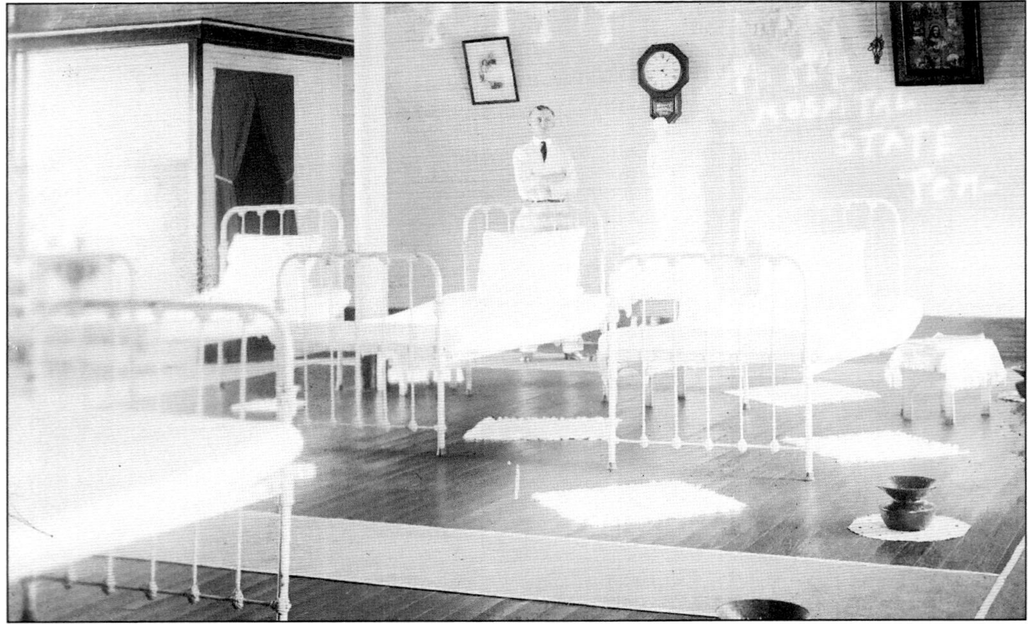

Illness of a prisoner might have placed him into one of these narrow iron beds in the state prison hospital. The bare fixtures include a religious picture on the wall and a row of spittoons, each placed on a circular mat to protect the floor. In 1910, the prison was relocated to Cummins Plantation south of Pine Bluff, to take advantage of the hundreds of acres of cotton land where the inmates could earn their keep. The prison remains on the site today. (*c.* 1905.)

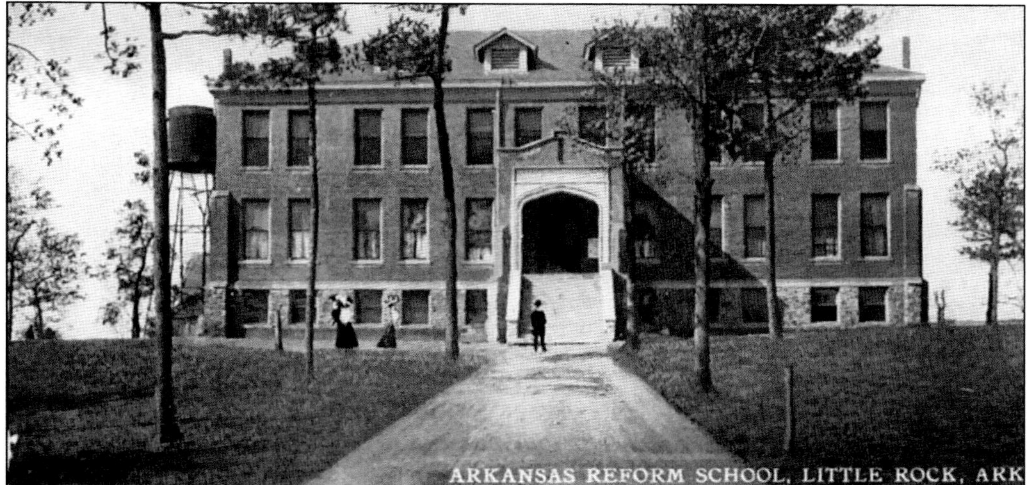

The State stepped into the domain of juvenile justice in 1905 with the construction of the Arkansas Reform School (for boys *and* girls), which was located 4 miles west of Little Rock. The cost of the facility, appropriated by the Arkansas Legislature, was $35,000 for the land and the building. The annual salary for the superintendent was set at $1,500. In 1917, the facility's name was changed to the Boy's Industrial School. (*c*. 1910.)

In an editorial on the institution, the *Arkansas Gazette* reported the following: "The Reform School is located about four miles from the end of the Highland Park car line. It consists of about 200 acres of land, which is said to be of about as poor a variety as can be found in Arkansas. Imagine what could be done by such a school of boys upon rich soil." The attitude that youthful offenders should be productive farmers led to the relocation of the boys' portion of the school to Pine Bluff in 1918, to take advantage of more productive crop land.

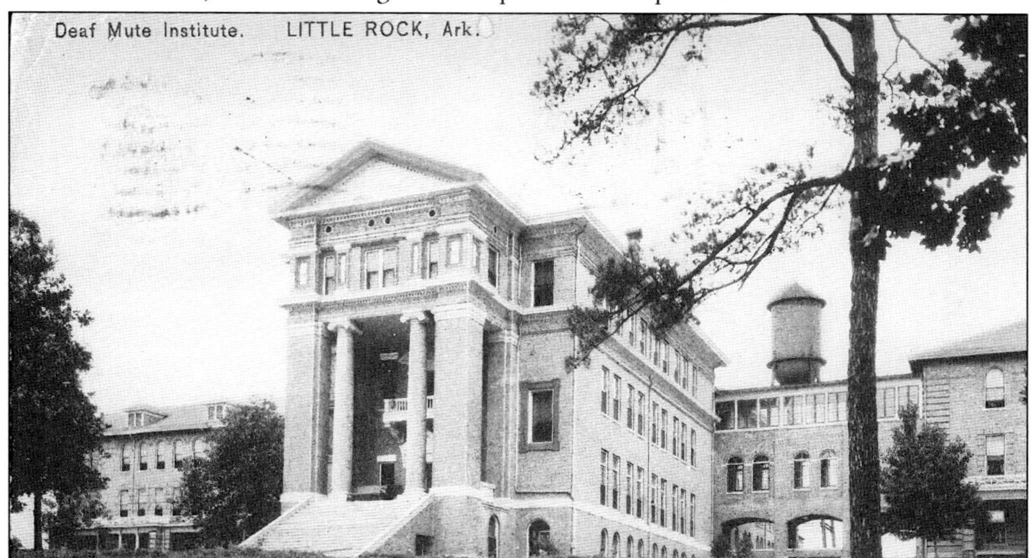

Initial efforts to run a school for deaf children failed, first at Clarksville in 1851, and then at Fort Smith in 1860. Success came when the School for Deaf Children was established at Little Rock in 1867 by Joseph Mount, a deaf man who trained at the Pennsylvania Institute for the Deaf. The State of Arkansas took over the facility in 1868, and at the turn of the century built this imposing central building on West Markham Street. The school still serves children today, but in more modern buildings on the original campus. (*c*. 1910.)

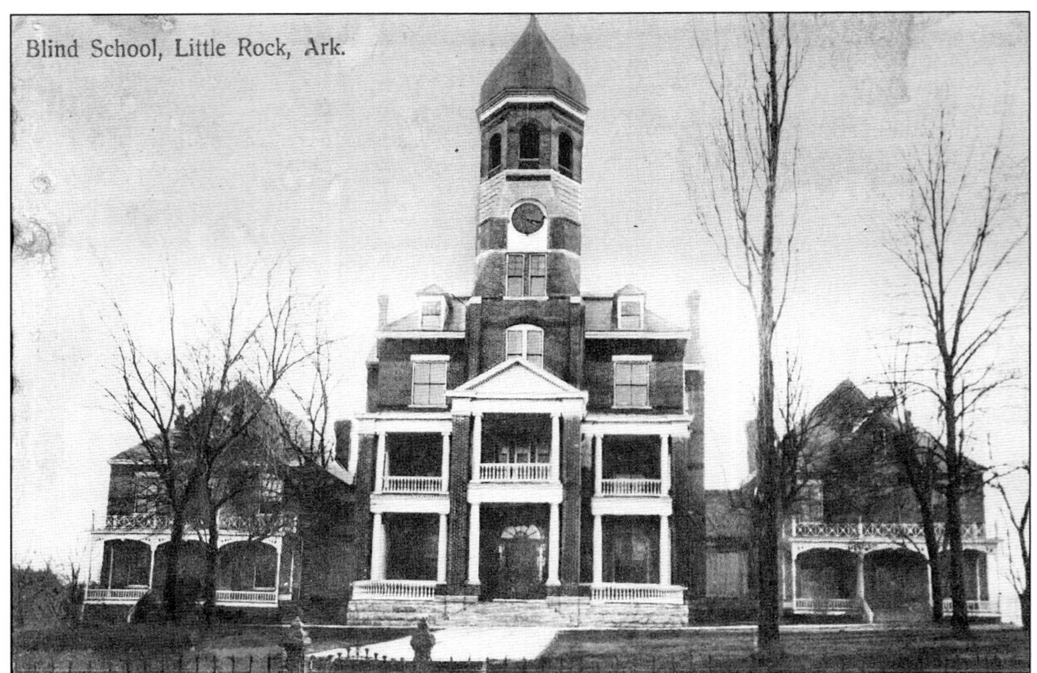

Efforts to educate the blind children of Arkansas began in 1850, when Rev. James Champlain, a blind Methodist minister, opened a school in Clarksville consisting of five pupils. After five months, the school was forced to close due to a lack of financial support in the remote location. In 1858, a blind Baptist minister, Reverend Haucke, along with local citizens, established the Arkansas Institute for the Education of the Blind in Arkadelphia. In 1868, the school was moved to Little Rock and taken over by the State. The school relocated to this building in 1885, where its distinctive center tower, a common feature of institutional buildings erected in that era, offered a panoramic view over all of Little Rock from its location in the 1800 block of Center Street. (*c.* 1905.)

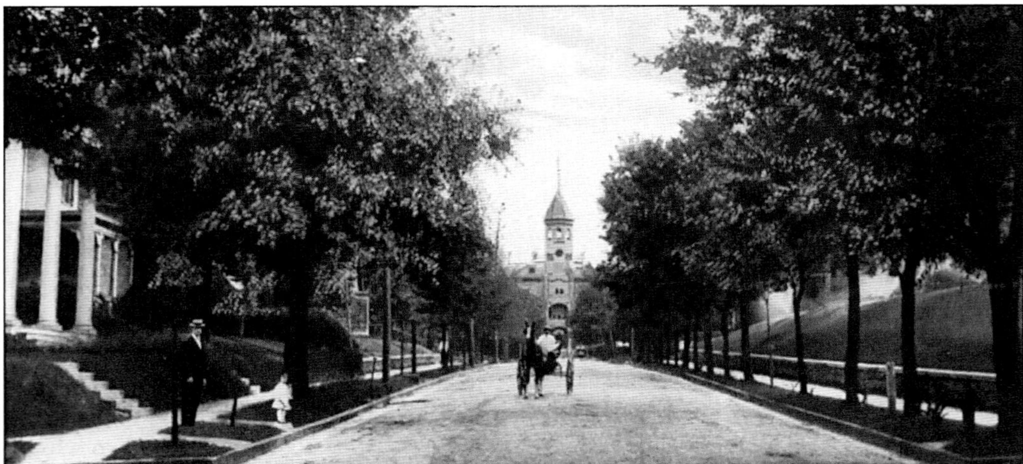

The Blind School's commanding presence at the intersection of Eighteenth and Center Streets is clearly evident from this 1908 card. The street leading up to the school was lined with large homes which still stand today. The school, however, was relocated to its present location on West Markham in 1939, and the towered building was torn down in 1948 to make way for the construction of the new governor's mansion.

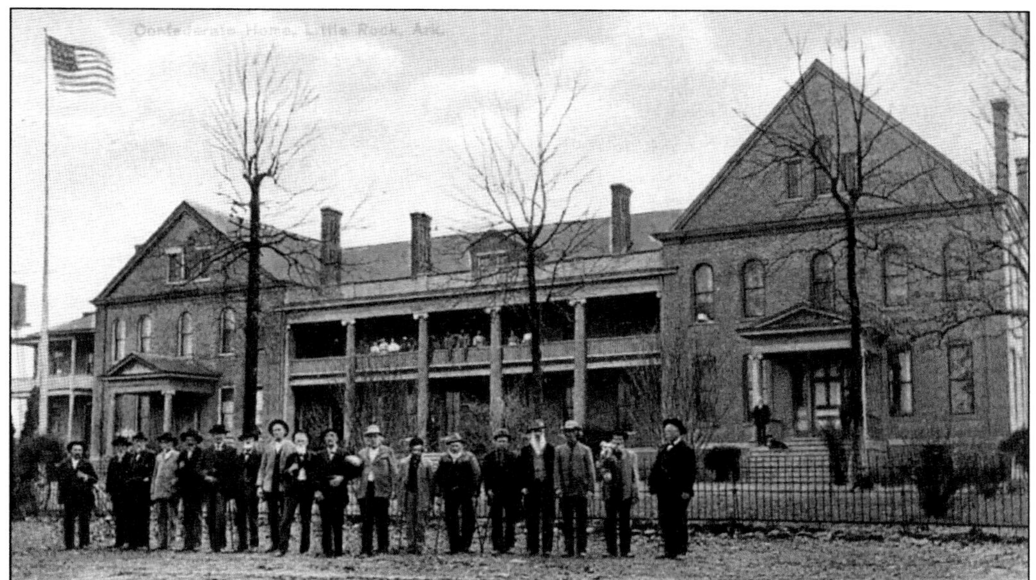

The State-funded Confederate Soldiers' Home, before which a line of grizzled veterans posed, was located in the Sweet Home community east of Little Rock. In 1890, the war had been over for 25 years, and the need to care for the aging veterans began to weigh on the conscience of the state's citizens. With a legislative appropriation, the building seen on this card was erected in 1892 and became a new state institution. As years went by, the veteran soldiers passed away, and today no trace of the building remains.

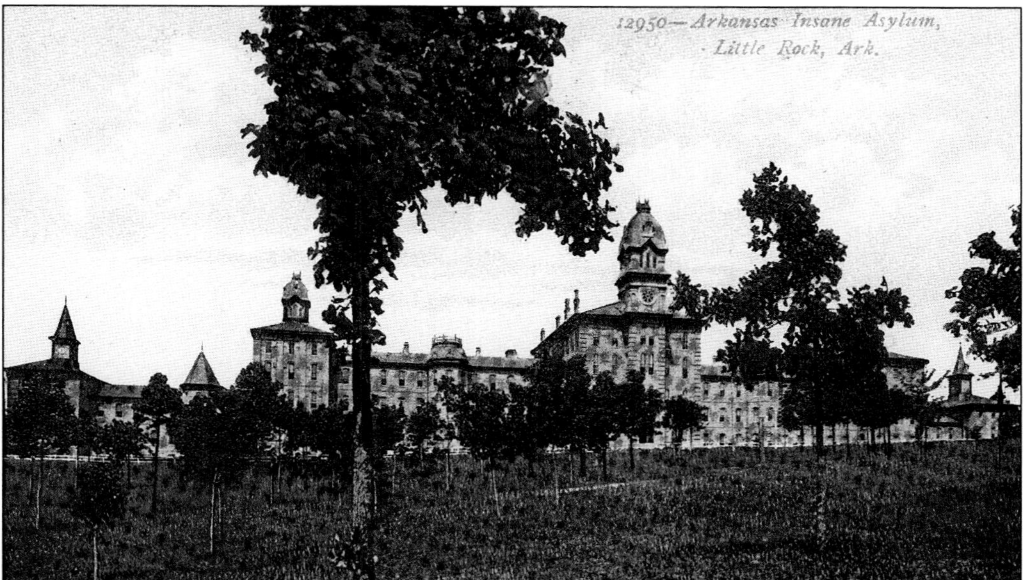

"What do you think of this hotel? I tried to get a room here and they wouldn't have me," reads the message on a 1907 card of the Arkansas Insane Asylum. The State first funded the establishment of the "Arkansas State Lunatic Asylum" at Little Rock, on what is now West Markham Street in 1873. The *Arkansas Gazette* reported in 1911," Arkansas is not only caring for all its insane, but is making splendid progress in restoring to usefulness those persons who can be cured by proper medical treatment." The buildings shown here would be replaced in the 1950s by what is now the Arkansas State Hospital.

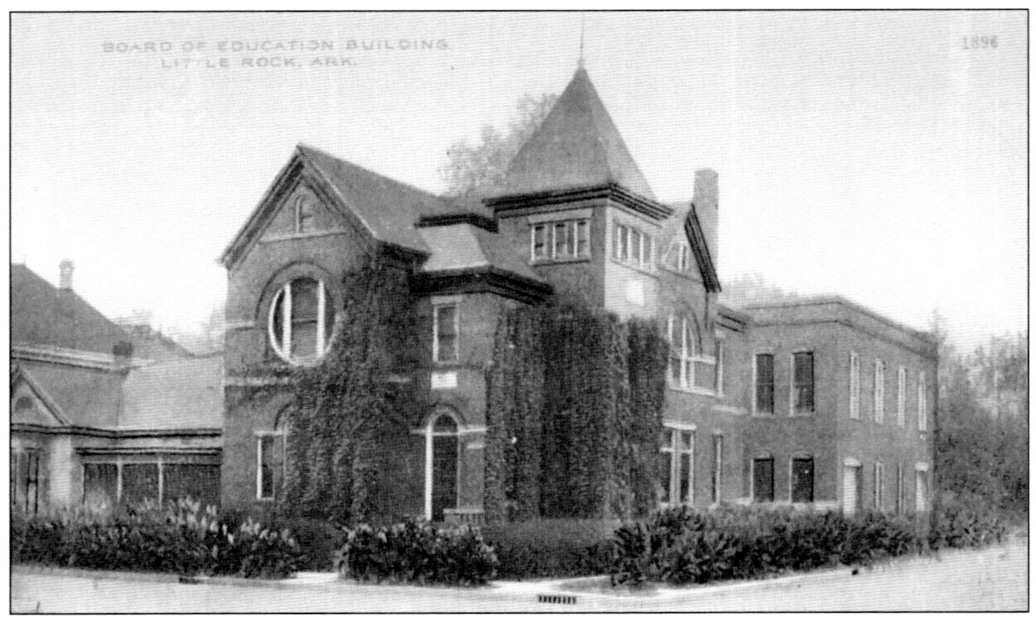

From this ivy-covered structure photographed in 1908, the state's board of education faced a formidable challenge. In 1900, the length of the school term was only 69 days per year. At the time, 170,000 Arkansas children of school age were not even enrolled in any of the state's schools; only about 40% of the state's school-age children could be counted among daily attendance figures. The average annual Arkansas schoolteacher's salary in 1900 was $166, with raises to only $273 in 1910 and to $476 by 1920.

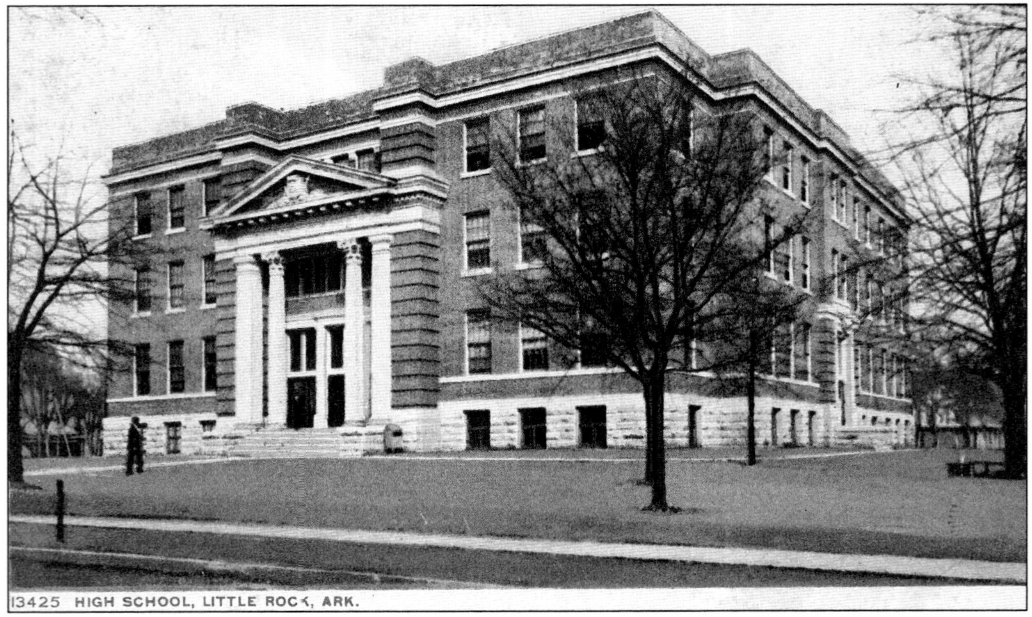

The Little Rock High School was built at the turn of the century, at the corner of Fourteenth and Scott Streets. The school served as the city's high school for white students until the opening of Central High School in 1927. In later years, the school served various other purposes, including use as an adult vocational school. As of 1997 it was closed, but continues to await a hopeful future of service. (*c.* 1910.)

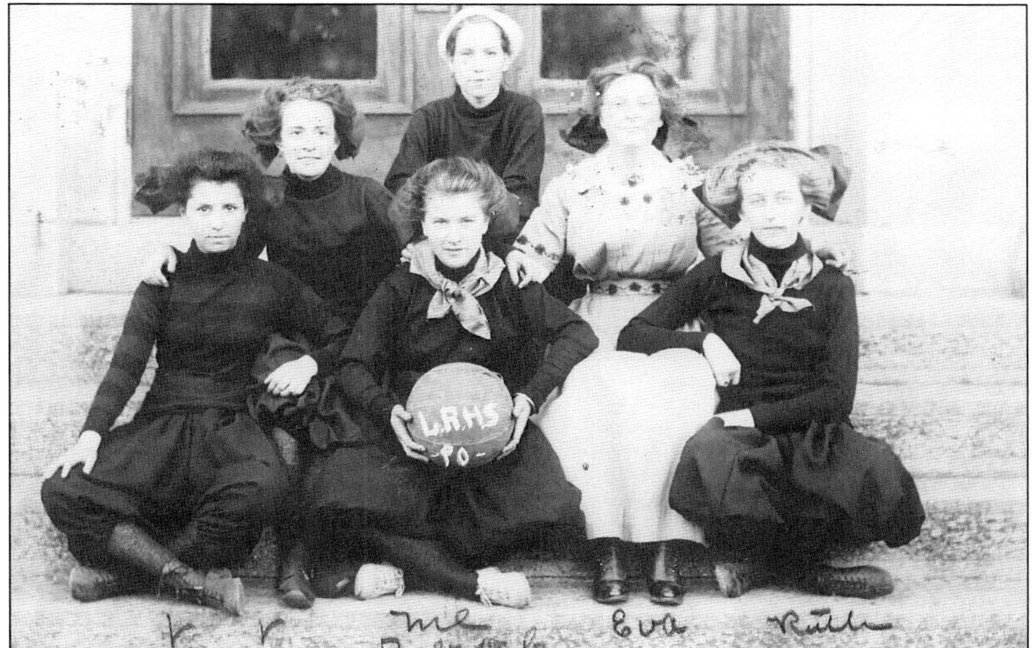

The girls of Little Rock High School could claim their share of athletes, as witnessed by the five basketball players who posed with their coach on the front steps of the school. In a message sent to Hot Springs in 1909, one of the girls wrote, "What do you think of this picture? Isn't it queer looking? Gee! You seem to be in an awful big hurry to answer that letter, am beginning to think something is about to happen."

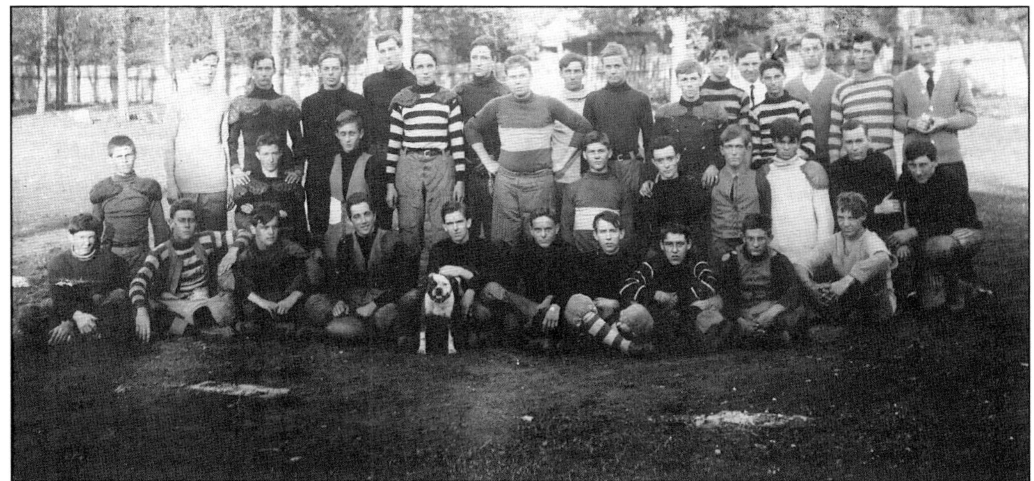

The boys' football team posed with what seems to have been a mascot bulldog. The 1908 message written to an Atlanta cousin was from an aspiring future player who wrote, "This is the team I hope to make. Why don't you write? Don't be so lazy."

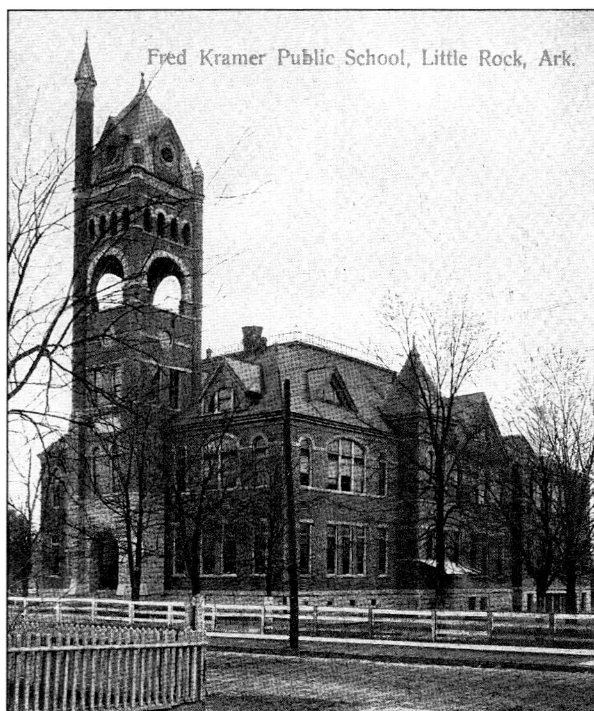

The Fred Kramer School was erected in 1895 on Sherman Street between Seventh and Eighth Streets. The distinctive tower would be removed some 50 years later, and the entire building would teeter on the brink of demolition as it sat boarded and decaying for much of the 1980s and 90s. This oldest surviving public school building in Little Rock was saved and restored as a resident artists' gallery in 1997. (*c.* 1908.)

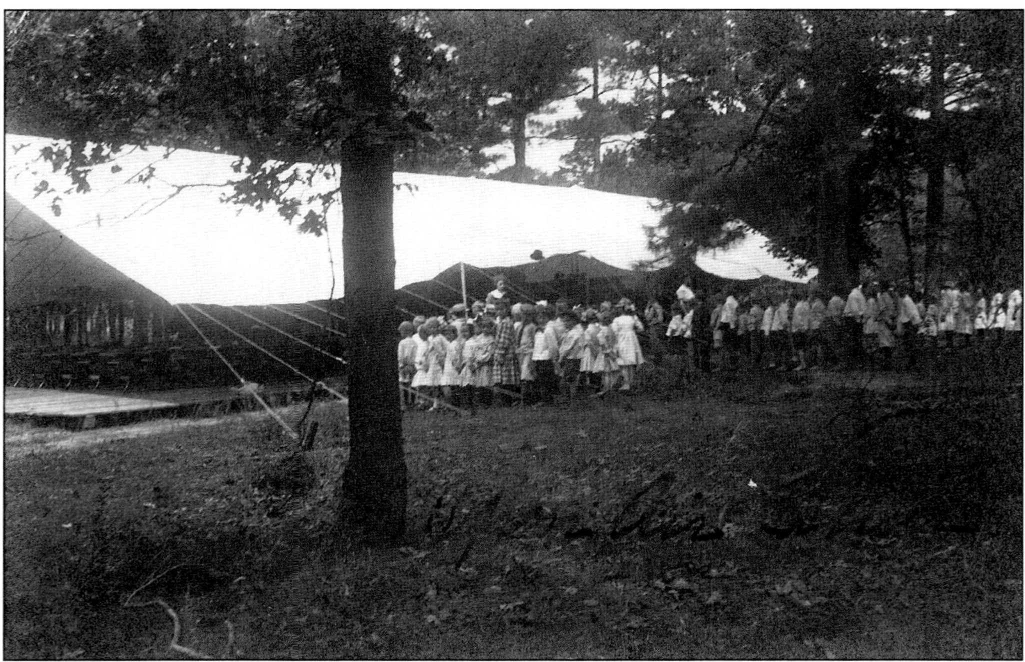

"Open air school" is penned on the front of this 1911 card of a group of children and their teachers preparing to hold class under a large tent. The back of the card reads, "The teachers of the William Woodruff School will hold an evening with the patrons Friday 8 to 10 pm. Will be delighted to have you all with us. The Prin." Now Woodruff Elementary, named for the founder of the *Arkansas Gazette*, the school still stands on West Seventh Street, and continues to educate the children of Little Rock.

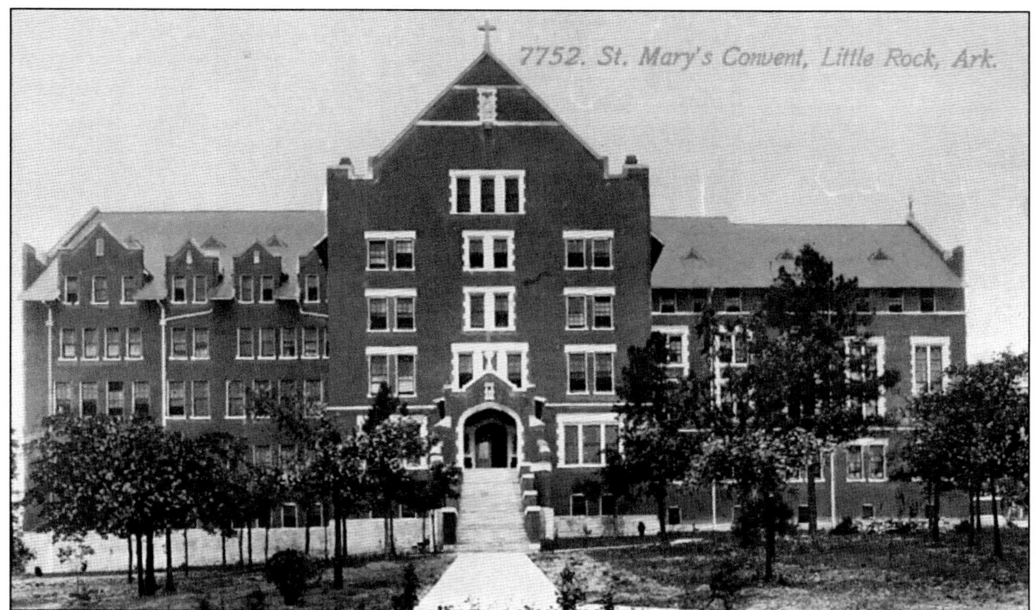

Little Rock's small but growing Catholic population got a boost in 1904 when the Sisters of Mercy decided to relocate their convent and girls' school to what is now the corner of Kavanuagh and Van Buren Streets. The school building was a Little Rock landmark for 75 years. It was removed to make way for a student parking lot in the late 1980s. (*c.* 1910.)

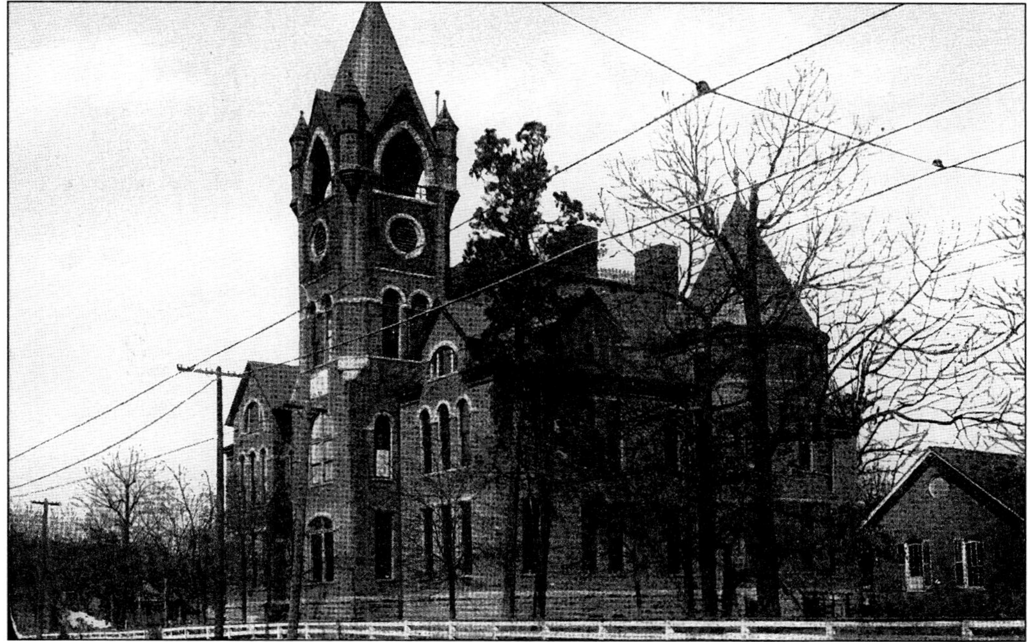

"Am writing this on the front porch of the Hotel Astor at Benton, Ark. 20 miles south of Little Rock and just as I looked up I saw three hogs promenading on the hotel lawn. Evidently this is great country for hogs." Peabody Public School, the city's first brick school building, was built in 1887 on Capitol Avenue. It was named for philanthropist George Peabody, who donated $2 million to advance education in the South. The structure was torn down in the 1950s to make way for a new federal building. (*c.* 1909.)

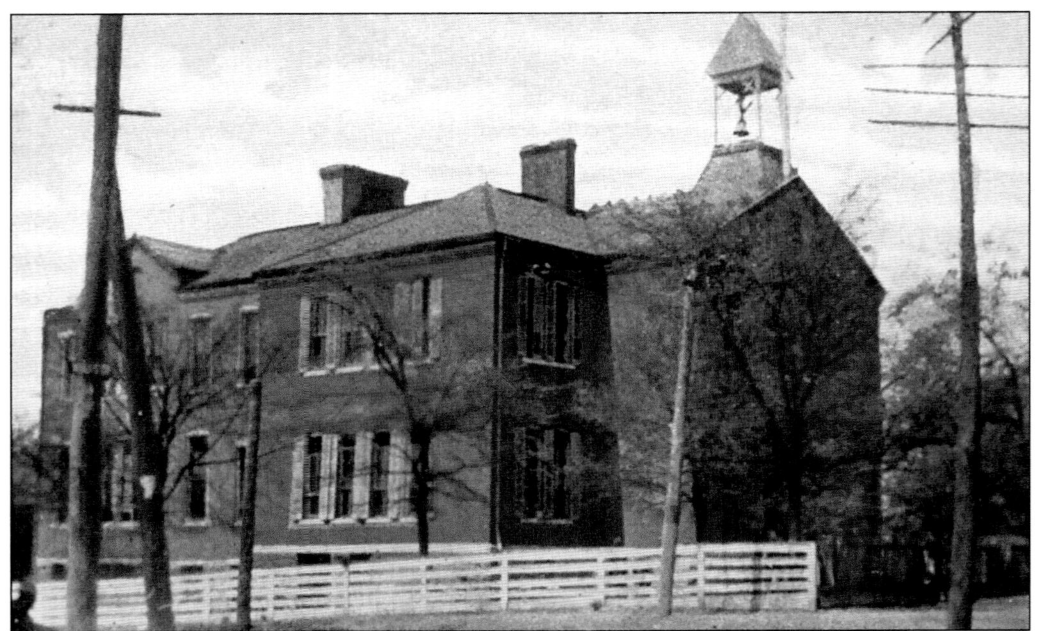

In comparison to the larger, more impressive towered schools for the white children of Little Rock, the small bell-topped Capitol Hill School served many of the city's black children. The school was located at Thirteenth and Wolfe Streets, behind what is now Arkansas Children's Hospital. A fire destroyed the building in 1966. (*c.* 1910.)

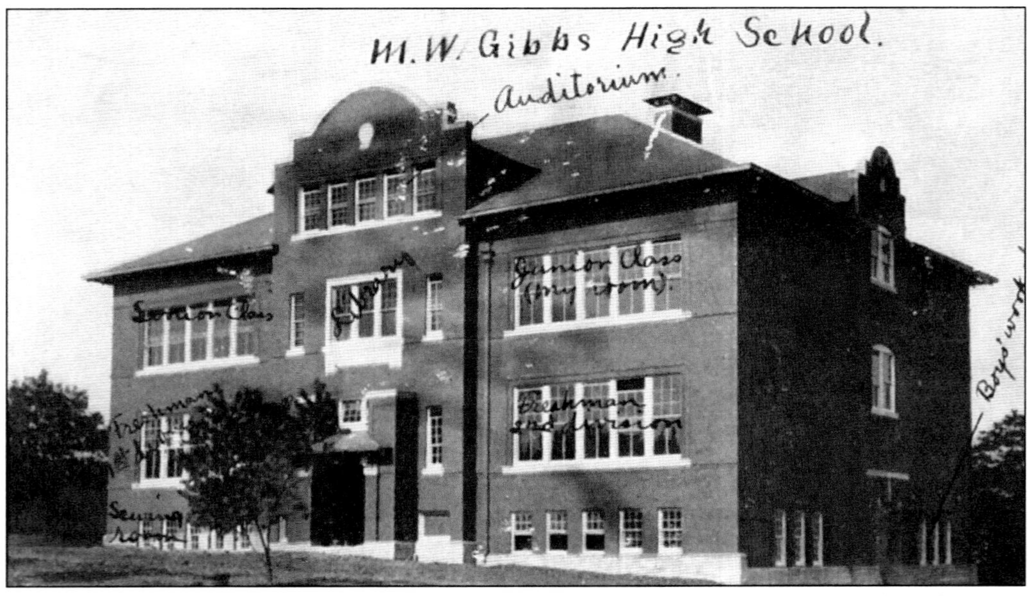

Little Rock's W.W. Gibbs High School, which was once located at Eighteenth and Ringo Streets, provided an education for the black children of the area. One of these students, junior Joe Elsberry, mailed this 1909 card to his aunt Lalla. Young Joe's penned notes on the card reflect how compact the school was; he labeled the locations of the auditorium, library, workshop, classrooms, and dining room. The school was razed years ago, and a much more modern Gibbs School operates today for elementary children of all races on West Sixteenth Street.

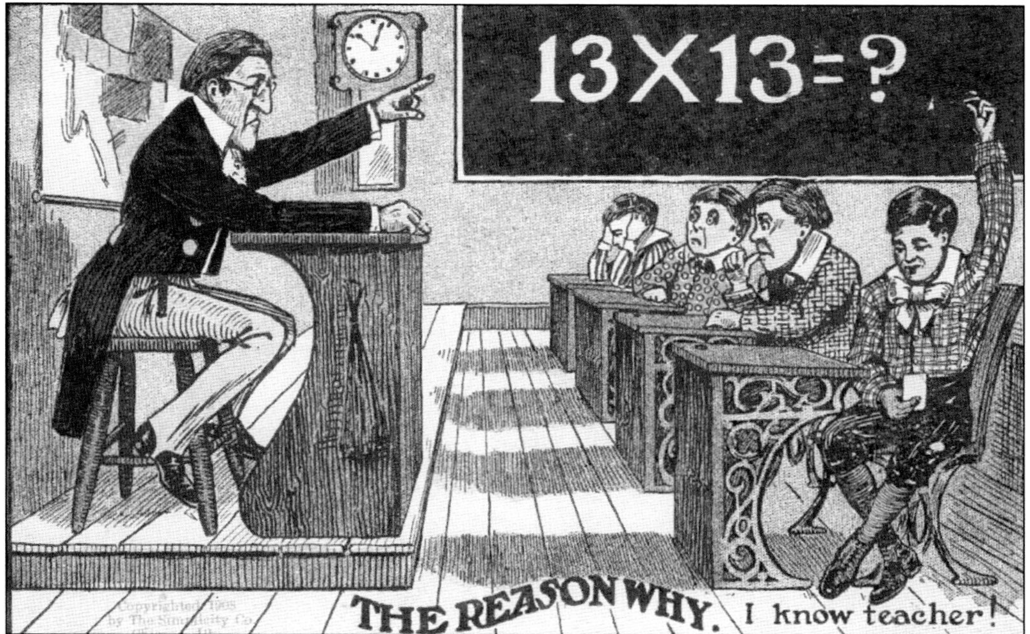

Coy and Miller, a pool hall and cigar store located at 215 West Second Street, printed this very rare postcard in 1908 as a promotional tool. The card is actually made in pocket style and holds a pull-out "lightning multiplier" card intended to help students with their multiplication tables. This convenient calculator listed equations through 25 x 50=1250. How teachers and parents viewed such a device, published by a business promoting cigars and pool, can only be surmised.

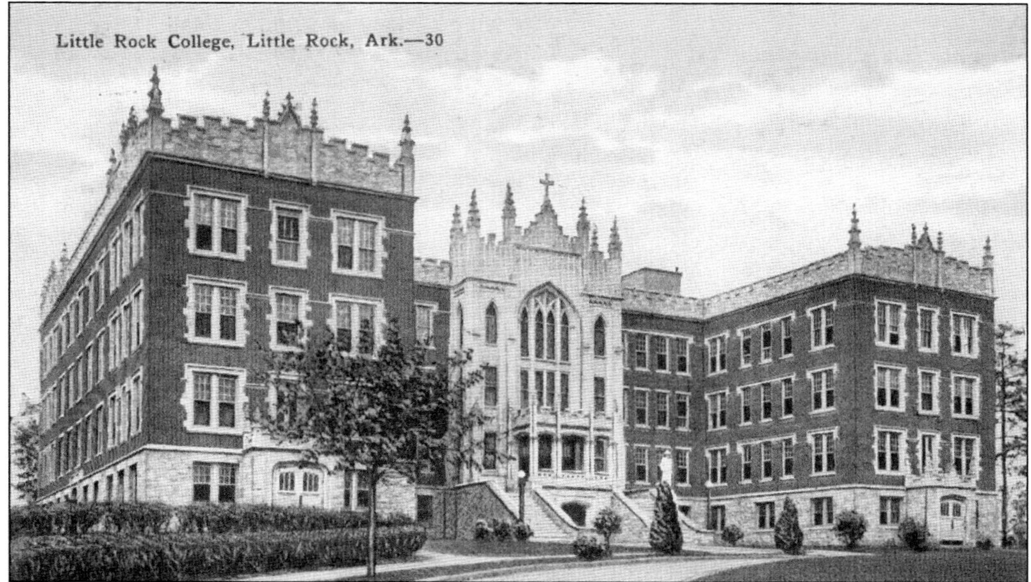

Under the leadership of Bishop John Morris, the Catholic Diocese opened Little Rock College, initially on State Street, in 1908. An increase in enrollment led to a move in 1916 to this building, shared for a time with the Seminary of St. John the Baptist. With the coming of WW I, the campus was home to a large ROTC program. By 1919, the college offered programs in pre-med and pharmacy. The Great Depression led to the closing of the college in 1930. The building still serves today, housing offices for the Diocese of Little Rock.

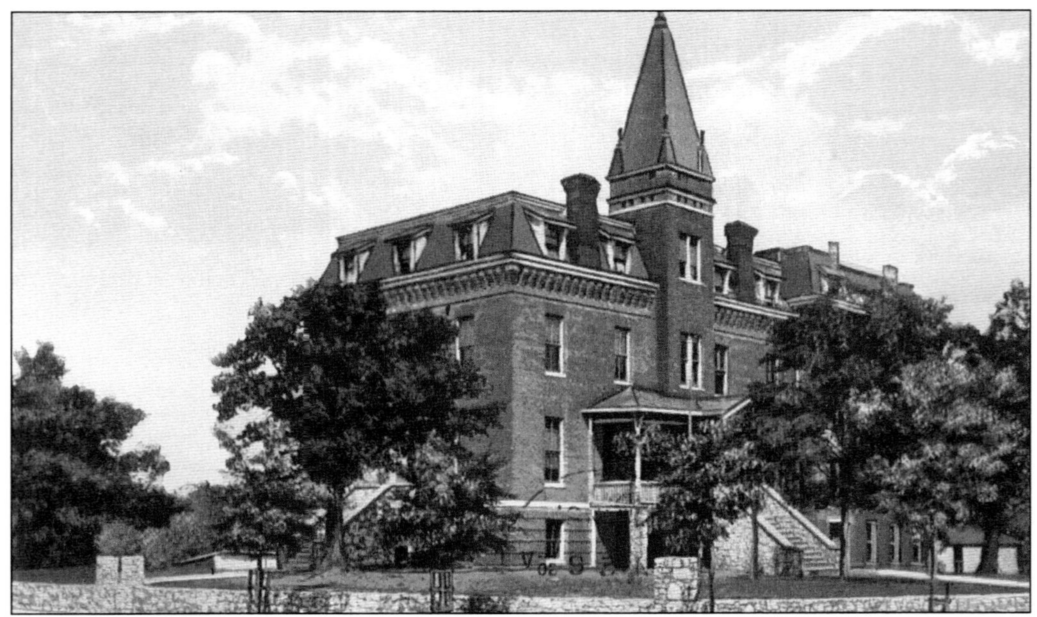

Philander Smith College, a historical black school, had its start in 1866, through the assistance of the Methodist Episcopal Church and its founding of the Freedman's Aid Society. Initially called the Walden Seminary, the school became Philander Smith College in 1883, about the time this building was erected. The construction of the building was made possible by a gift from the widow of Mr. Smith, a native of Chicago. Now located on Thirteenth and State Streets, the school still serves today, more than a century after its founding.

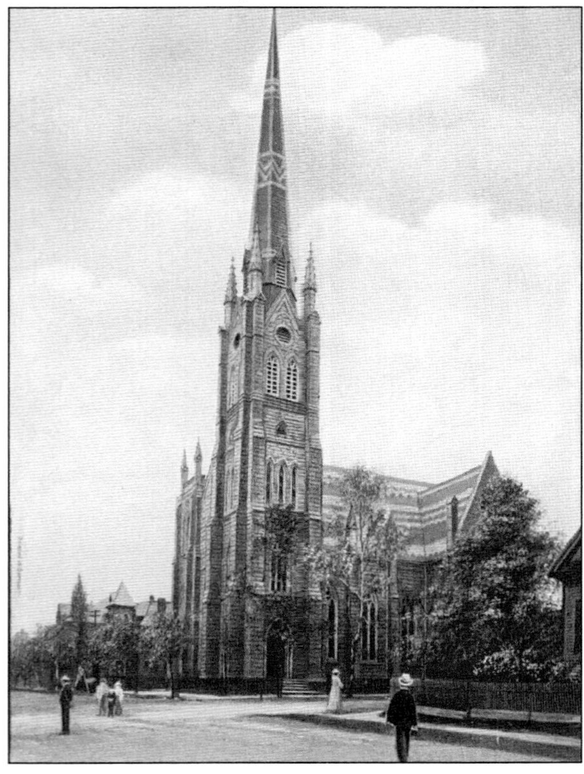

In 1878, the cornerstone was laid for St. Andrew's Cathedral at Seventh and Louisiana Streets; the building was constructed of local blue granite. When the cathedral was dedicated three years later, it still lacked a spire, a condition which would not be remedied until 1887. One story was that Bishop Edward Fitzgerald delayed the erection of the steeple while he monitored the construction of the Masonic Temple going up nearby at Fifth and Main Streets because he wanted to make sure that the steeple on the Catholic cathedral was taller—as indeed it was when the structure was finally completed. A report in the *Arkansas Gazette* at the time noted that the steeple compared equally to the height of the Washington Monument, then the tallest man-made structure in the nation.(*c.* 1905.)

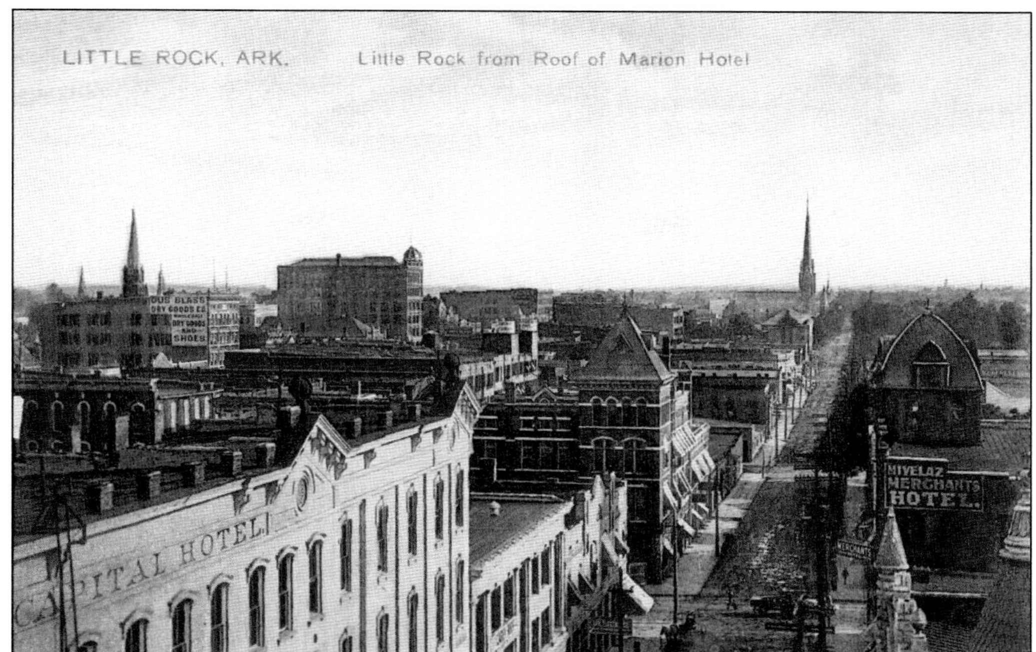

"You can see the Masonic Temple, Catholic Cathedral and some other churches which we have. The spire to the left is Christ Episcopal." This message was on the back of a 1905 view, most likely taken from atop the Hotel Marion, looking over the Capital Hotel toward the church spires of the Little Rock skyline.

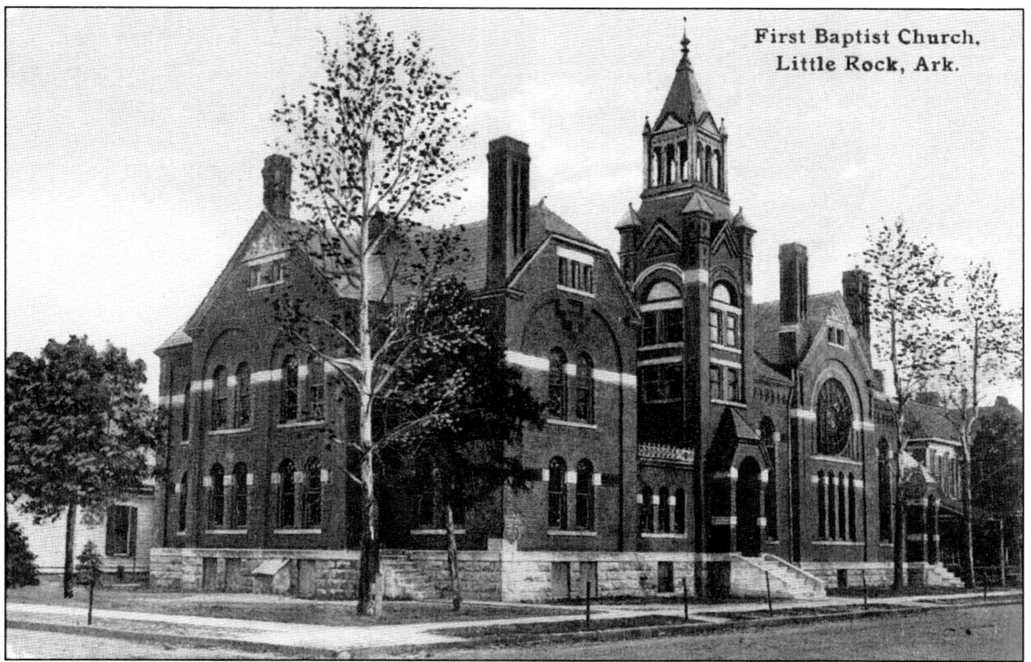

"I feared you were suffering greatly from rheumatism," was the message sent to Virginia on the back of a 1911 view of First Baptist Church. The church was erected in 1889 at Twelfth and Louisiana Streets. It was removed and replaced with a new building sometime around 1940; in the 1970s, the congregation left downtown and relocated to western Little Rock.

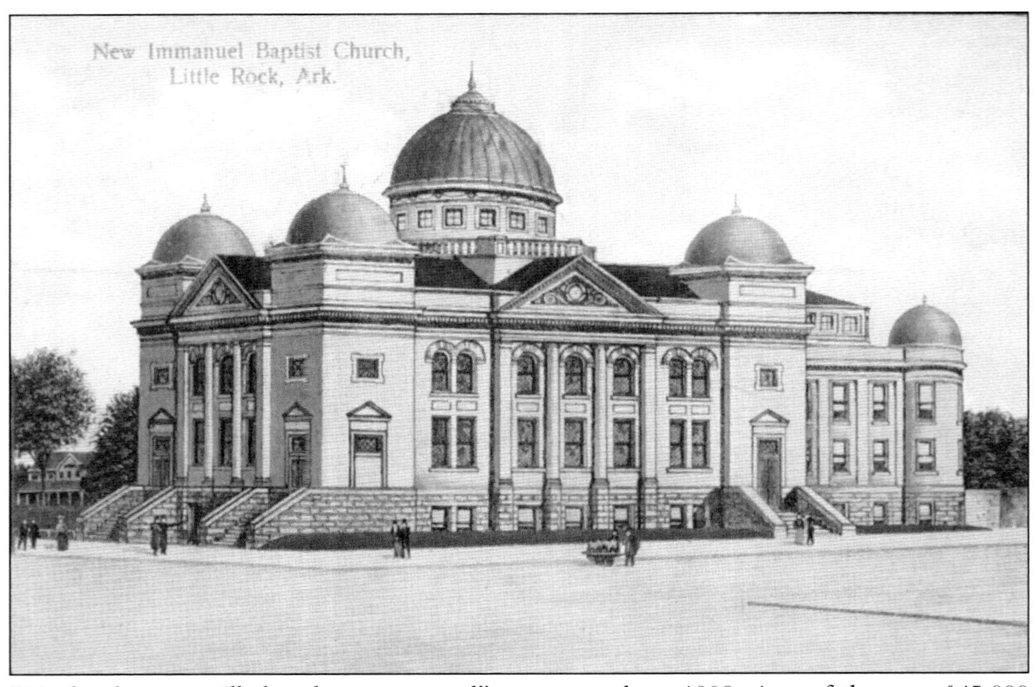

"My headquarters till the plate was passed" was penned on 1908 view of the new $45,000 Immanuel Baptist Church at Tenth and Bishop Streets. The grand church was largely destroyed by a 1926 fire and replaced by the present-day Immanuel Baptist Church, which claimed among its members Arkansas Governor Bill Clinton prior to his election as president in 1992.

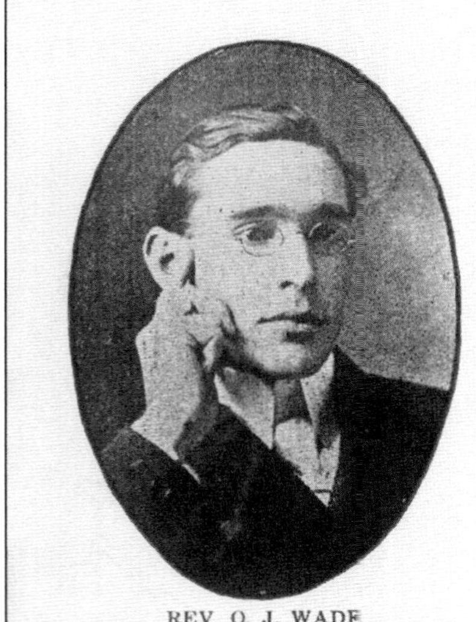

REV. O. J. WADE
PASTOR IMMANUEL BAPTIST CHURCH
LITTLE ROCK, ARKANSAS

DEACONS

W. E. BERTHE
T. H. DUGGER
D. F. DOBBINS
J. H. ESTES
W. S. FARMER
J. F. HAMMETT
I. H. KING
C. H. MCGUIRE
J. H. REYNOLDS
S. P. VAUGHTER

WOMEN'S SOCIETIES

Circle No. 1, MRS. M. B. LOTT
Circle No. 2, MRS. J. D. BRUMBELOW
Circle No. 3, MRS. J. A. WOODALL
Circle No. 4, MRS. W. E. BERTHE
President Ladies Aid Society, MRS. O. J. WADE.
Girls Aid and Sunbeam Societies.

Sunday School Superintendent, W. E. BERTHE

Immanuel Baptist Church used this 1907 card to share the names of its deacons and Women's Societies, including the Ladies Aid Society, Girls Aid, and Sunbeam Societies. Pictured, looking quite reflective, is Rev. O.J. Wade, the congregation's pastor.

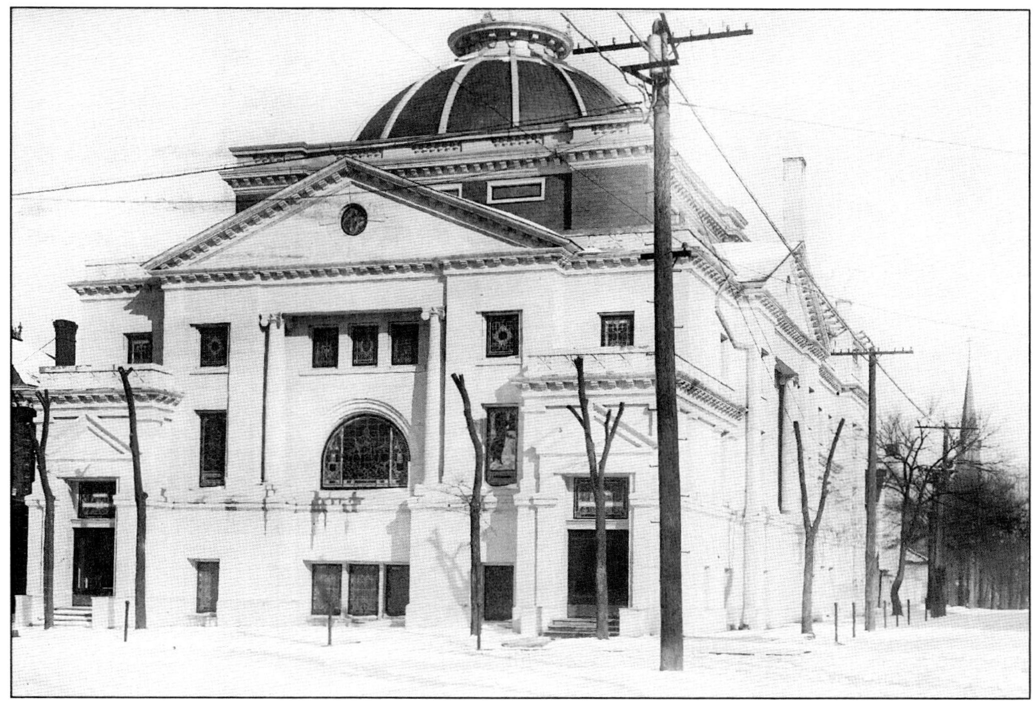

Second Baptist Church members erected this marble-laden, domed sanctuary at the turn of the century on the northeast corner of Seventh and Scott Streets. The church was torn down in the 1950s and a new sanctuary was built nearby. The congregation continues to thrive in downtown Little Rock. (*c.* 1910.)

The First Presbyterian Church, founded in Little Rock in 1828, may be the oldest continuously functioning church in the city today. The building shown on this 1908 card was built in 1868 at the corner of Fifth and Scott Streets, and it was the first church erected after the Civil War. Its architectural design set a style for others to emulate. The building on the left is the back of the Masonic Temple. The church itself is long gone; a newer replacement serves at a different location. The site of this view is now a parking lot.

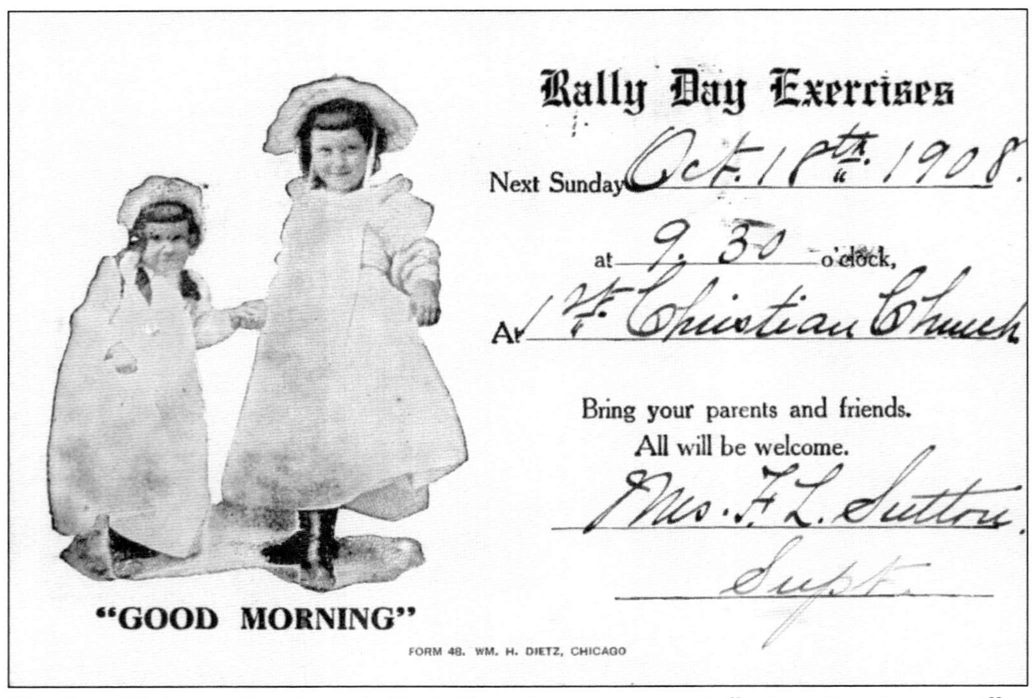

The First Christian Church used this 1908 card to announce Rally Day Exercises, an effort planned to boost attendance at Sunday school and worship services. This card was obviously directed at children, with the call to "bring your parents" to church.

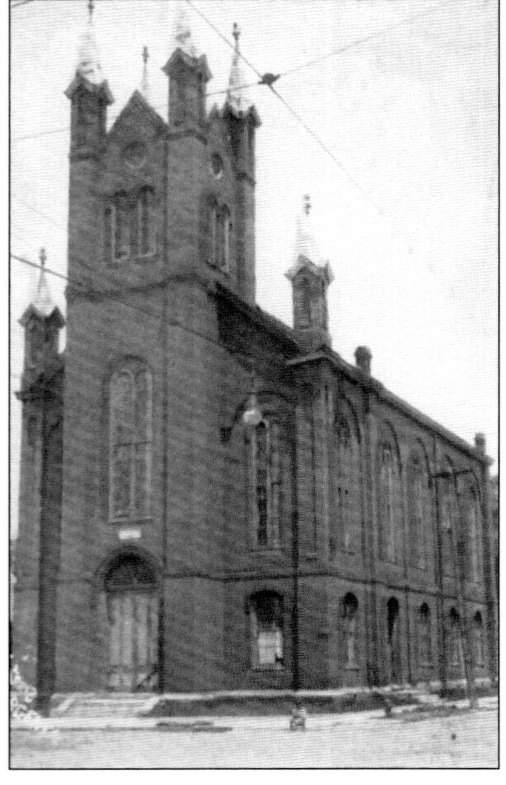

Although not as prevalent on postcards, churches were an integral part of Little Rock's black community in the early years of the century. Perhaps the most prominent was Bethel A.M.E., located at Ninth and Broadway Streets. What is presently Shorter College, a historical black college located in North Little Rock, began as the Bethel Institute in this building in 1887. The building is long gone, but the congregation relocated to a site on Izard Street. (*c.* 1909.)

Christ Episcopal Church was built in 1886 at the corner of Fifth and Scott Streets and added its soaring steeple to the others reaching for the skies above Little Rock. The sender of this 1908 card exhibited a sense of theological humor, having drawn a stick man diving from the steeple into a washtub and adding, "This will make him a good Baptist." The church was destroyed by fire in 1938 and was replaced by a new church building near the same site.

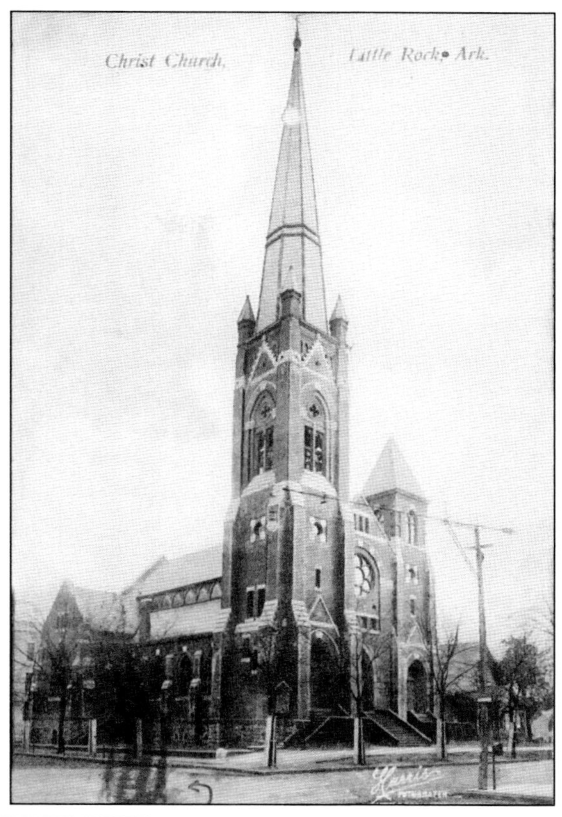

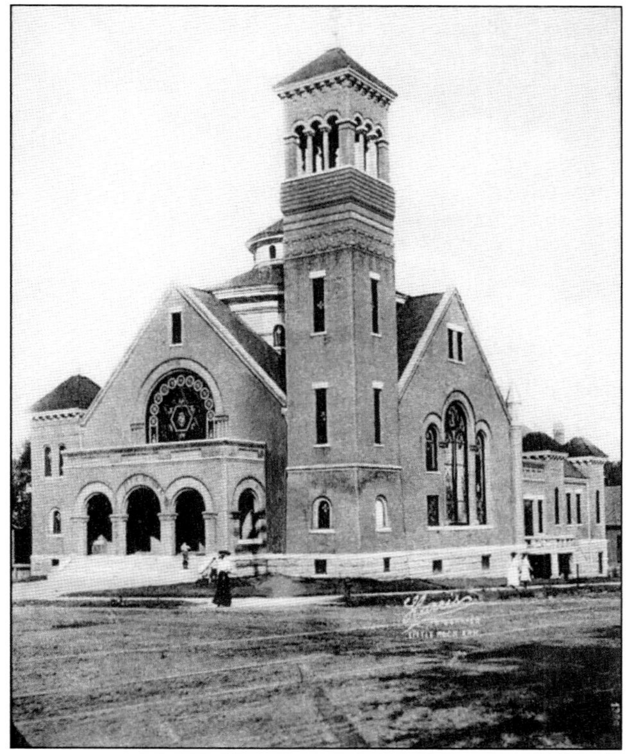

In 1866, a group of Jewish Civil War veterans formed the Temple B'nai Israel congregation. This distinctive temple was erected in 1897 at the corner of Fifth and Broadway Streets, to replace a smaller temple located on Center Street. The Romanesque-style building served until 1972, when it was demolished to make way for the 30-story First Commercial Bank building. The congregation relocated to a modern house of worship in west Little Rock. (*c.* 1905.)

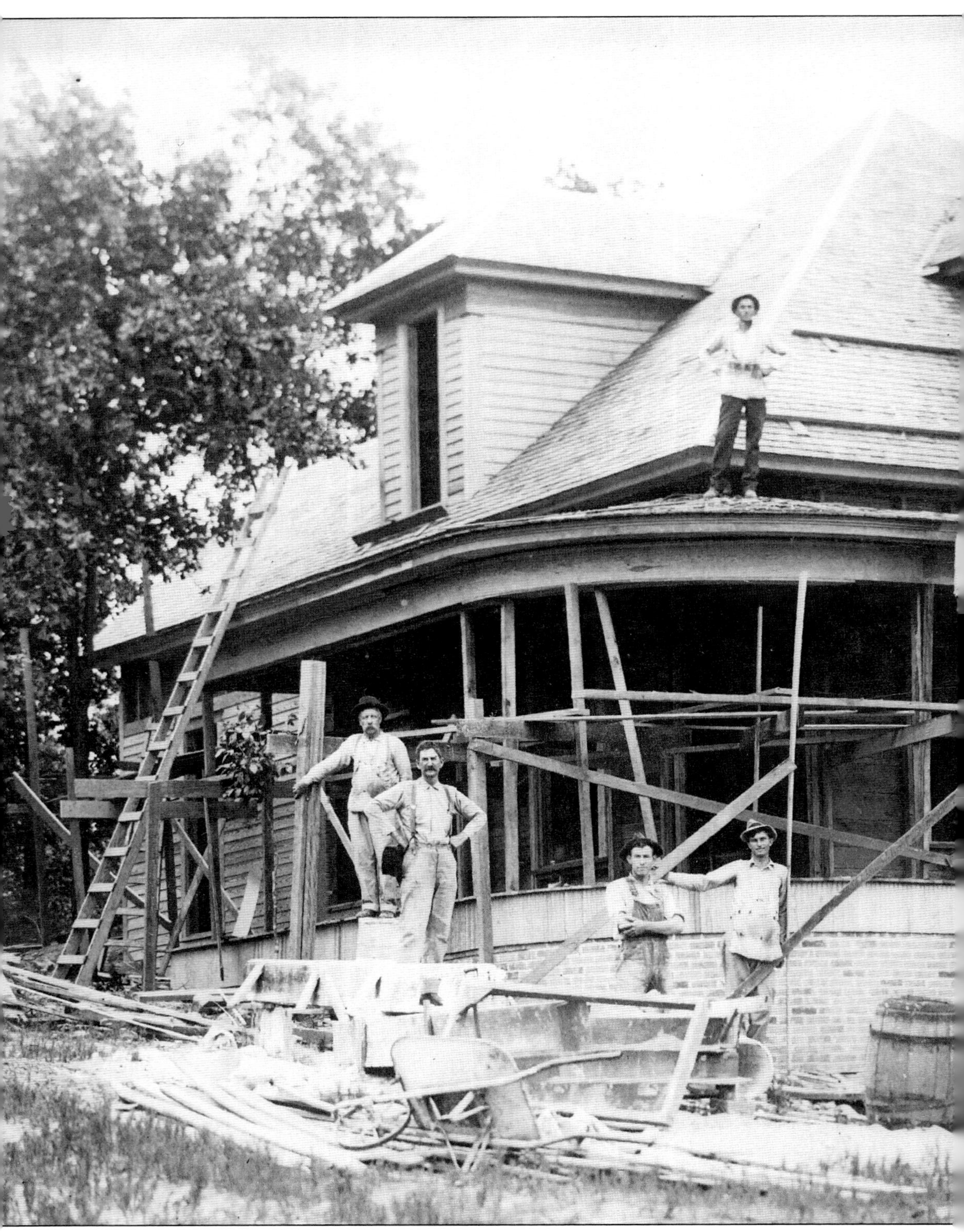

The relatively modest home of a Little Rock family was photographed during its construction at 1424 West Fourth Street. The labor-intensive nature of construction in the era before power tools

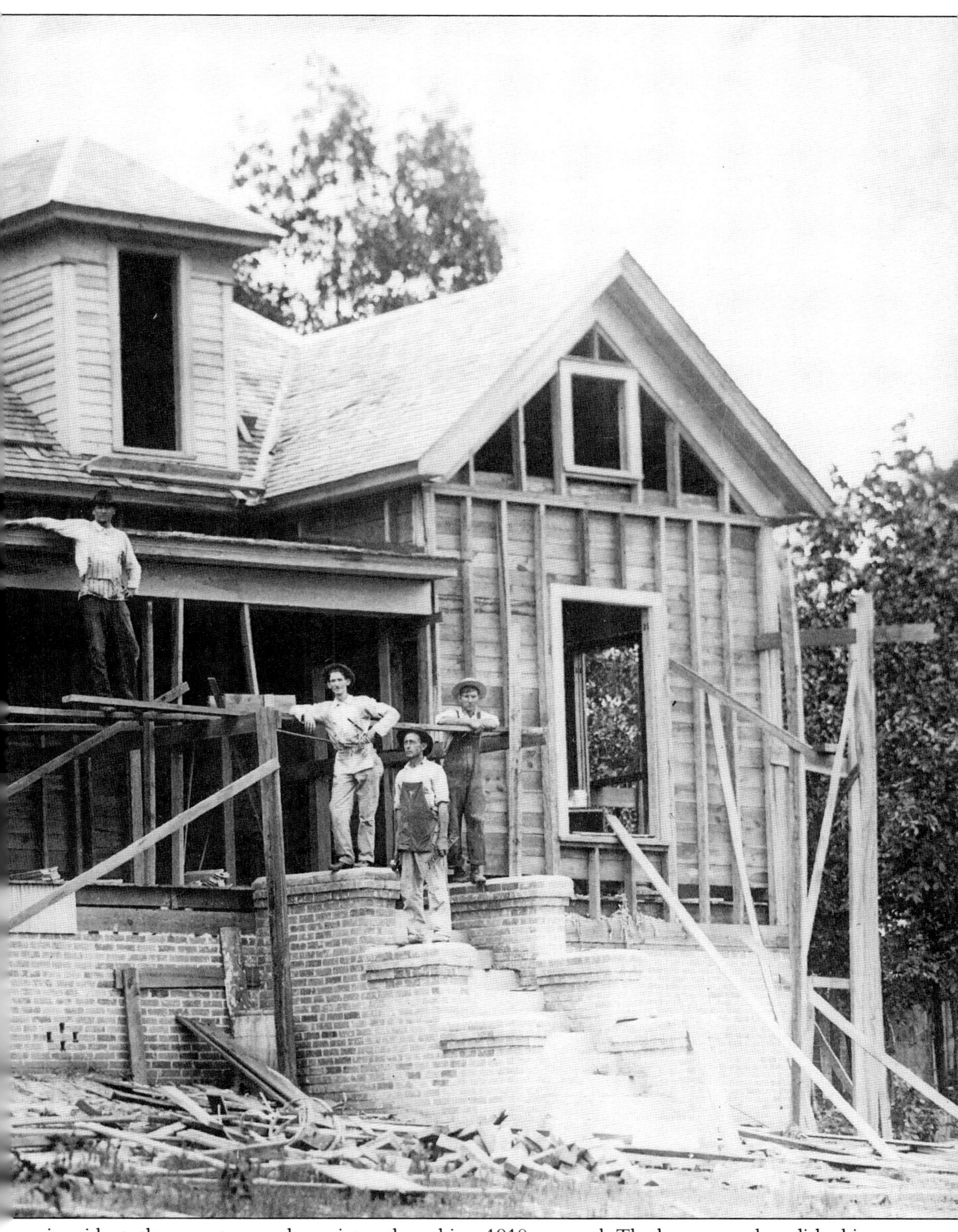

is evident; there are ten workers pictured on this *c.* 1910 postcard. The house was demolished in the 1960s.

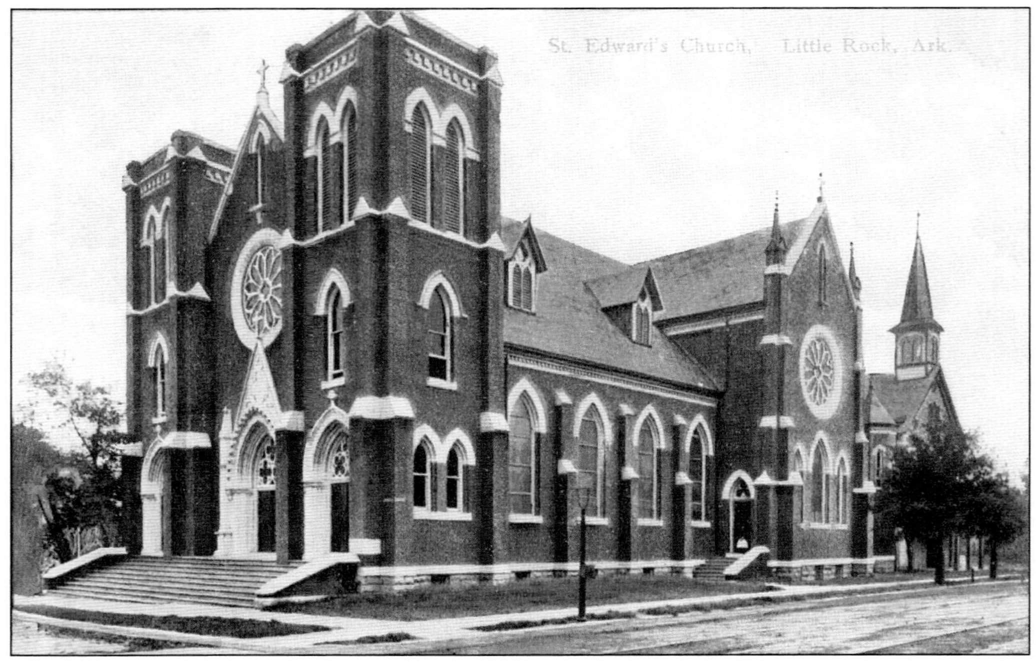

St. Edward's Catholic Church was formed in 1885 to serve the growing German Catholic population. The parish's first wooden frame church building was replaced by this structure, built between 1901 and 1905 at a cost of $114,000. It still serves today at Ninth and Sherman Streets, its congregation bolstered by an outreach to the city's Hispanic population. (*c.* 1910.)

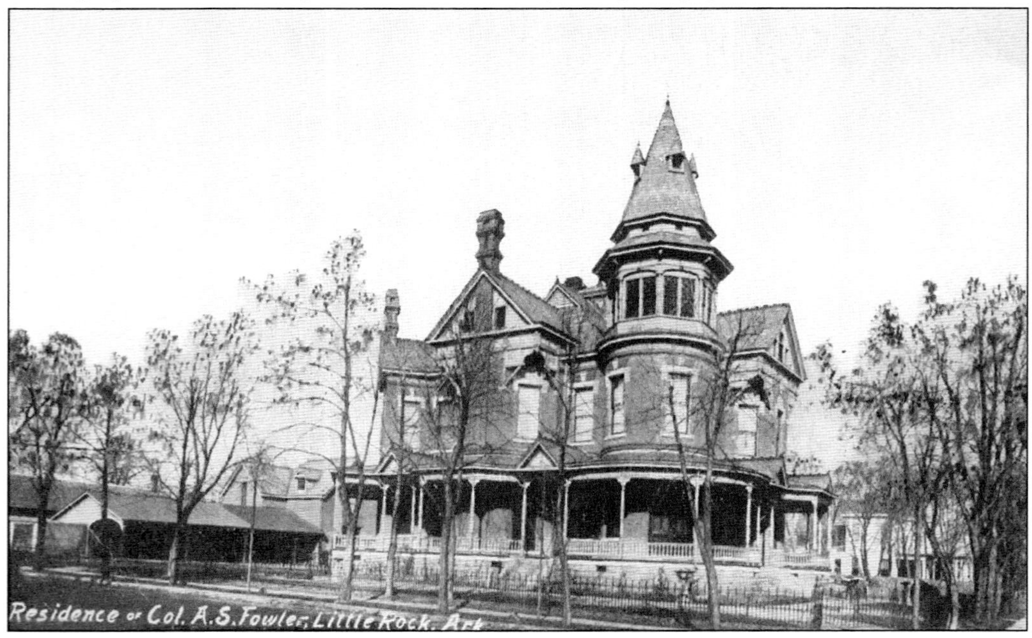

James H. Hornibrook erected this magnificent Queen Anne–style house at the corner of Twenty-second and Louisiana Streets in 1888. In 1890, after returning from a party he hosted at his saloon, Mr. Hornibrook suffered a stroke and was found dead at his front gate by a butcher's delivery boy. The home later became the home of Col. and Mrs. Asbury Fowler. Today, after having housed various businesses, including a nursing home, it stands restored. (*c.* 1905.)

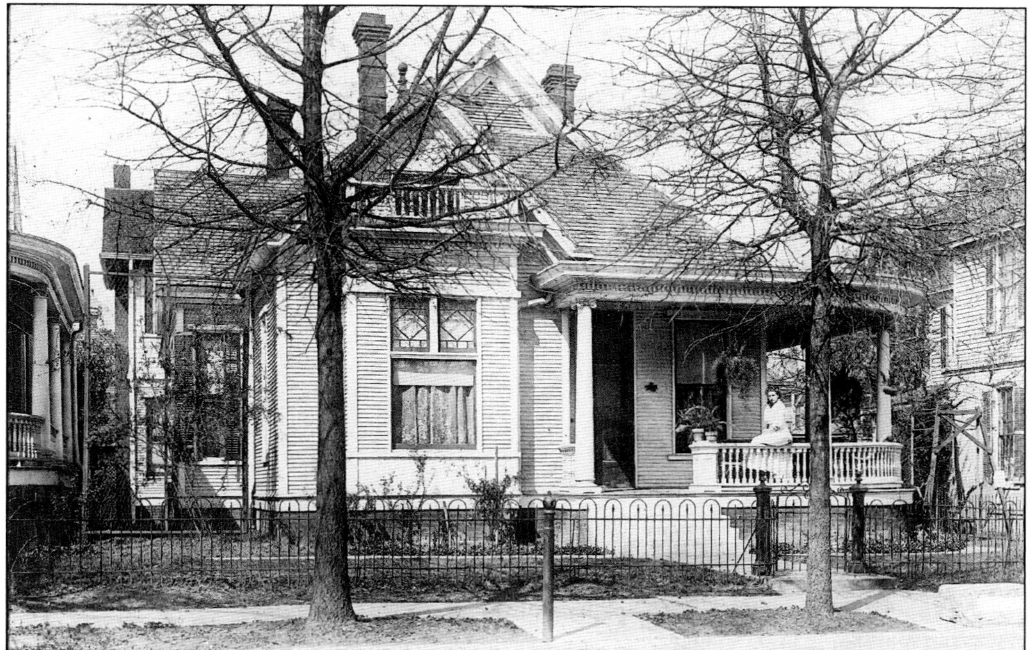

"Here is your cousin setting [*sic*] on the rail looking for the postman with a letter from you—but he cometh not! Are you so busy eating you have no time to write?" The woman sending this 1911 card to Ohio is actually in the photo; the house is restored and still stands today near the Arkansas Governor's Mansion.

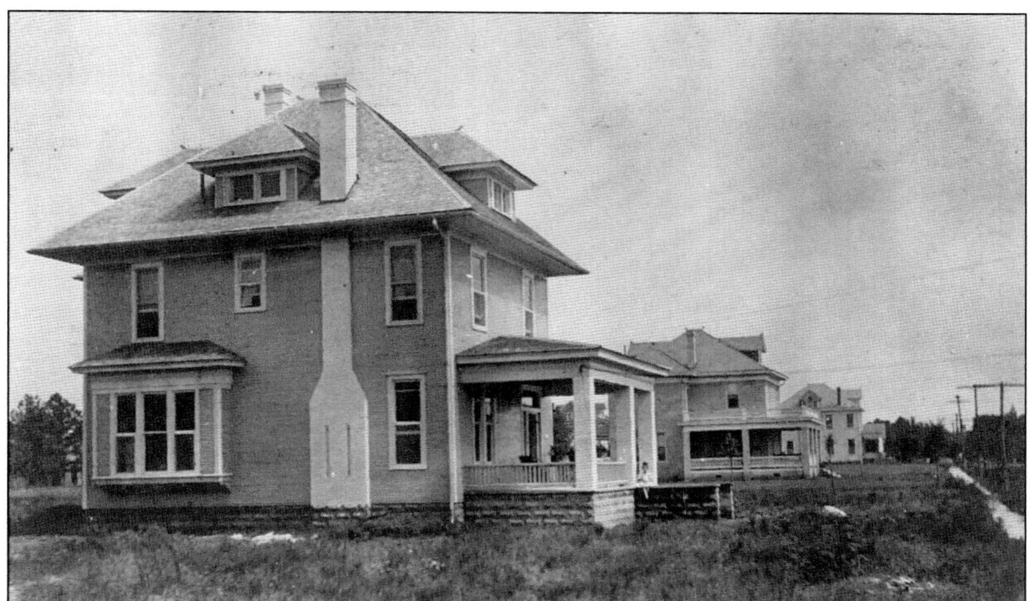

"We moved in three weeks ago and are so comfortable we do not object to a summer in Arkansas. Lawn will look better in six months," wrote a proud new homeowner in the 2300 block of Battery Street in 1909. The large house with multiple fireplaces was one of a line of similar homes erected together, seen stretching down the block. Today the homes still stand amidst tall trees, though some are in a state of disrepair brought on by the shift of the city's population to distant suburbs.

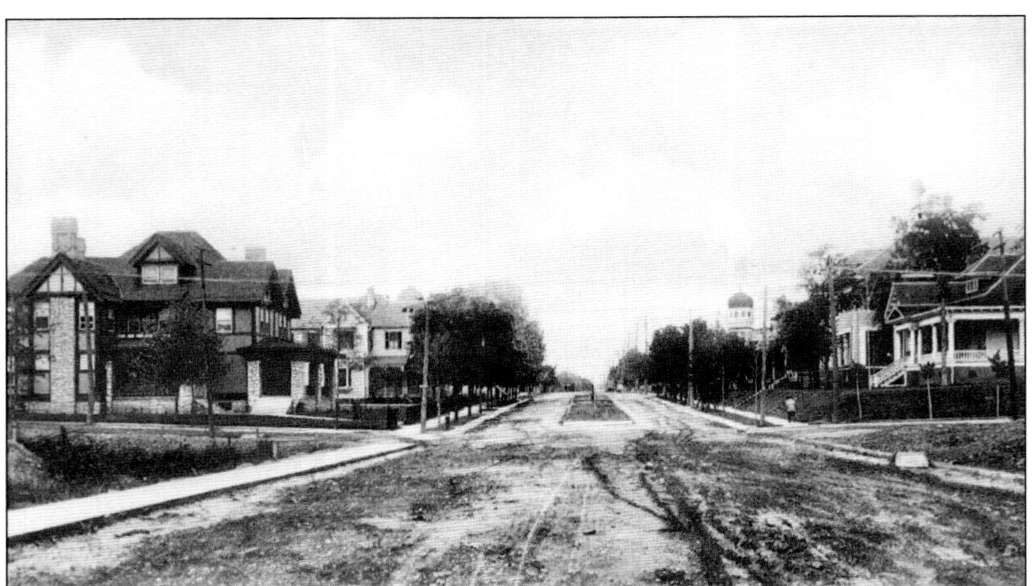

These two cards offer a look at what may have been Little Rock's most stately boulevard of homes. Broadway stretched for more than 20 blocks, running parallel to Main Street before intersecting Markham to meet the Arkansas River near city hall. The first card (above) reflects huge homes recently built on a wide (but still muddy) street in 1905. By the time the second card (below) was mailed in 1908, the street's island had been landscaped and numerous young trees had been planted on lawns sloping to the sidewalks. Today many of these homes are gone. A few have been restored, and more stand in need of such salvation. The upper ten blocks of Broadway have given way to commercial development and contain no residences.

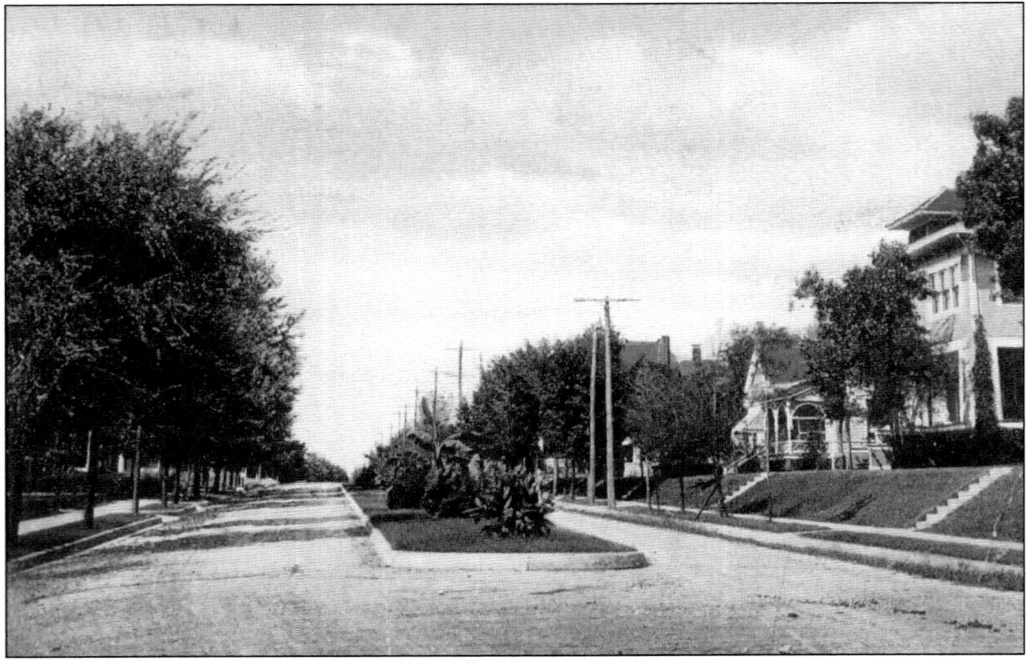

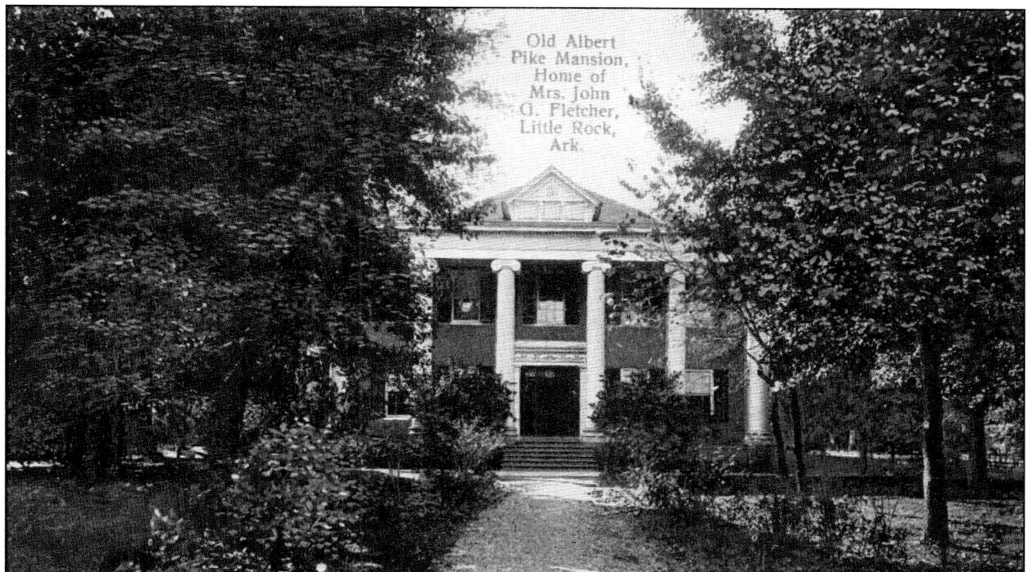

"I will send you a picture of this old southern mansion. Notice the large pillars," wrote a young man. One of Little Rock's oldest and finest homes was built in 1840 by Albert Pike, a lawyer of literary talents who served in both the Mexican and Civil Wars. During the 1870s, after Pike sold the home, it served for a time as the Arkansas Female College. The home is noted on this *c.* 1909 card as belonging to Mrs. John Fletcher. In 1976, the house became the property of the City of Little Rock, and is today the home of the Arkansas Decorative Arts Museum.

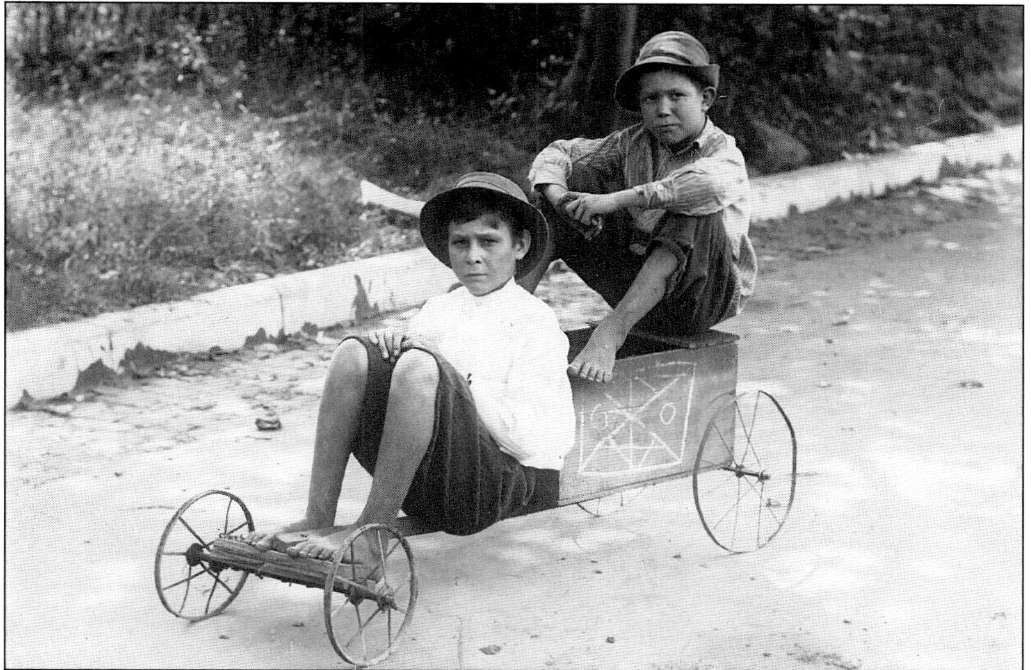

The street in front of the Kennedy home at 1221 West Sixth Street was the testing ground for brothers Norman and Robert to launch their homemade car. These children, who lived in a working-class neighborhood, were shoeless but had their hats on, ready to ride a vehicle with few safety features. (*c.* 1908.)

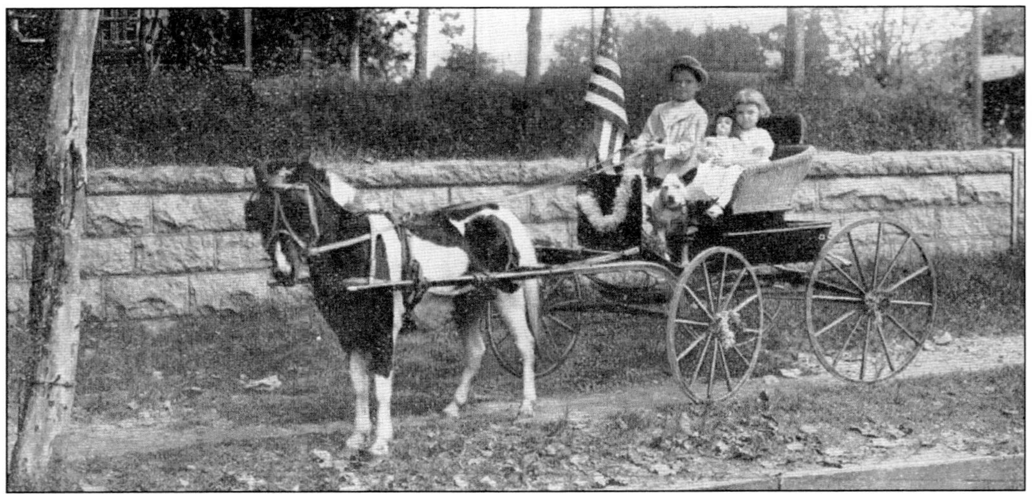

Two lucky children posed before their home with a new pony, "Bob," that had been awarded by the Webb Publishing Company. The most likely explanation for the caption is that children won some sort of contest, perhaps for selling papers. As with many postcard images, the modern-day viewer is left to wonder about the "rest of the story." (*c.* 1905.)

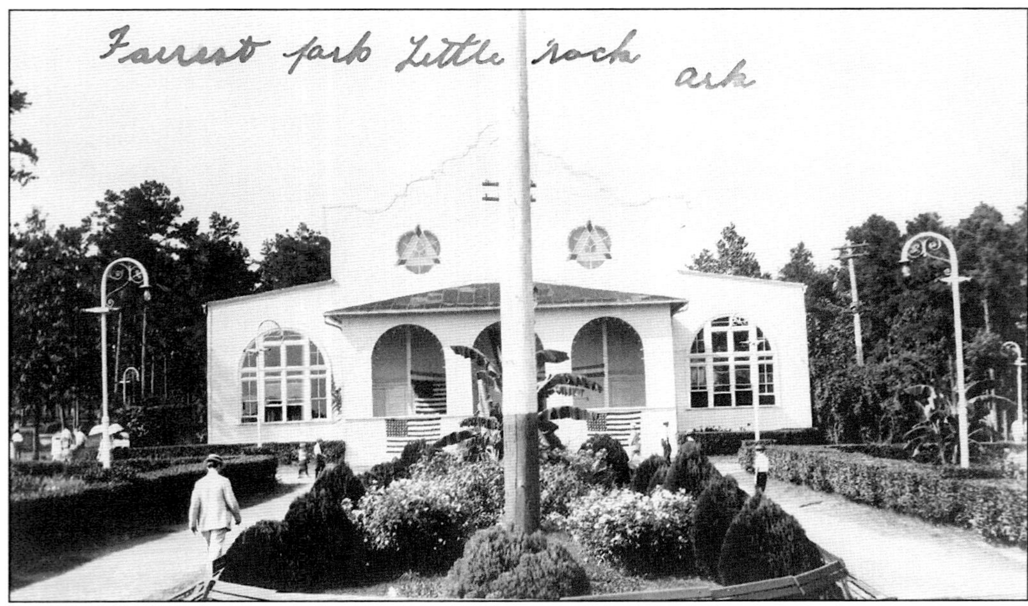

Forest Park was created to promote the streetcar company's new line into distant Pulaski Heights, a separate developing city until its annexation to Little Rock in 1916. One of the attractions found along the streetcar route was this theater at the park, which hosted minstrel shows and silent films for an admission of 10¢. (*c.* 1905.)

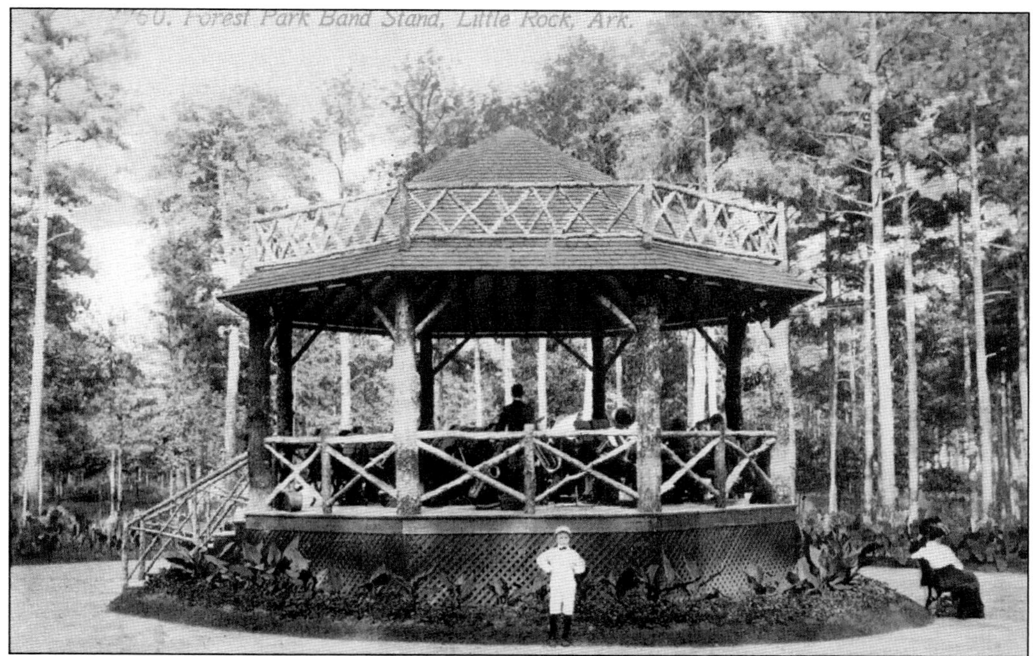

Forest Park featured this circular bandstand and a dance pavilion, as well as a variety of activities, including Sunday balloon ascensions. The Pulaski County Fair was held in the park and offered many attractions, including dog shows and harness racing. The rapid spread of automobiles and roads contributed to the decline of the park, as housing and commercial enterprises bought up and developed the park land. The park area is now occupied by the homes and businesses around the upper section of Kavanaugh Boulevard. (*c.* 1910.)

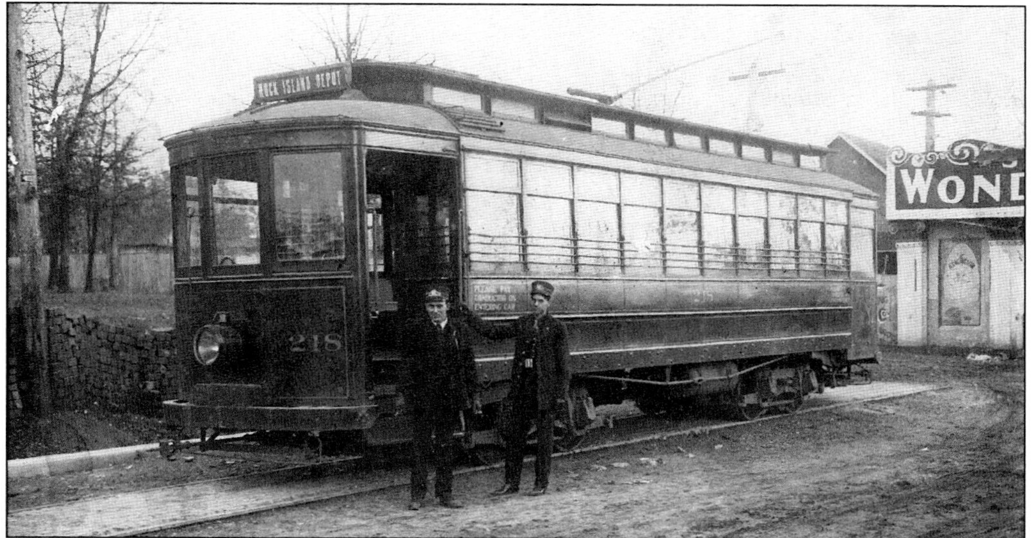

Boulevard Park, later renamed Braddock's Park, was another private park built in part to boost business for the streetcar company. The park's "Wonderland" amusement area, the entrance of which is seen at the end the streetcar in this *c.* 1905 view, ran from Thirty-sixth Street southwest to the Choctaw (later Rock Island) railroad tracks, near today's state fair grounds. The area is reserved as a park today. In this card's view, the two conductors had stopped their car where the tracks ended at the park gate.

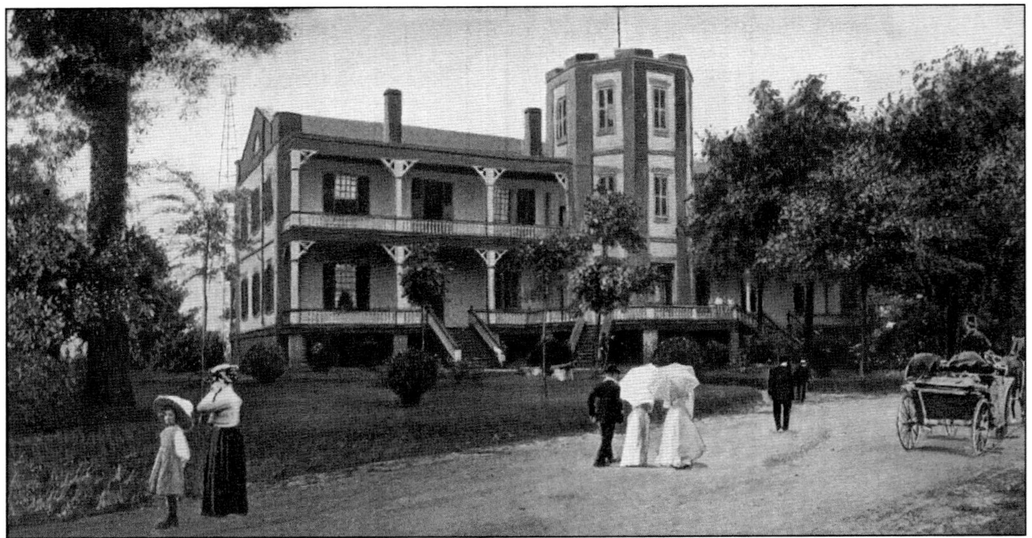

The most popular public recreation area in Little Rock was City Park, at the center of which stood the historic Arsenal building dating from 1840. The building changed hands twice during the Civil War. At the turn of the century, band concerts were held in the park; ice skating was enjoyed in rare cold winters, on a lake that once graced the park. Today the park still serves the city as MacArthur Park, so named because of the birth of the famous general in this building in 1880. (*c.* 1905.)

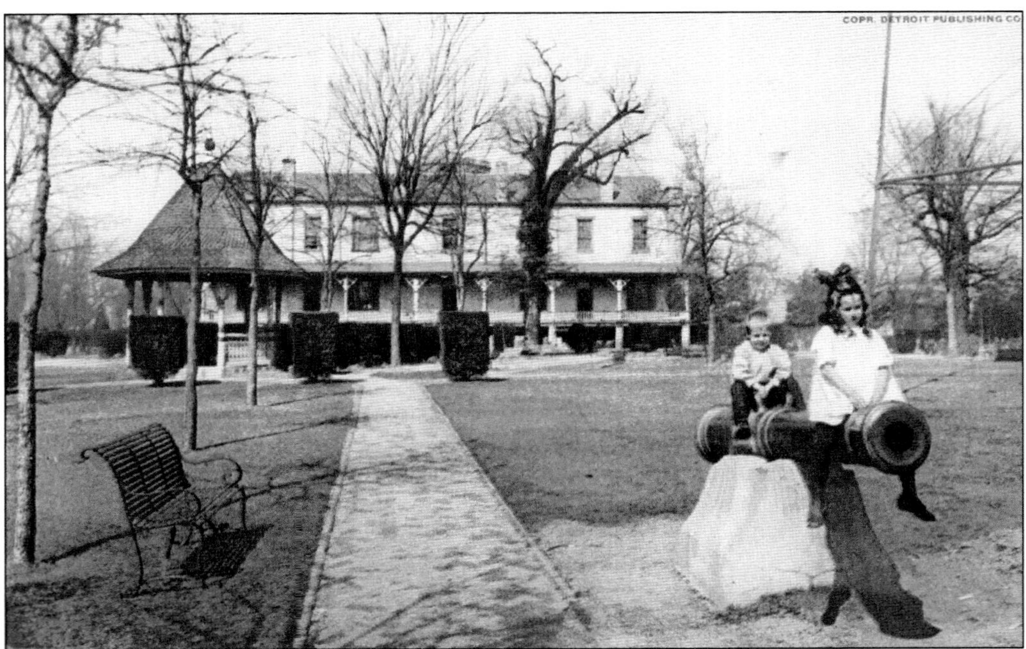

One of the attractions in City Park was a 12-foot brass cannon, forged in Spain in 1796. It had been captured in Cuba during the Spanish-American War of 1898. The cannon was among a number of military weapons taken to New York after the war, but was later sent to Little Rock as a gift to the city. During WW II the cannon was donated to the war effort and melted down for use in more modern weapons of war. (*c.* 1905.)

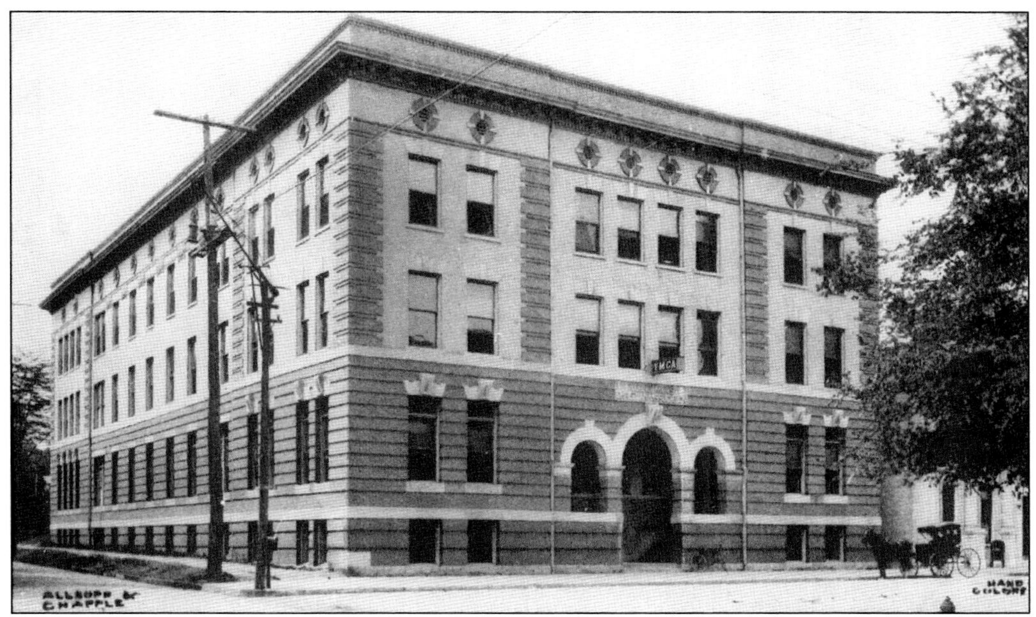
Not all recreation was outdoors, and the YMCA located at Fifth and Scott Streets was a popular draw after the $100,000 building opened in 1905. The first Little Rock chapter of the YMCA was organized in the 1880s. The building shown in this *c.* 1905 photo served until 1928, when a new, larger "Y" was built. This building stands restored today as the home of the *Arkansas Democrat-Gazette*.

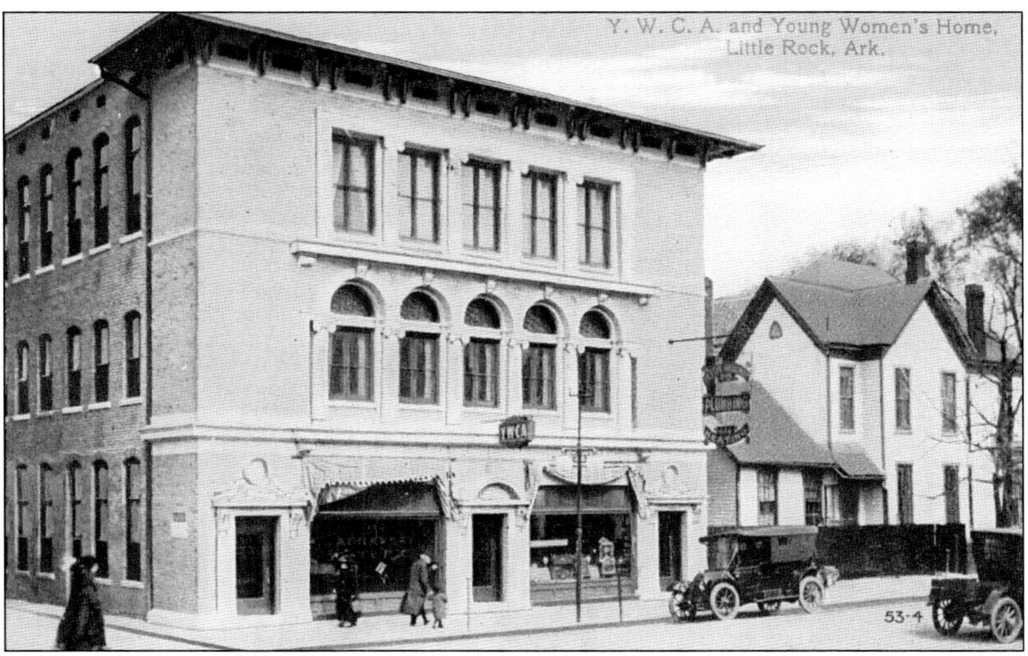

The YWCA was located at 114 East Seventh Street, its lower floors leased to such businesses as the Home Water Company. Lodging for young women was apparently available in the adjacent house. The building is long gone, having fallen victim to the great fire of 1911. The site is presently occupied by a seven-story parking deck. (*c.* 1915.)

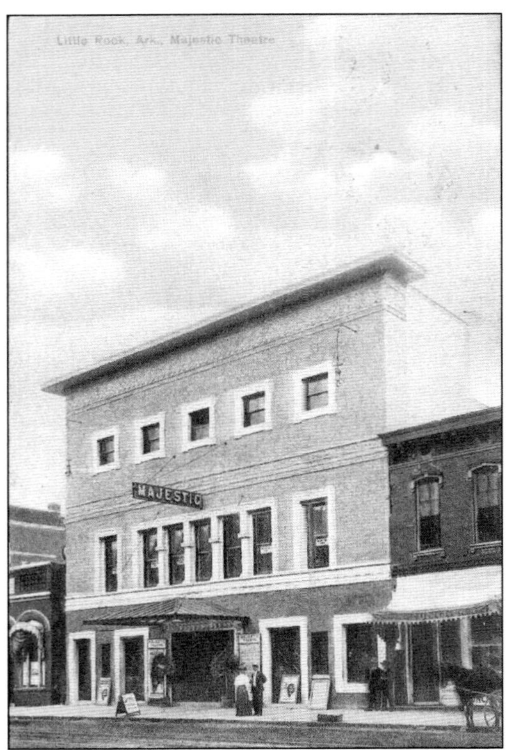

"Guess who I am," was the only message to "Baby Anne" of Atlanta, from the sender of this 1910 card of the Majestic Theater. The small playhouse was located on the 800 block of Main Street and was styled after European theaters, decorated in bold red, white, and gold. Humorist Will Rogers was among the many musical and comedy acts to appear on the Majestic's stage. The theater burned in 1930, and today the entire block is a parking lot.

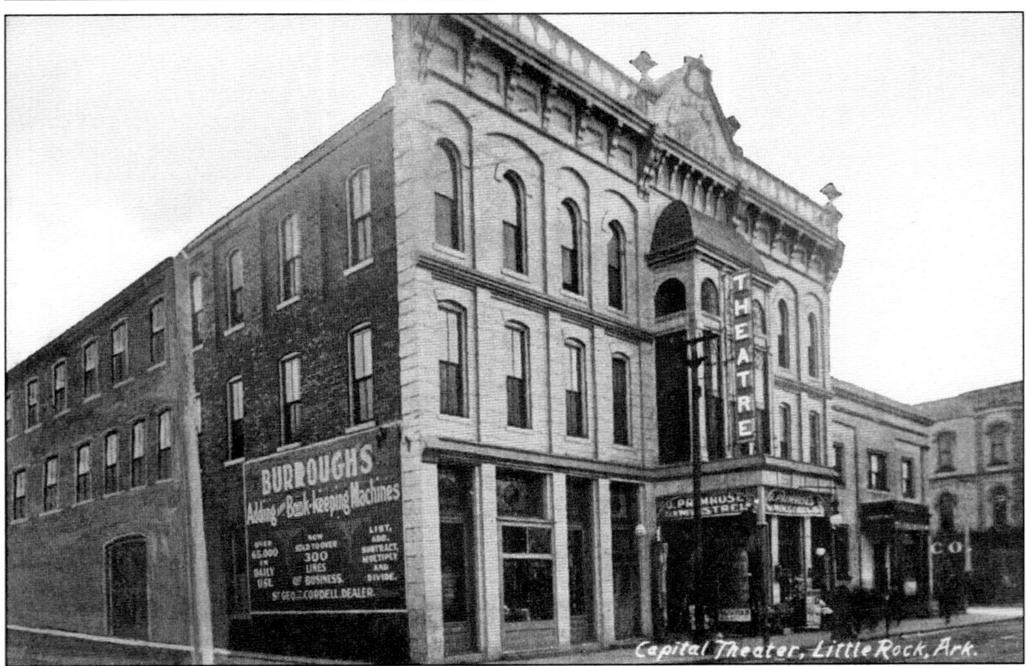

The Capital Theater was built on Markham Street in the 1880s, across the street from the early state capitol building (today's Old State House), and just down the block from the Capital Hotel. The theater hosted many silent movies and vaudeville acts. According to the marquee, the featured act at the time this *c.* 1905 photo was made was "The Primrose Minstrels." The theater burned in 1913, and the site is presently occupied by the Stephens Building.

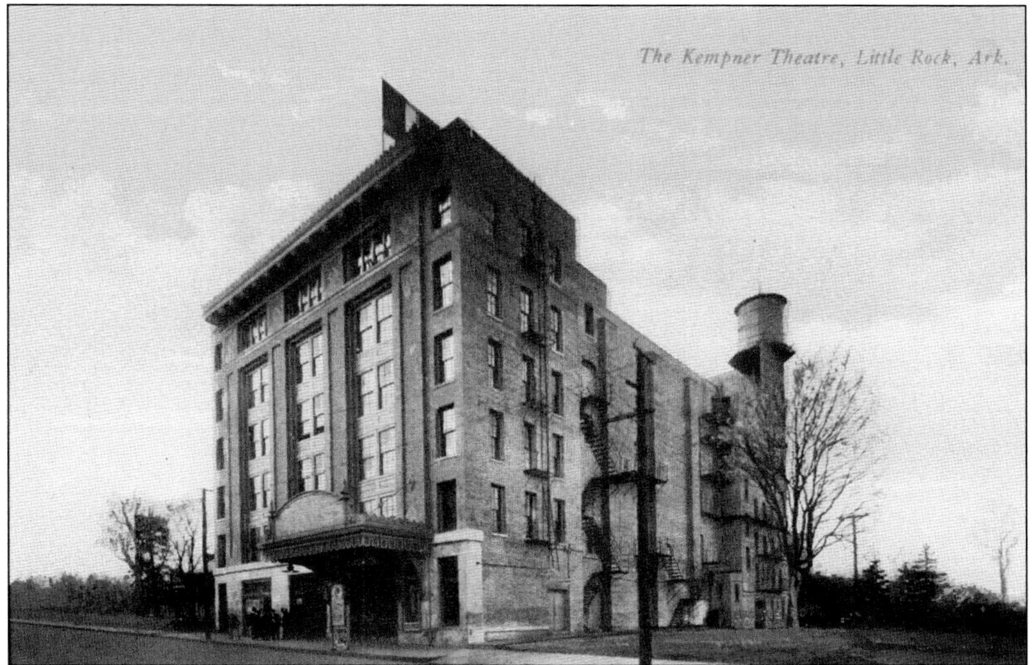

The Kempner Theater, named for a prominent Jewish family who immigrated to Little Rock in the 1800s, was located in the 600 block of Center Street. While other local theaters favored silent films, the Kempner was partial to lectures and plays. The Kempner later became a movie theater and was renamed the Arkansas Theater. It was active during the 1960s and '70s, and then stood boarded in decay for a decade before being razed in 1997 for the site of a parking lot. (*c.* 1900.)

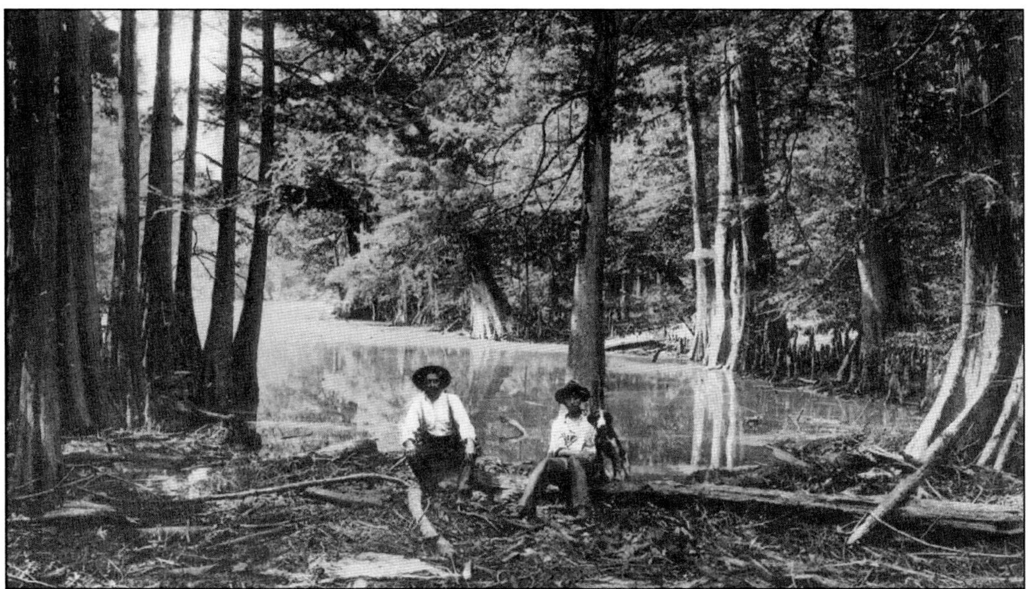

Little Rock was bounded on the east and south by vast wetlands of huge cypress trees and the bottomland swamps of Fourche Creek. These wild areas have survived many years, due in part to the difficulty of extracting the timber. In early days the wetlands provided a sportsman's refuge near the city. In this *c.* 1908 card, a father, son, and their dog pose in a cypress brake.

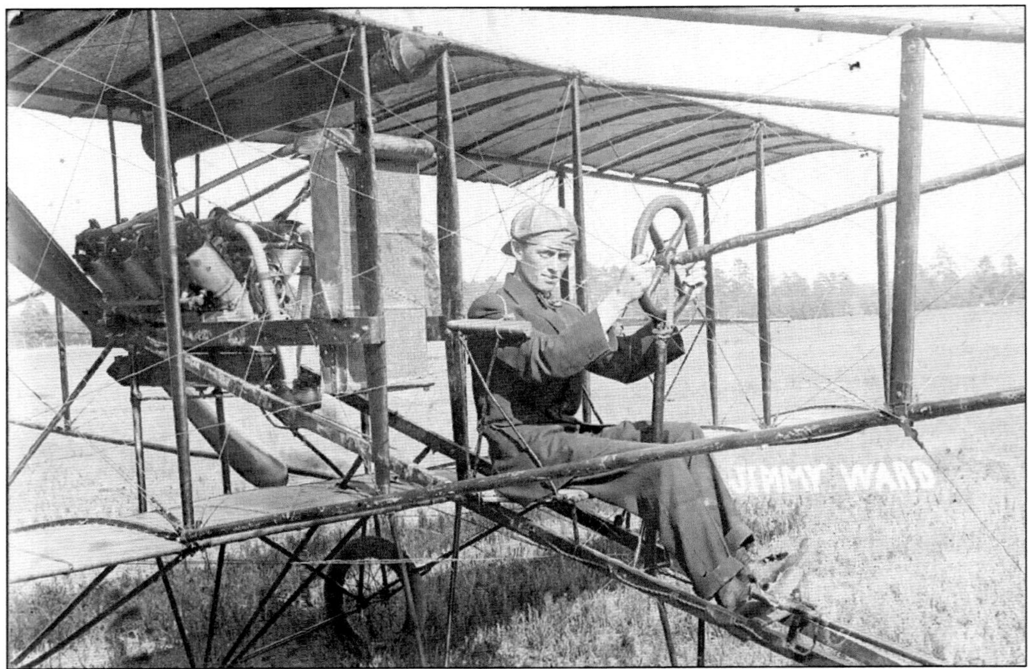

"Witnessed this June 3, 1911," were the words about 19-year-old Jimmy Ward penciled on the back of this card, which was made the same year. Newspaper records describe the exploits of the young aviator: "BIRDMEN MAKE FOUR FLIGHTS" was the headline for the front-page story in the *Arkansas Democrat.* Ward and his older partner, Hugh Robinson, thrilled crowds with performances for three days on the grounds of the Country Club. Thousands of Little Rock residents paid 50¢ each to watch the men's aerial feats, only eight years after the Wright brothers made the first manned flight.

Press accounts spoke of Ward hovering in the atmosphere before ascending to 900 feet, exclaiming the following:

> . . . no automobile, no express flyer of the steam railroad ever acquired such remarkable speed as his ship attained. The spectacle was superb. . . The personnel of the gathering at the Country Club was unique. It brought together people from every latitude of life. Clergymen were there; senators and representatives from the legislature, prominent merchants and manufacturers and bankers were at the scene, and the plain but hardy and honest mechanic could be found in the crowd. More than 100 automobile parties whizzed to the place in their speedy cars.

On the last day of the three-day event, Ward became even more daring in repeated flights which lasted 15 to 20 minutes each. The newspaper recounts the following: ". . . he gave an exhibition of fancy driving, making the figure eight twice, and dipping and soaring all the while, until he was about 1,600 feet above the spectators, when he began to descend in graceful circles, and once he leaned forward and waved his cap at the crowd, and then made his landing."

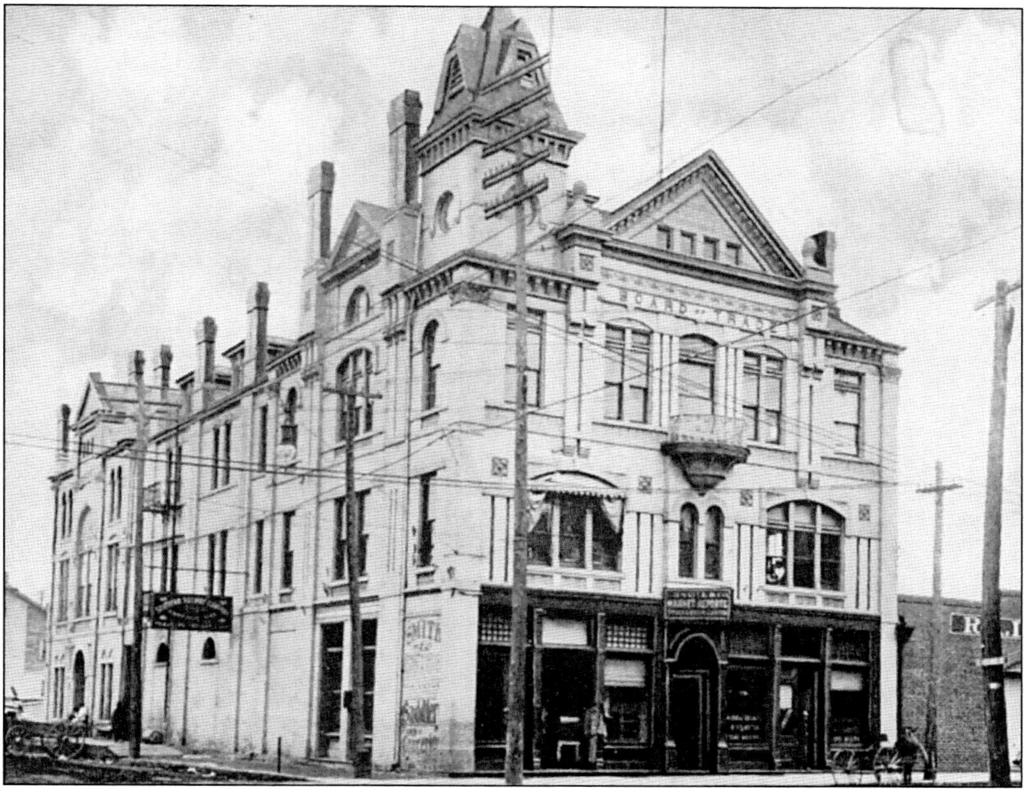

The board of trade, an early version of the chamber of commerce, was organized in 1886 "to more thoroughly organize the commerce of the city." The Queen Anne-style building erected in 1887 at the corner of Second and Scott Streets was adorned with multiple chimneys. The building contained a large room, two stories high, which was used by the Little Rock Cotton Exchange. Apparently, the building was removed by 1920. (*c.* 1905.)

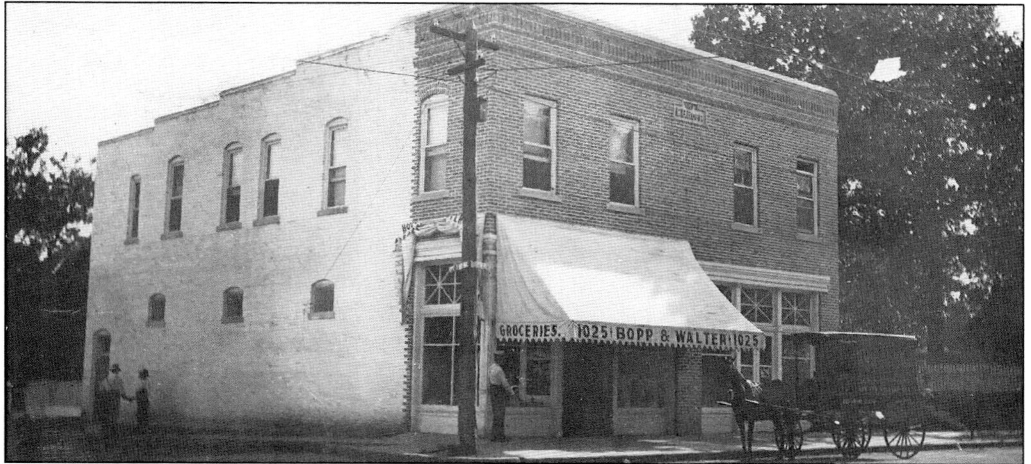

Bopp and Walters' Grocery store operated at 1025 East Ninth Street as a neighborhood fixture common before the rise of the modern supermarkets. The vehicle parked on the street appears to be a delivery wagon. Note the two men standing with their backs to the photographer, as they shake hands near the store's rear door. The building still stands today, but operates as a liquor store.

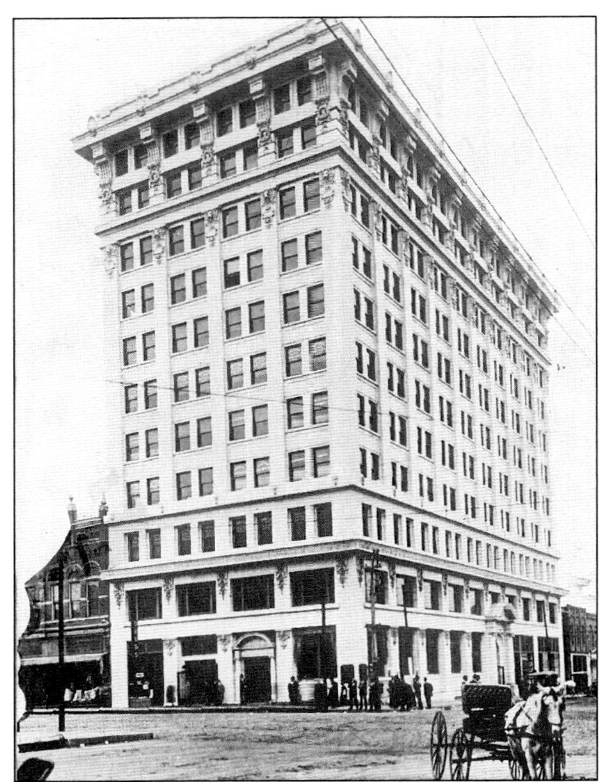

The State National Bank Building was erected in 1910 at the corner of Fifth and Main Streets, only a year before this card was mailed. It surpassed the Southern Trust Building as the city's tallest building, with its soaring 11 floors. The structure was among several steel-framed "skyscrapers" to rise in Little Rock during the era. A basement power plant furnished heat, electricity, and power for the elevators. The building became the Boyle Building a decade later and still serves the downtown area.

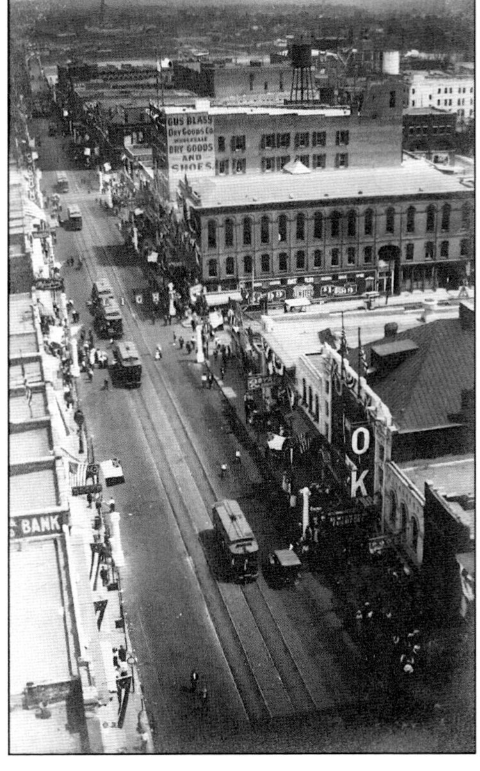

A testament to how the new State National Bank towered over its neighbors is offered in this 1911 view taken from the roof of the building, looking north on Main Street. In the view are multiple streetcars which would have been in place to carry extra passengers, as the United Confederate Veterans' annual meeting was being hosted by Little Rock at the time.

The Southern Trust Building, which opened in 1907 at Second and Center Streets, was the city's tallest building. Among the most noted attractions were a summer garden on the roof and a weather observatory. The arrow drawn in by "Pete," the sender of this *c.* 1915 card, is explained in his message: "You asked about our building, here is a picture, with the usual arrow pointing to the approximate location of my desk." Writing to a lady named Virginia, Pete continues: "After my miserable letter last night, I started to write again, but it was so late when I came to myself I postponed it. . . . I told Chas. about our engagement and the long wait. Hope I made no mistake". Another mystery lost in postcard history—what became of the young banker Pete and his love Virginia?

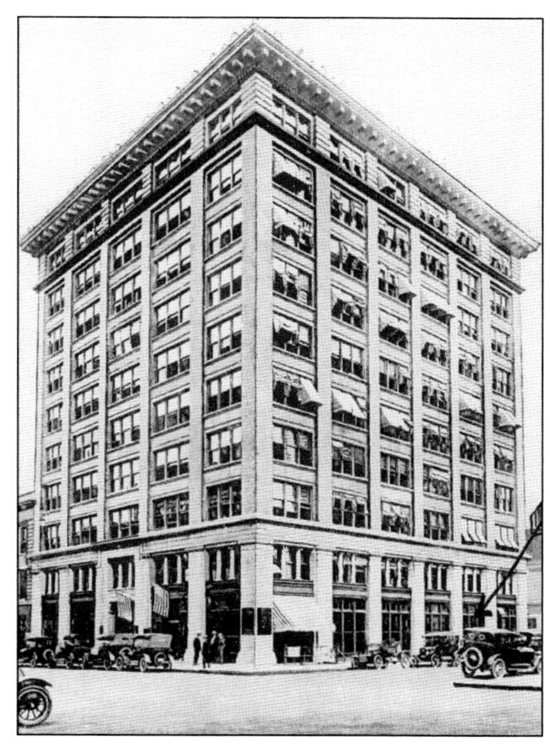

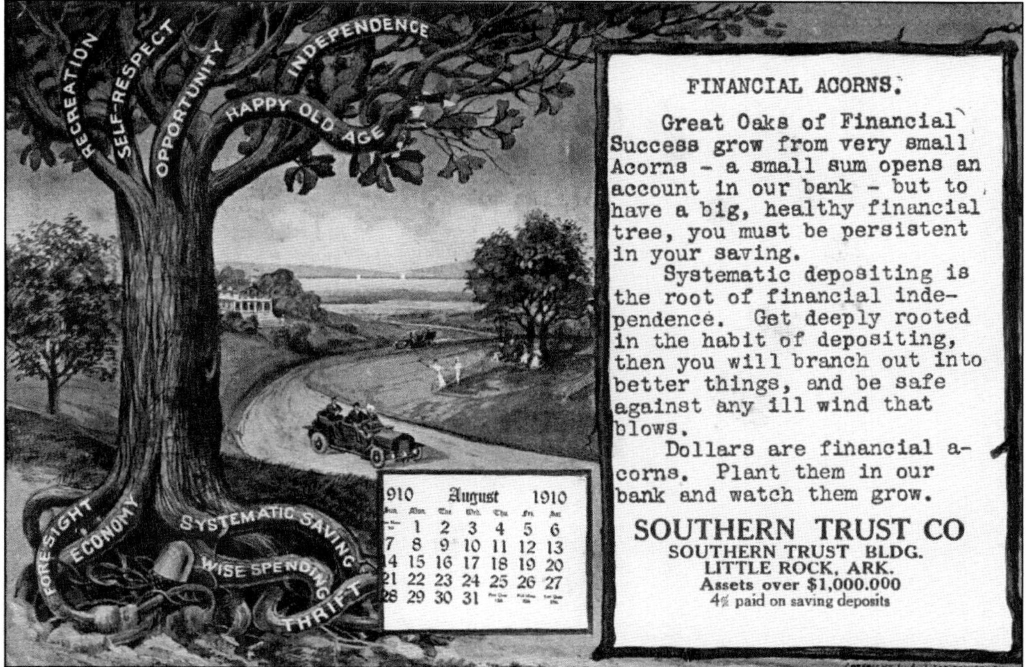

The Southern Trust Company, like other banking institutions, relied on postcards with creative messages to encourage new accounts. This card from 1910 proclaimed assets of over $1 million and a 4% interest to be paid on deposits. "Dollars are financial acorns. Plant them in our bank and watch them grow." The branches proclaim reasons to save, such as "independence" and a "happy old age," which would spring from roots such as "foresight" and "systematic savings."

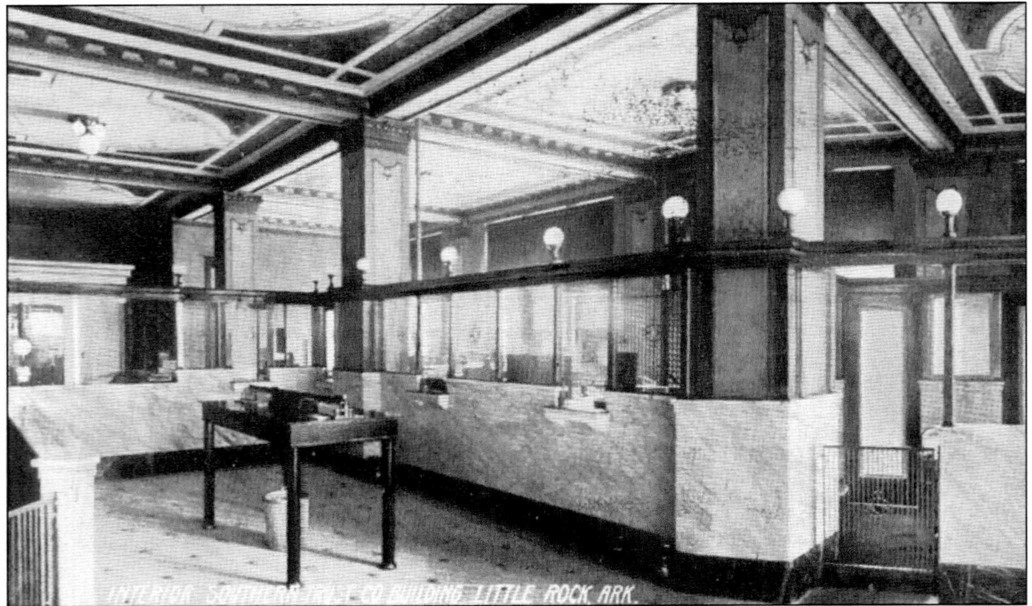

"You will find a cordial welcome always at [the] first window whenever you honor us with a visit" was the message of a bank teller on this 1908 card, the year after the Southern Trust Company opened its building. The banking area on the ground floor was considered very striking, with embellished steel, Italian marble, bronze, mahogany, and mosaic tile floors. The building is today known as Pyramid Place, providing office space to attorneys and other professionals.

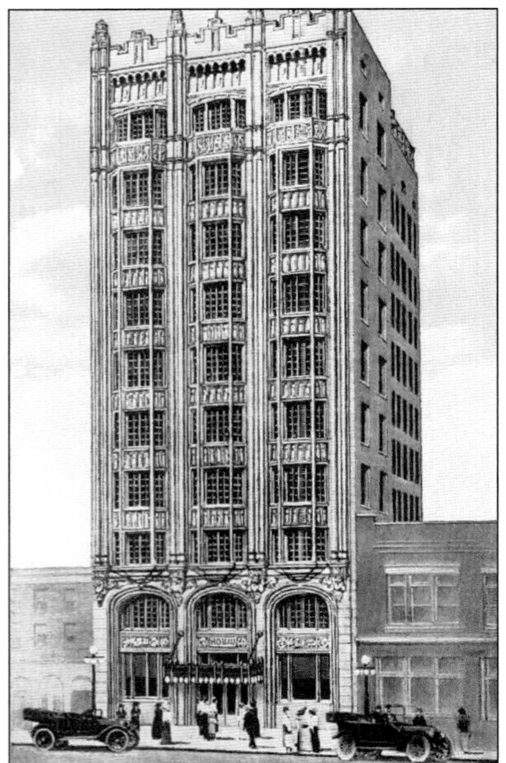

"We have several big buildings like this here, and this is a very busy city. . . Saw watermelons today for $1.10 each but they will soon be cheap" reads the message on a 1919 card of the very striking Ancient Order of United Workmen (AOUW) building. When work began at 212 Center Street in 1911, the building was designed to have six stories. Work halted, however, in 1912 for financial reasons, with only a steel framework finished. The incomplete building was purchased in 1917 by the AOUW, which designed and erected a ten-story building. The gothic ornaments, high speed elevators, and filtered ice water to all ten floors were among the bragging points for the completed building's owners and tenants.

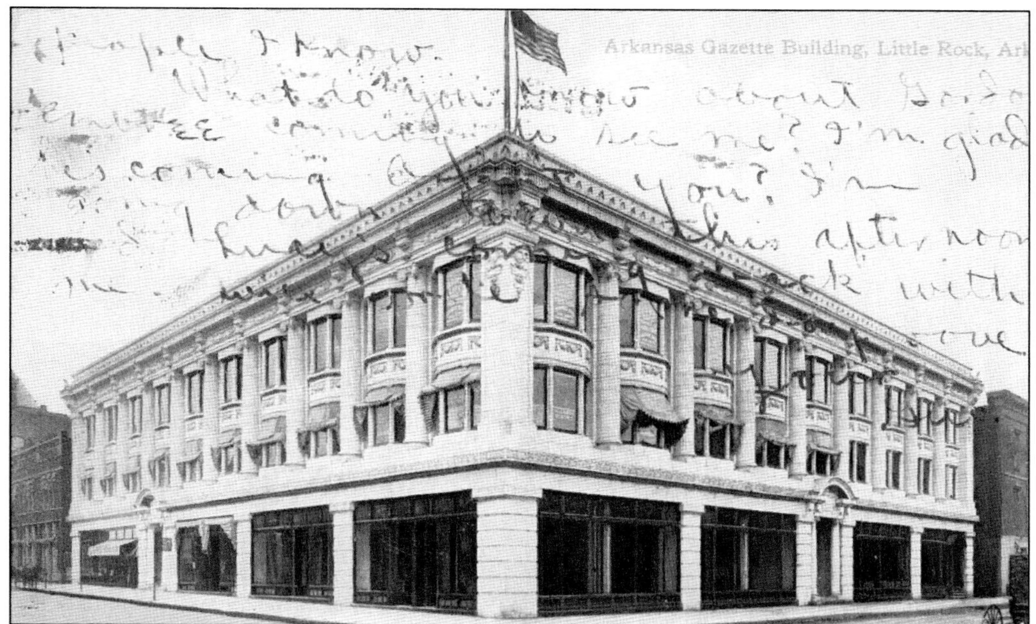

"Would have written sooner but was too lazy to go downtown to get some cards" was penned on the back of a 1910 view of the *Arkansas Gazette* building. The paper was, for many years, the oldest continuously published newspaper west of the Mississippi, having been founded by William Woodruff in what was Arkansas Territory in 1820. This classical building was completed in 1908 and was home to the *Gazette* until 1991, when it was sold by the Gannett Corporation to the rival *Arkansas Democrat*. The building served in 1992 as the national headquarters for the successful presidential campaign of Arkansas Gov. Bill Clinton.

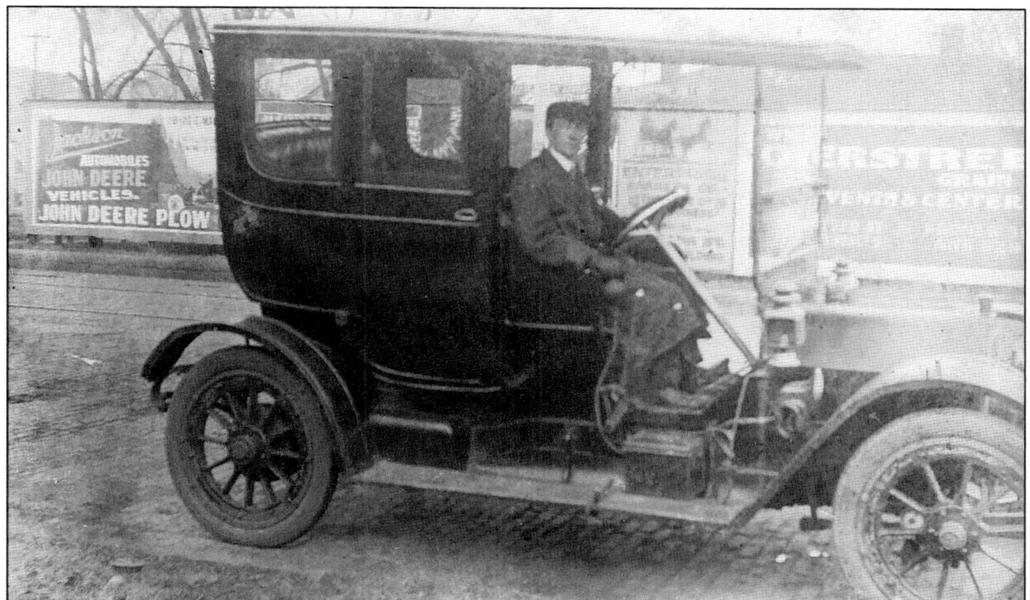

While most people still preferred streetcars and horse-drawn rigs, the automobile was beginning to emerge. The Stearns Taxicab Company was one of the first in Little Rock to start a business with the "horseless carriage." The taxi was powered by a 30-horsepower engine, according to a notation on the back of this 1911 card.

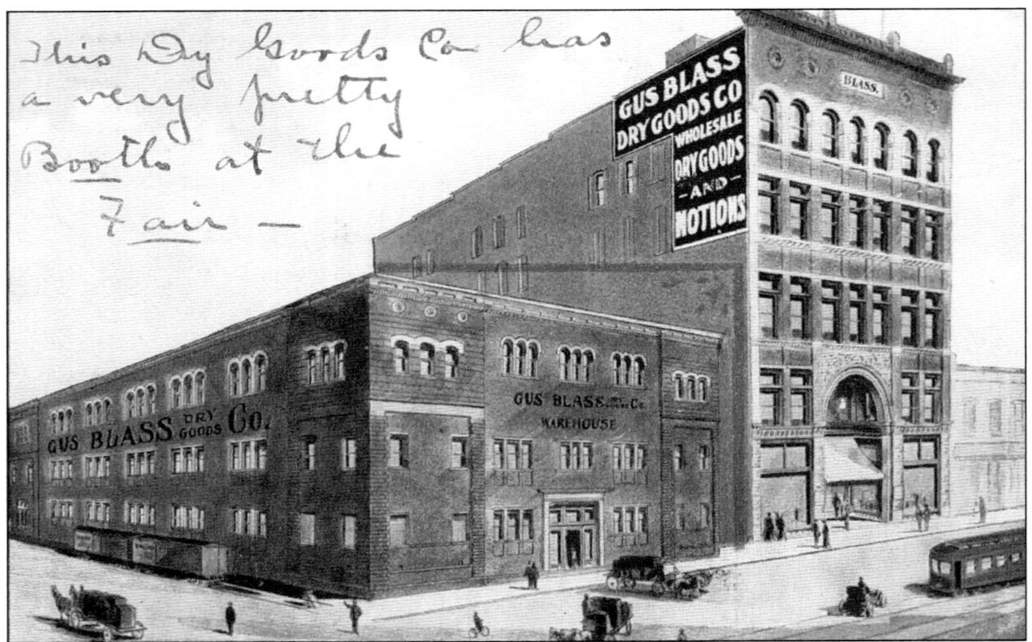

This 1908 card of the Gus Blass Dry Goods Company was penned by Gus himself, proclaiming, "a very pretty Booth at the Fair." On the back, Mr. Blass continued, "Our 'Big State Fair' opened Monday, my but it is fine, much better than ever before, Love to all, Gus." Blass was almost surely the best known and most successful of early-20th-century Arkansas retailers. Blass founded his first store in Little Rock in 1871, and later moved to this Main Street location.

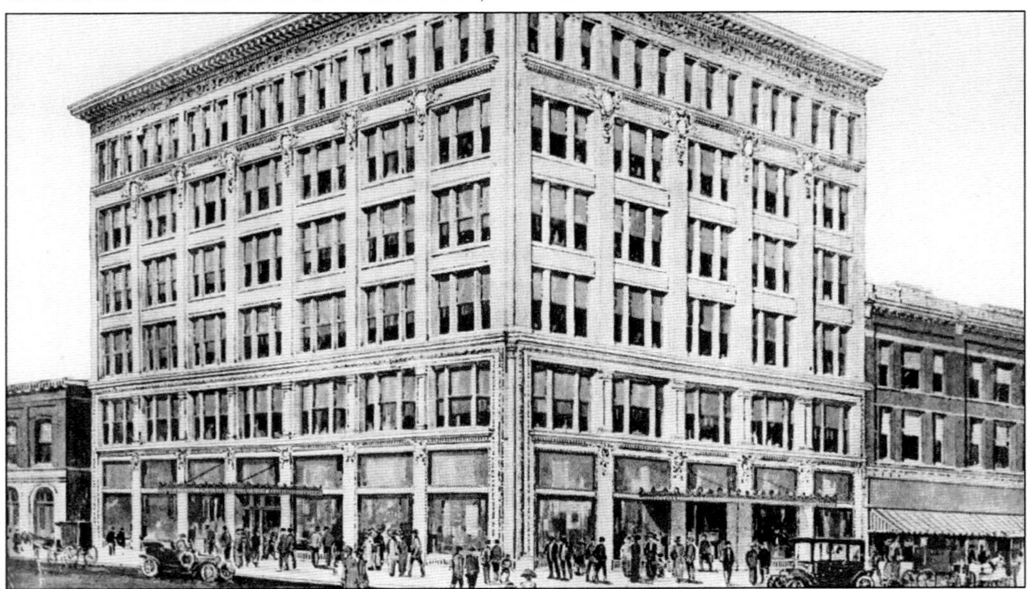

Blass Dry Goods Company maintained dominance of the Little Rock retail scene when it moved into its new seven-floor building and came to be considered a city landmark. Gus died in 1916, but the company prospered and further increased its fame with the leadership of his son, Julian. The store was fully air-conditioned by the 1940s and became one of the first Southern department stores to install an escalator. The Gus Blass Company was sold to Dillard's Department Store chain in 1964. Today the building houses only offices. (*c.* 1915.)

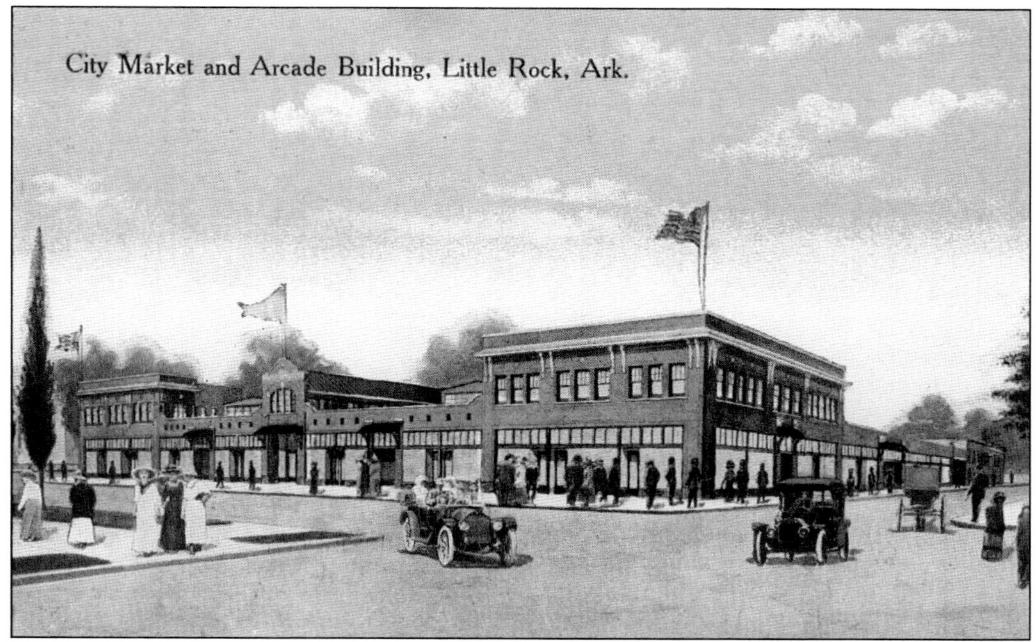

Little Rock's first shopping mall was the City Market and Arcade Building, which opened on Louisiana Street across from St. Andrew's Cathedral in 1914 at a cost of $137,000. It had a vaulted roof which arched over a long hallway of shops that included greengrocers, jewelers, candy shops, bathhouses, cobblers, and merchants offering fine meats and groceries. Apartments on the second floor were often rented to stock company actors who worked for the nearby Kempner Theater. The building was demolished in 1959. (*c.* 1915.)

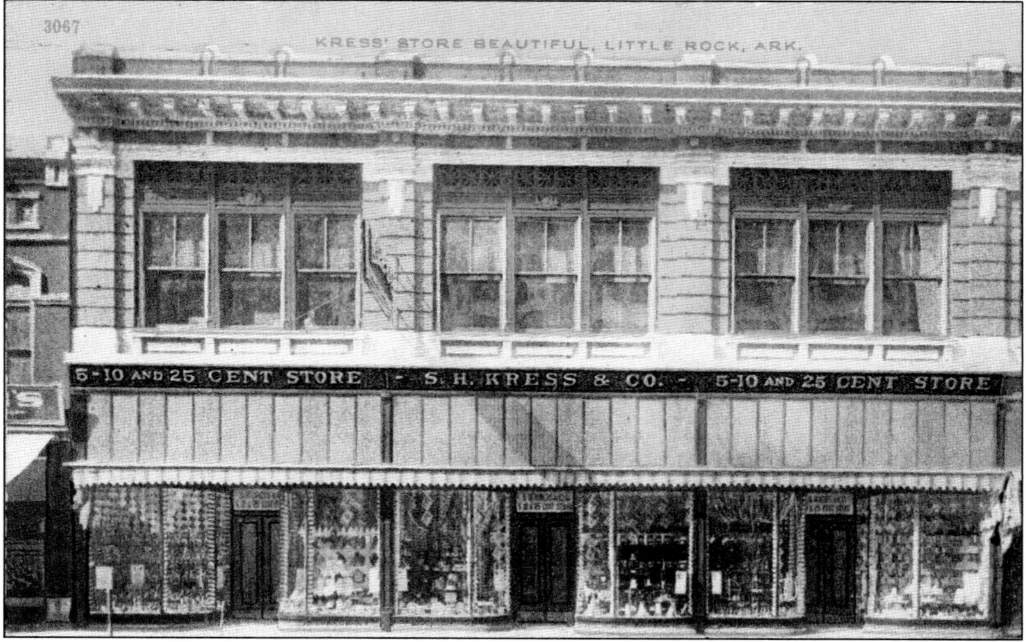

Little Rock's Main Street was home to the store of at least one national chain retailer. The S.H. Kress and Company's 5-10-25 Cent Store was a fixture for many years before the rise of other national chains. It has been gone from downtown Little Rock for over two decades. (*c.* 1912.)

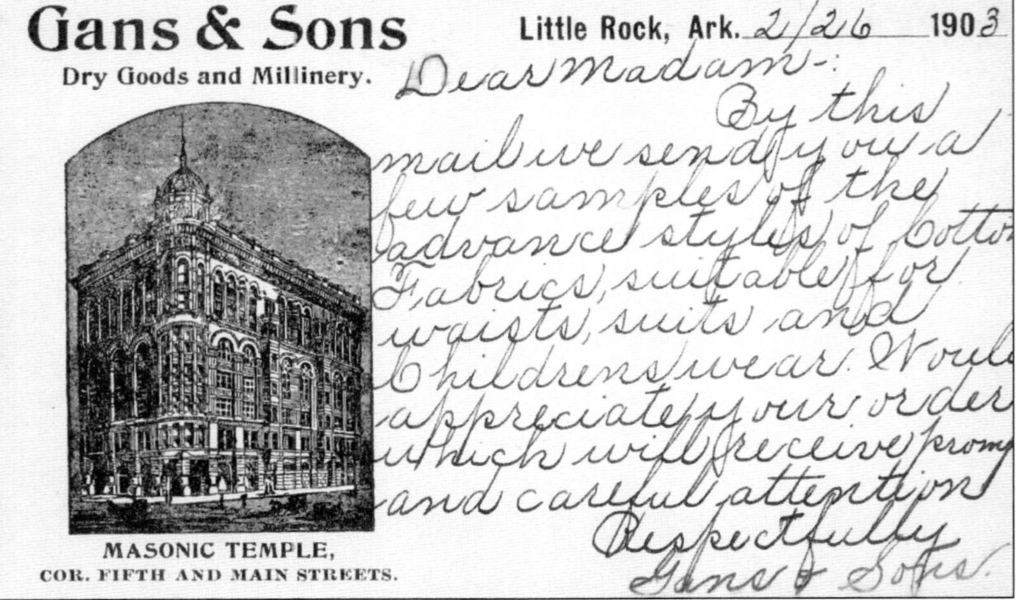
Gans & Sons

Dry Goods and Millinery.

Little Rock, Ark. 2/26 1903

Dear Madam-:

By this mail we send you a few samples of the advance styles of Cotton Fabrics, suitable for waists, suits and Childrens wear. Would appreciate your order which will receive prompt and careful attention

Respectfully

Gans & Sons.

MASONIC TEMPLE,

COR. FIFTH AND MAIN STREETS.

An employee of Gans and Sons used a 1903 card, with an image of the towering Masonic Temple at Fifth and Main Streets, to advertise to women customers with the words, "By this mail we send you a few samples of the advance styles of cotton fabrics, suitable for waists, suits, and children's wear. Would appreciate your order, which will receive prompt and careful attention." In 1903 the store was housed in the Masonic Temple in rented space. The building burned in 1919.

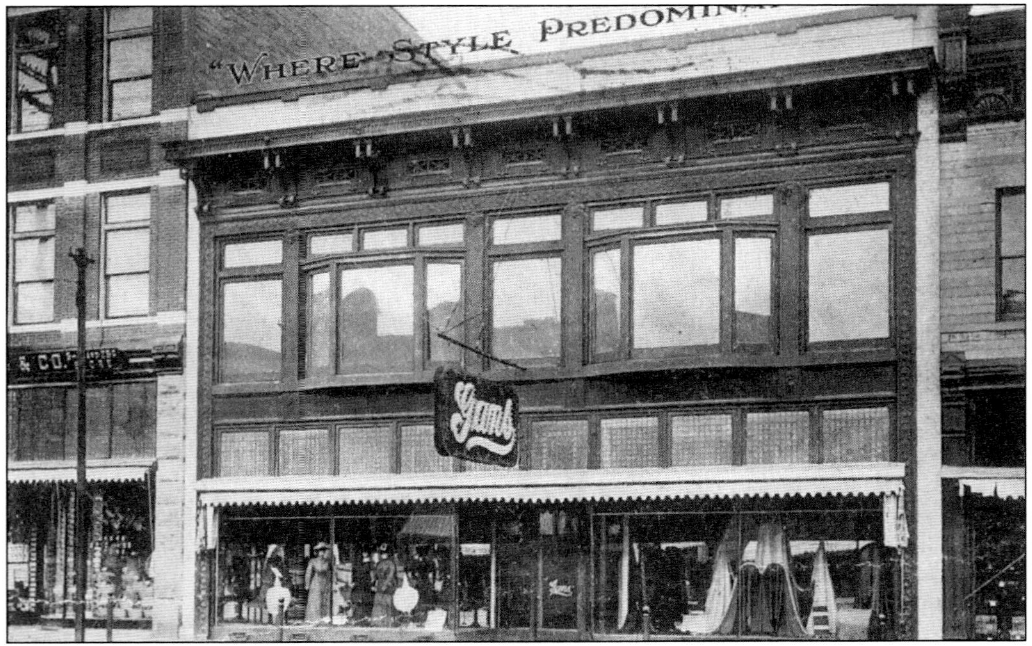

"Where Style Predominates" and "Outfitters to All Womankind" were the mottoes of Main Street merchant Solomon Gans, who catered to the upscale female clientele of Little Rock. Although the store has long since ceased business, the granite home it financed for Mr. Gans in 1896 still stands at 1010 West Third Street. (*c.* 1910.)

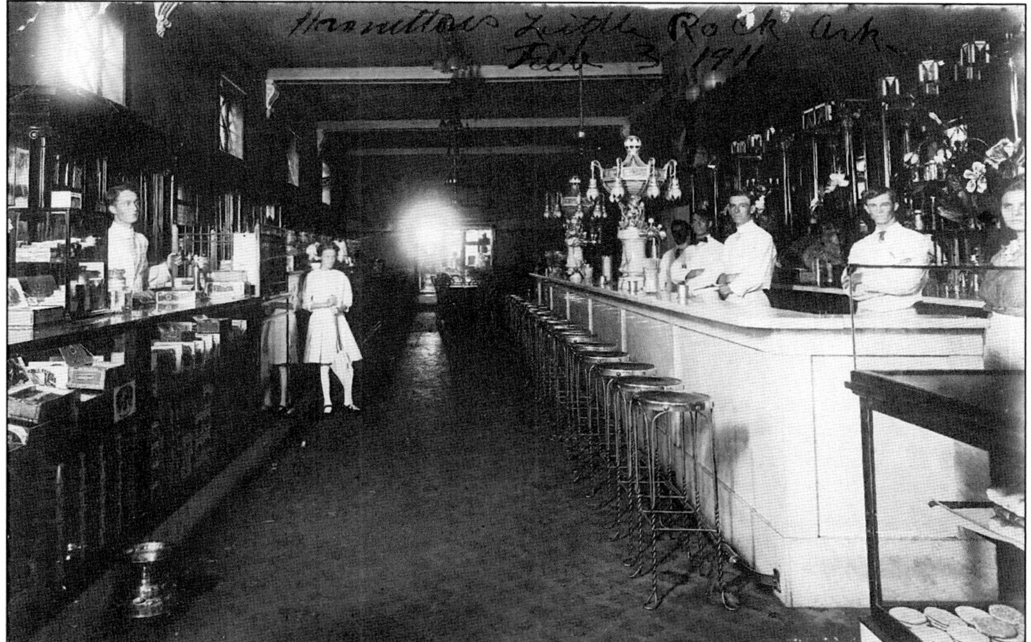

"Nat Plunkett, head man—and Dispensers, Hamilton's, My first job at a fountain" were the words penned on a 1909 card of the soda fountain at Hamilton's Drug Store located at 220 Main Street. Note the ornate fixtures, the baked goods on display, the many cigars in the case, and the gleaming brass spittoon. Reportedly it was the state's largest pharmacy at the time; both the business and the building are today only a memory.

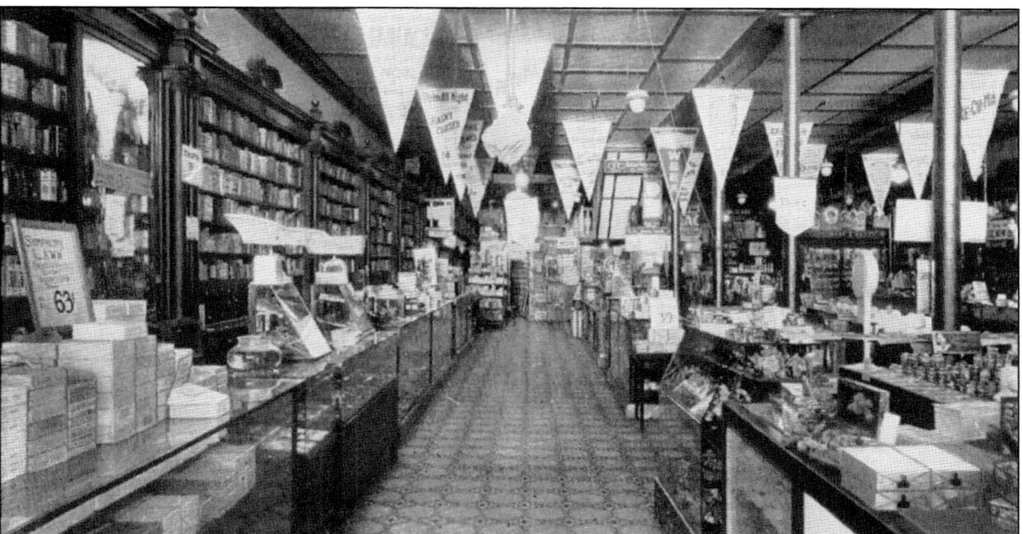

Modern consumers may assume that 24-hour pharmacies are a recent development in the American economy, but this *c.* 1915 card of Snodgrass and Brace's Rexall Drug Store in the 100 block of Main Street proves otherwise. "We never close," proclaims the front of the card; a pennant hanging from the ceiling reads, "Open all night—hasn't closed in 14 years." The store opened in 1899 at 100 Main, and by 1931 had ten different departments. The business even manufactured some products, including "Brain Storm Capsules" for dogs. Fire destroyed the building in the 1930s.

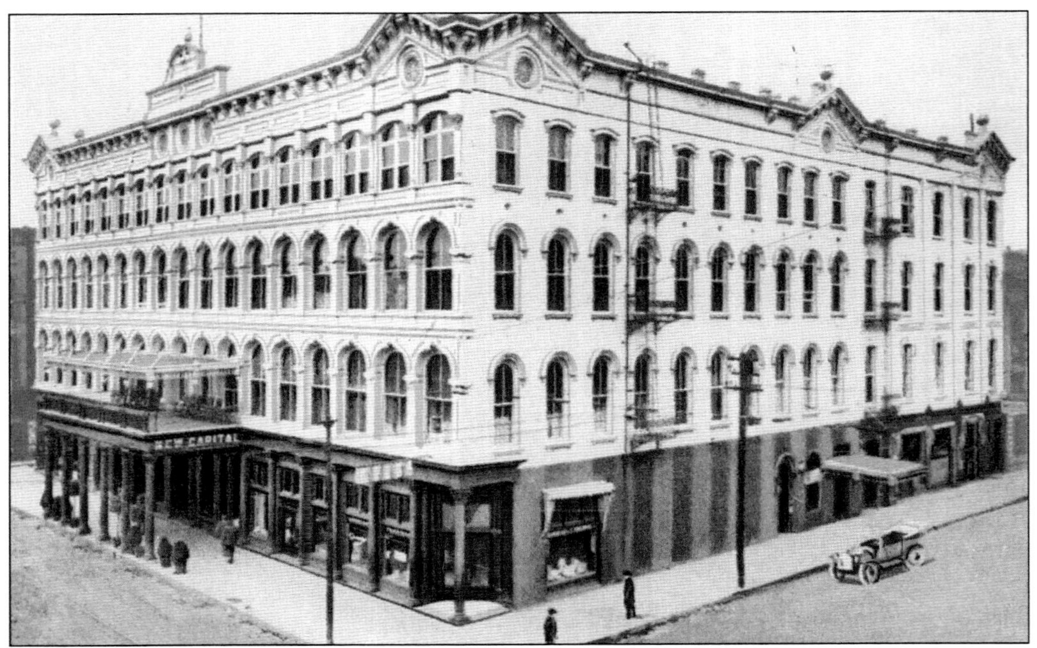

In 1873, a wealthy businessman named William Denckla erected this building, with its distinctive cast-iron front, to house offices. When fire destroyed the city's only first-class hotel, the Metropolitan, in 1877, Denckla converted his building to the New Capital Hotel. The hotel was in a prime location on Markham Street, across from the state capitol. The popularity of the hotel quickly led to an addition in back and the construction of a fourth floor in 1890. (*c.* 1905.)

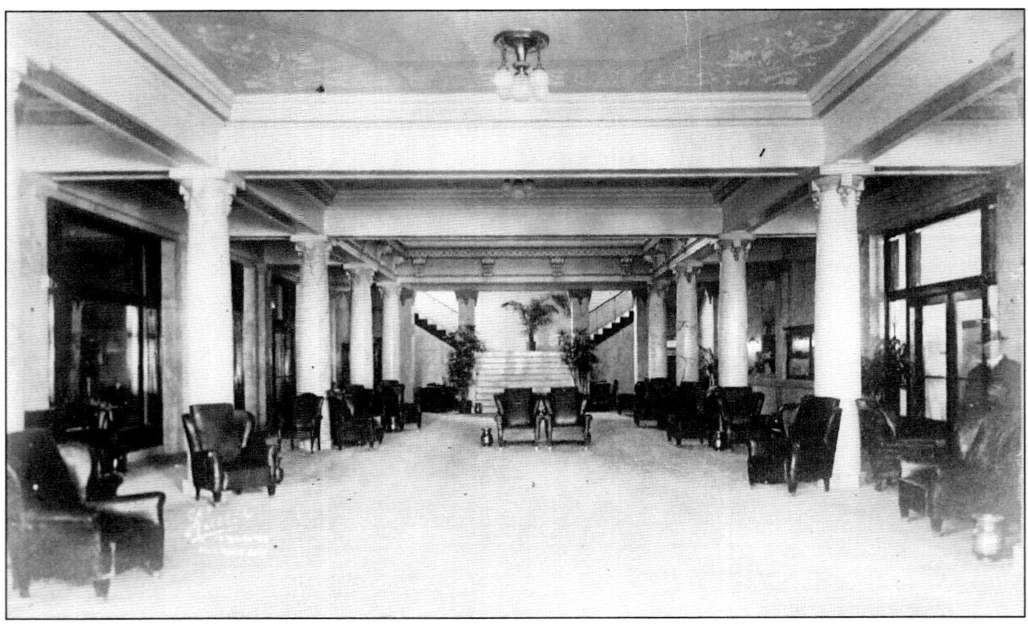

Pres. Ulysses S. Grant was among the many guests who were greeted over the years in the grand columned lobby of the Capital Hotel. As decades passed, the hotel fell into decline and was boarded up in the 1960s, just escaping plans to be demolished. Fortunately, the Lincoln Hotel Corporation purchased the hotel in the early 1980s and restored it to its former glory. (*c.* 1905.)

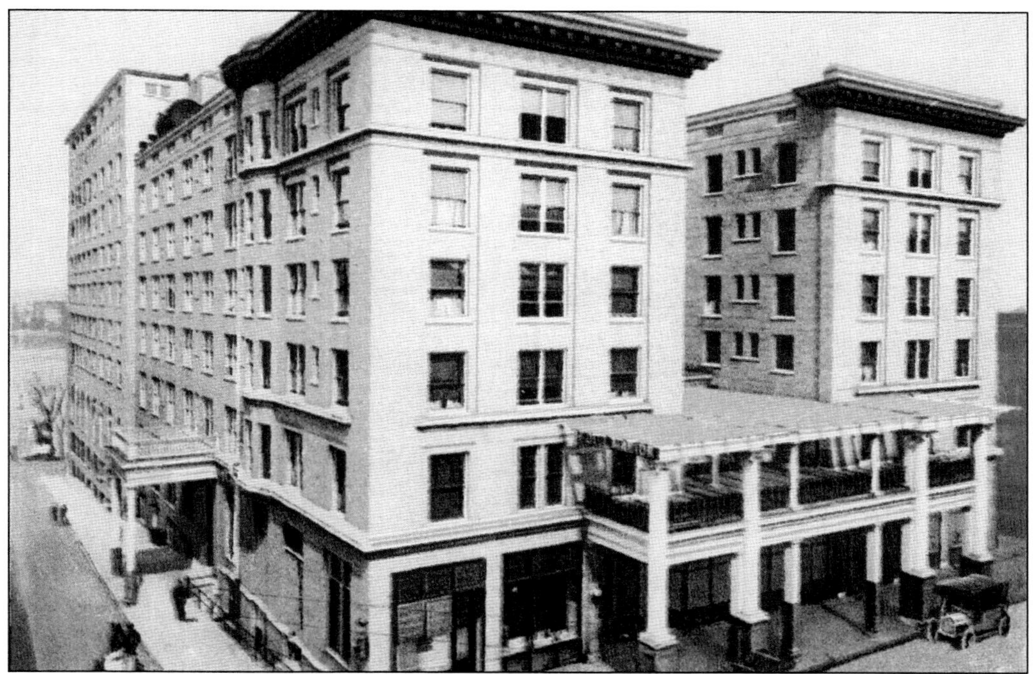

Demand for more first-class hotel space in Little Rock led to the opening of the Hotel Marion in 1907, adjacent to the old state capitol building and across from the Capital Hotel on Markham Street. The hotel's owner, Herman Kahn, named it for his wife, Marion, who surely shared her husband's pride in their new 175-room showplace on the river. (*c.* 1910.)

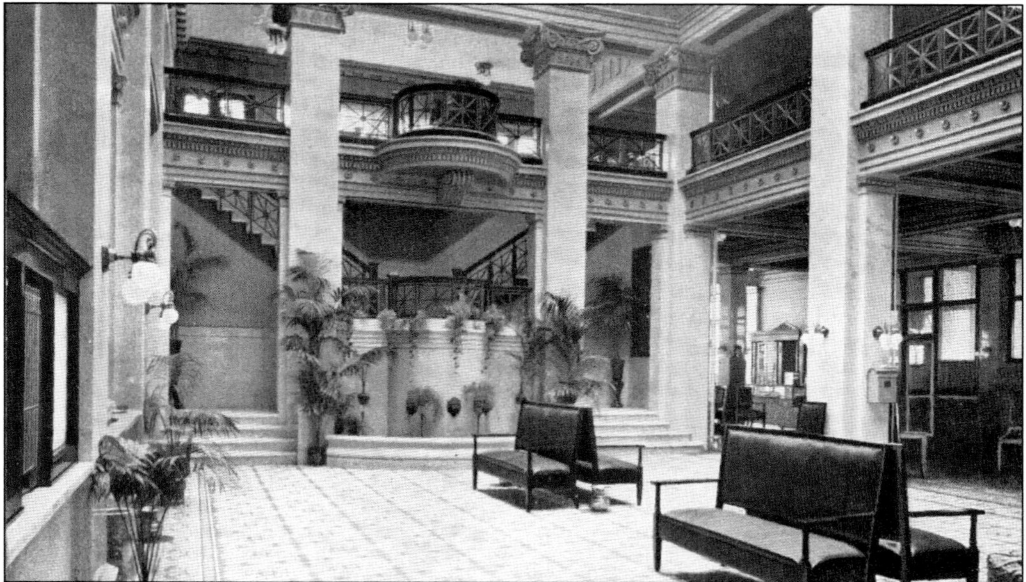

The Hotel Marion's greatest claim was its grand lobby, with features designed by architect George Mann, who also played a key role in designing the new state capitol. Famous guests of this hotel included Eleanor Roosevelt, Harry Truman, Douglas MacArthur, Will Rogers, Helen Keller, and Charles Lindbergh. The hotel, which stood closed and boarded up throughout the 1970s, was demolished in 1980 to make way for the Excelsior Hotel and the city's new convention center. (*c.* 1910.)

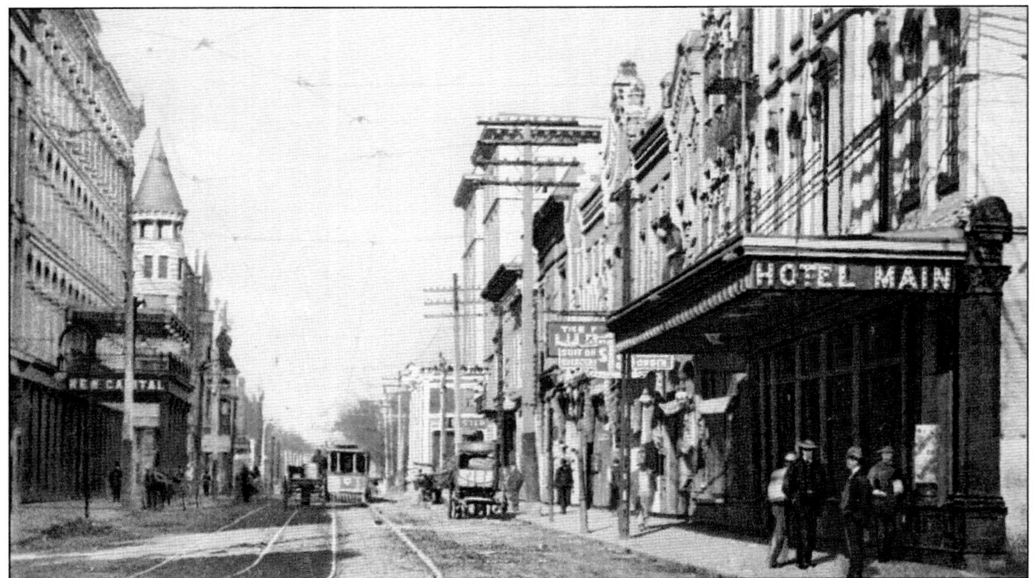

"I am on my way and very tired but leave here in one hour for St. Louis and then to Decatur" was the message on a 1913 card which documented "hotel row," the three blocks of Markham west of Main Street. The Hotel Marion can be seen on the right, the Hotel Main is in the foreground, and pictured on the left is the Capital Hotel. Twin sets of streetcar tracks carried guests around the corner to the left and up Main Street, where merchants would have welcomed out-of-town business.

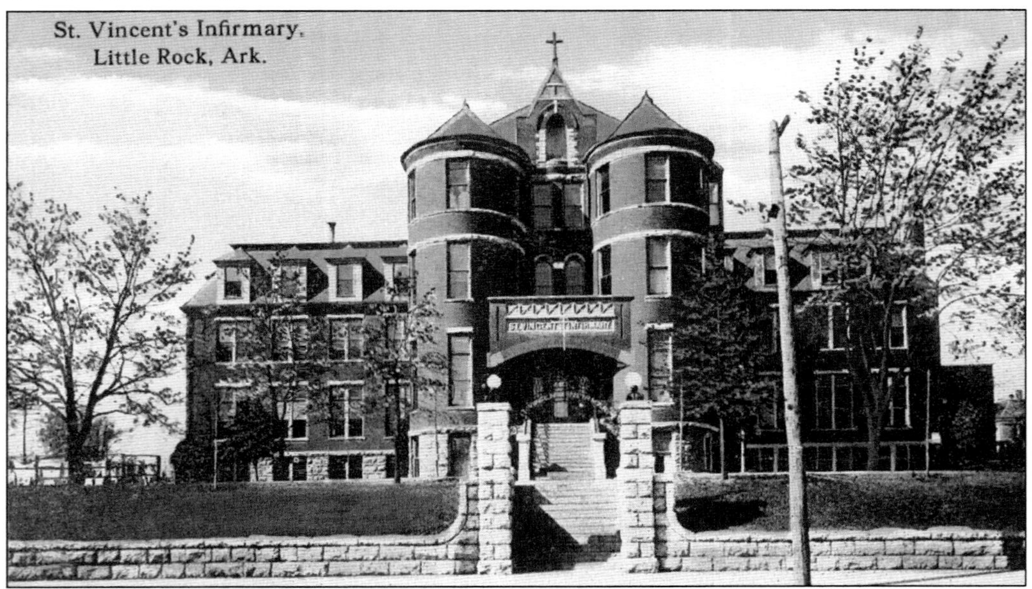

"Your postal received and in reply will say that we have 100 patients," from the St. Vincent's Infirmary located at Tenth and High Streets. The Sisters of Charity of Nazareth opened their first hospital with 26 beds in 1888, and moved to this building in 1900. In 1906 the hospital established the first nursing school in Arkansas and became one of the first dozen hospitals in the United States to be equipped with X-ray equipment. The hospital relocated in 1954 to a new facility near University Avenue. After serving as nursing home, the building was torn down in 1973. (*c.* 1909.)

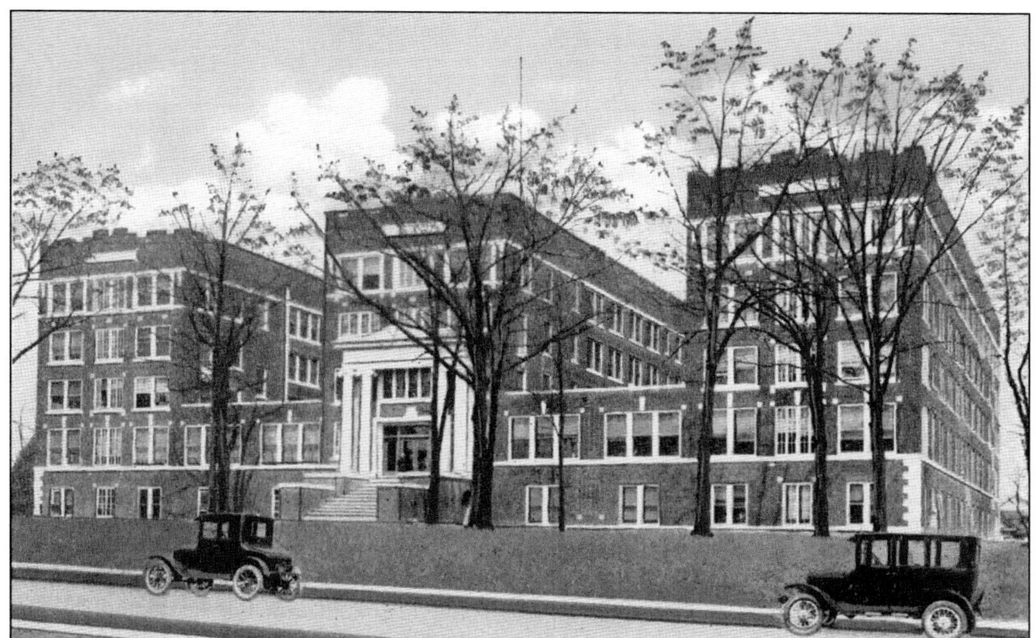

Today Little Rock's Baptist Medical Center is the state's largest hospital. The Baptist State Hospital located at Fourteenth and Battery Streets was the beginning of a massive medical complex, which is presently today housed on a west Little Rock campus with affiliated sites across the state. The Baptist Hospital moved from its Battery Street location in the 1970s. The building no longer stands, but its site now houses part of the expanded Arkansas Children's Hospital. (*c.* 1919.)

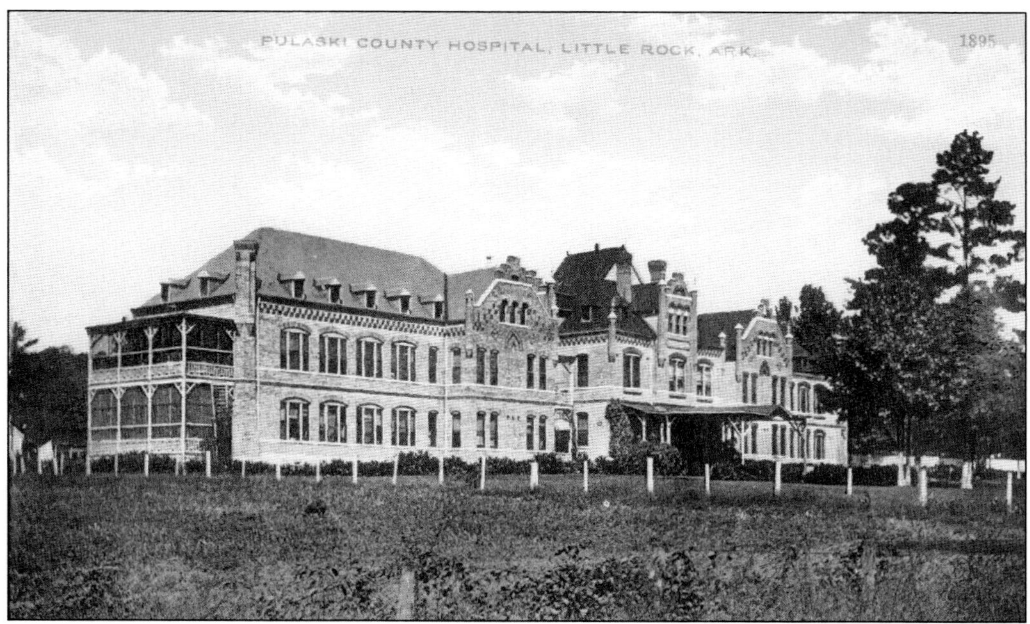

Looking more like an English estate, this building housed the Pulaski County Hospital on what is now Roosevelt Road. This hospital would have been the last hope for many of the area's indigent patients, in an era prior to public health care coverage. The building was removed many years ago. (*c.* 1910.)

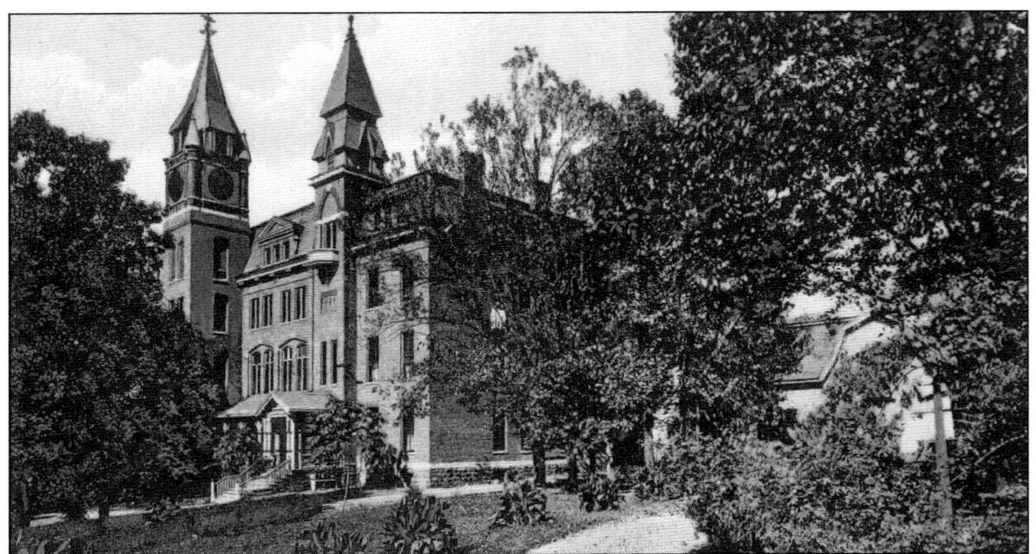

Among the area hospitals which are long gone is the Physicians and Surgeons Hospital, which was begun in 1906 on Lincoln Avenue (now Cantrell Boulevard). According to *Medical Education in Arkansas*, authored by W. David Baird, the hospital was created when a group of doctors felt slighted at the Arkansas University School of Medicine. The disgruntled doctors bought this building, which had been a seminary and a Methodist college in the years since its 1882 construction. The argument was resolved by 1914, and the faculties again merged at the University Medical School After standing vacant for several years, one of the towers of this building was struck by lightning. The edifice was remodeled into apartments, and was razed in the 1960s. (*c.* 1908.)

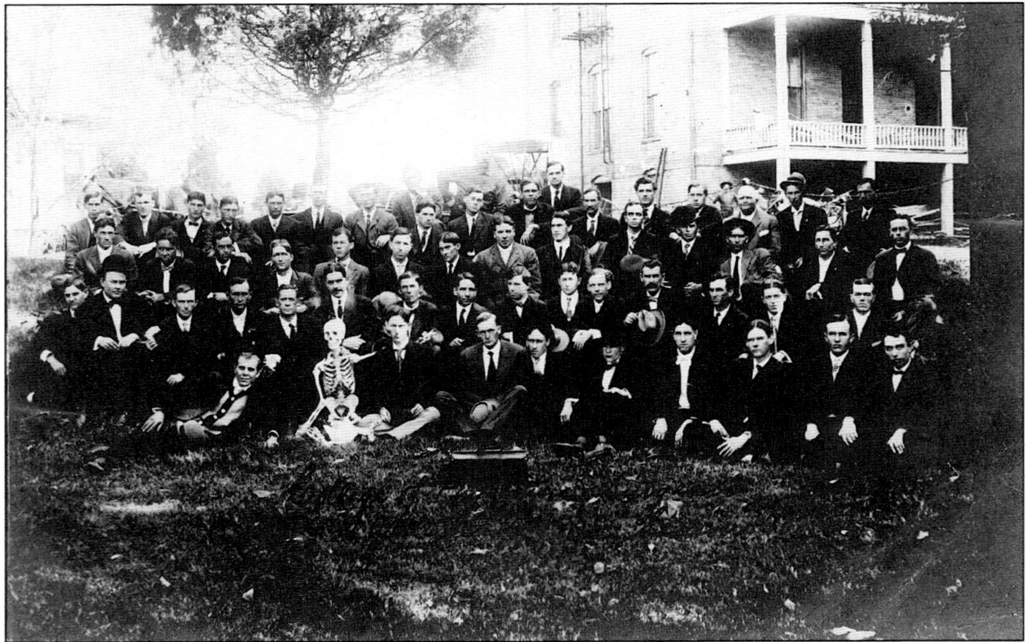

The University of Arkansas School of Medicine, located near City Park, educated most of the physicians who would serve the expanding hospital systems of Little Rock. A group of medical students pose with a skeleton and the physician's traditional black bag in this 1908 postcard.

Fraternal lodges were part of the fabric of Little Rock, and chief among them was the Masonic Temple. Completed in 1891 at its location on the corner of Fifth and Main Streets, the building laid claim to being the tallest commercial building in the city, topped only by the steeple of the Catholic Cathedral of St. Andrew. The Grand Masonic Lodge of Arkansas used a portion of the building, but most of it was leased as office and commercial space. An often faulty steam-powered elevator made it difficult to keep the upper floors rented. The building's wooden interior structure proved to be its downfall; an early morning blaze destroyed the landmark in 1919. (*c.* 1900.)

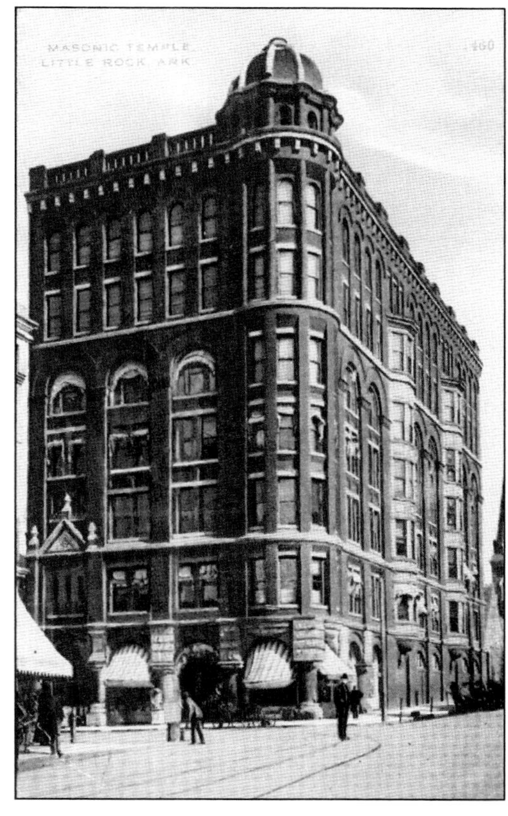

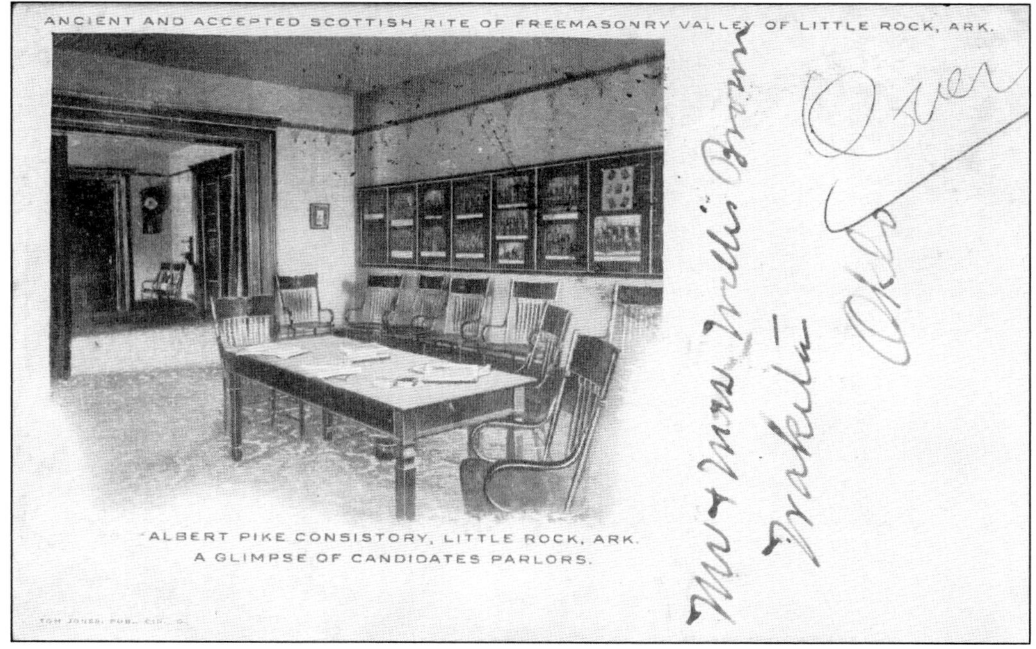

This rare 1911 card published by the Masonic Lodge shows an interior view of the "candidates parlor," presumably the setting for interviews of candidates seeking to join the "Ancient and Accepted Scottish Rite of Freemasonry Valley of Little Rock, Ark."

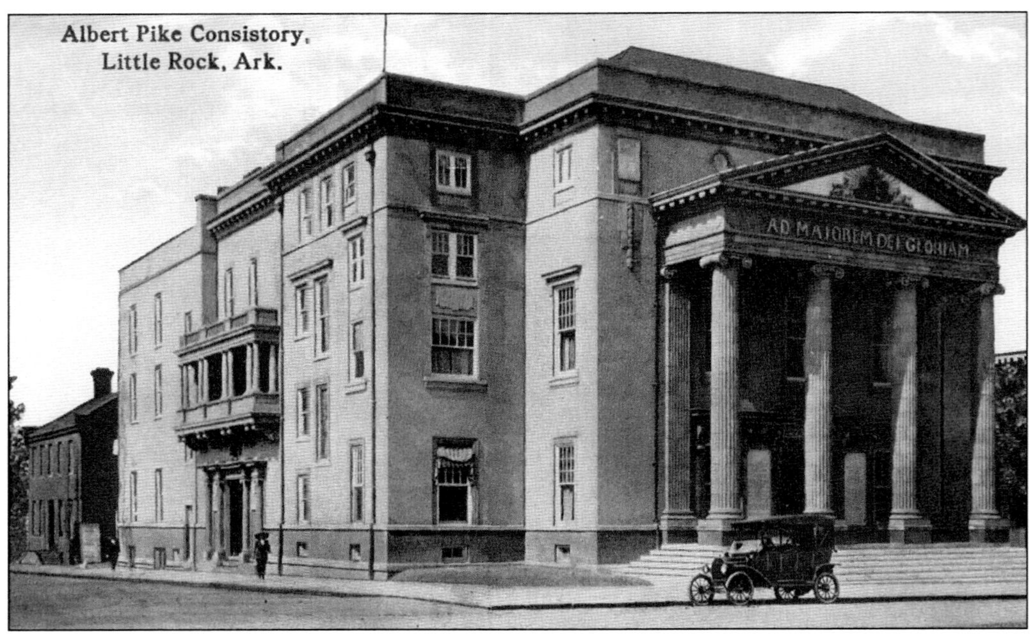

The Scottish Rite Consistory, named for Albert Pike, was erected at Seventh and Scott Streets at the turn of the century. Pike, who led Cherokee warriors against Union troops in the 1862 Battle of Pea Ridge, spent the latter years of his life writing books about freemasonry. This building was renovated in 1924 to create a grand new Masonic Temple, which still serves today. (*c.* 1910.)

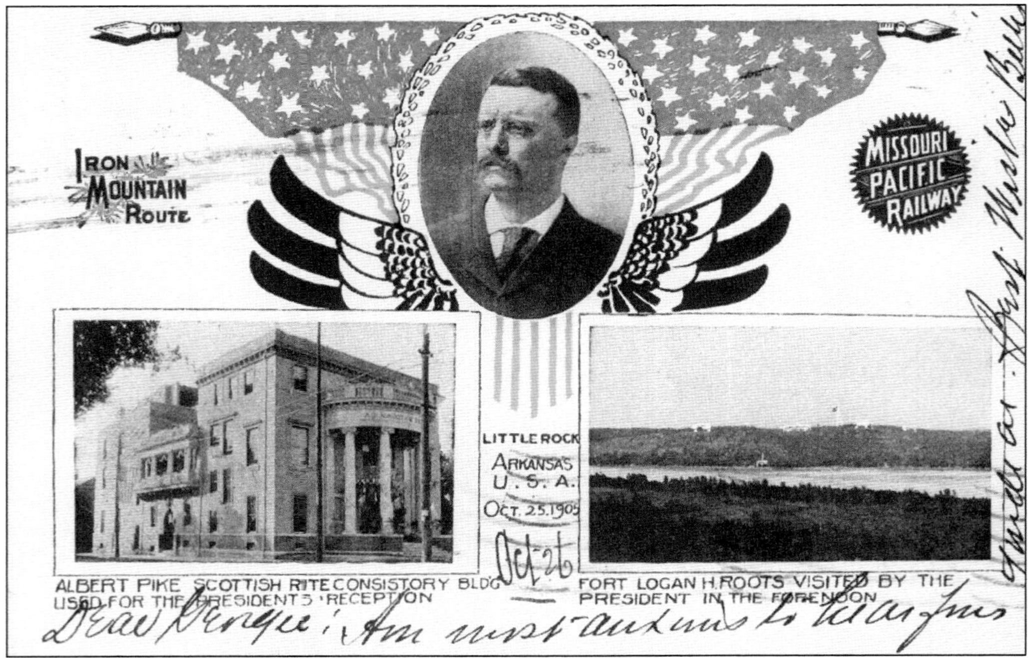

The Albert Pike Consistory played host to President Theodore Roosevelt when he spoke to a luncheon of assembled prominent businessmen during a visit to Little Rock in 1905. The vigorous young president stayed the night at the Marion Hotel, spoke in City Park, and visited nearby Fort Roots before making his address at the Consistory.

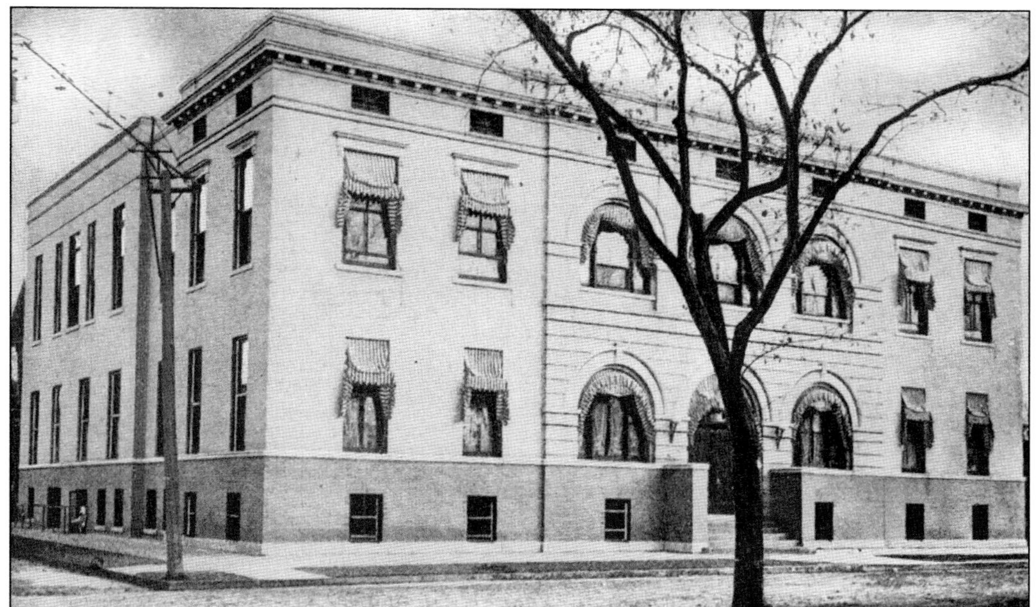

Little Rock's small but influential Jewish community formed the Concordia Association after the Civil War to serve as a Jewish men's club. Jewish residents of Little Rock were excluded from much of the community's societal affairs, despite the business success of some. The club members moved into this new building at Eighth and Scott Streets in 1904. The site became home to the Boys' Club in the 1920s. (*c.* 1910.)

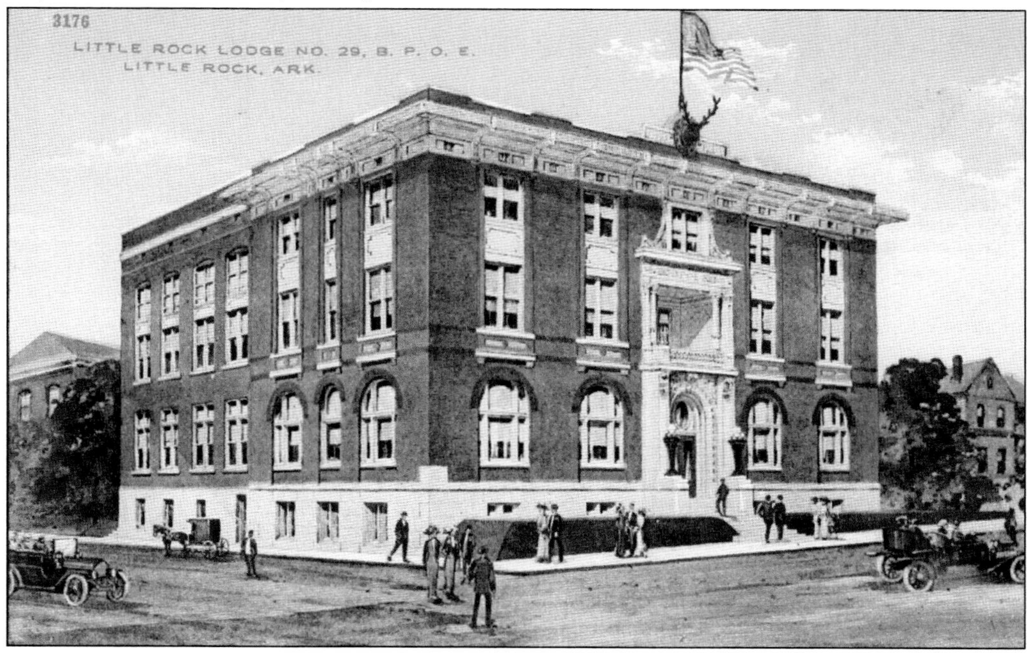

The Little Rock Lodge No. 29 of the Benevolent and Protective Order of Elks had its headquarters at Fourth and Scott Streets. The Elks were founded in New York in 1868 by the theatrical profession and were well known for charitable works by the time this building was erected at the turn of the century. The restored building is the present home to the Women's City Club. (*c.* 1910.)

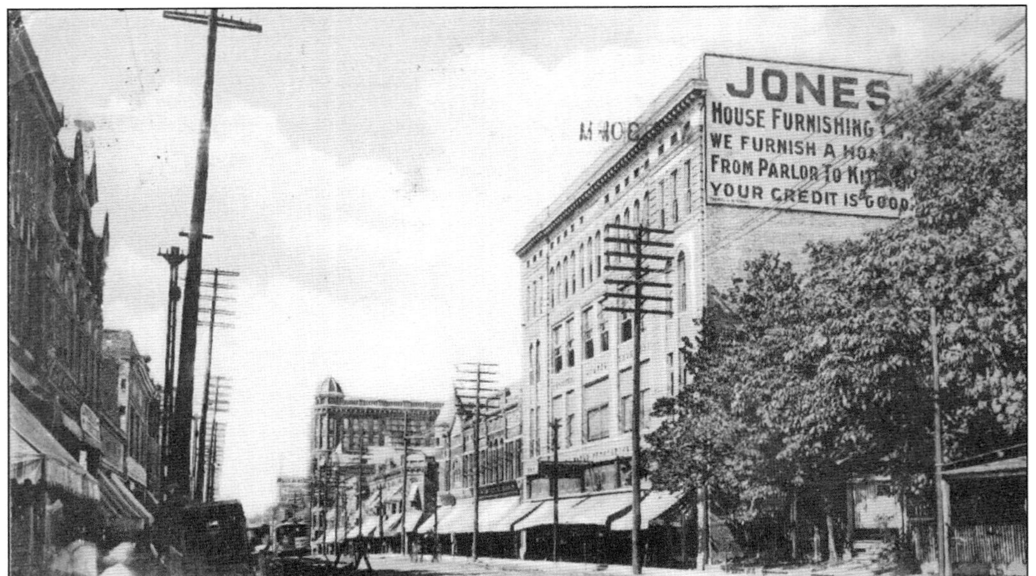

The Jones Furniture Company filled most of this building in the 700 block of Main Street, and advertised on January 1, 1911, a giant sale: "We're going to make things hum at this store in 1911 and start off with the greatest cut price sale ever. . . Destined to eclipse everything of its kind ever attempted in this town"—but such was not to be. Within 48 hours the store was destroyed by the great fire. (*c.* 1905.)

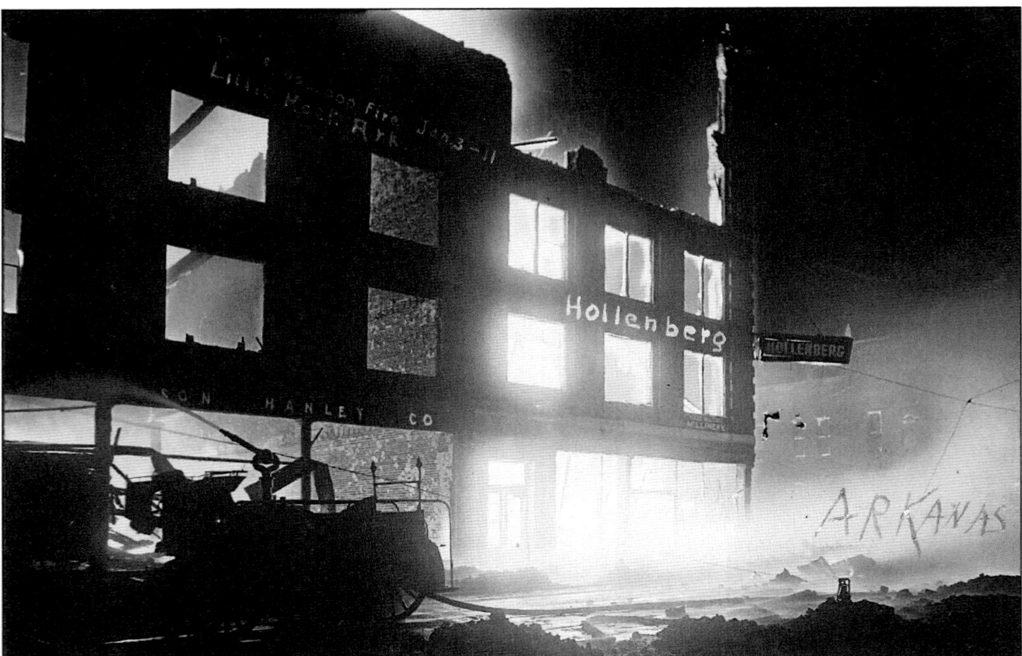

On January 3, 1911, the fire began on the upper floor of the Hollenberg Music Store (center), apparently from a discarded cigarette, and soon spread to the Jackson-Hanley Hardware store (left). The city's antiquated fire equipment is seen feebly shooting a weak stream of water onto the flaming holocaust. The City used the fire as support for its appeal to upgrade its firefighting equipment.

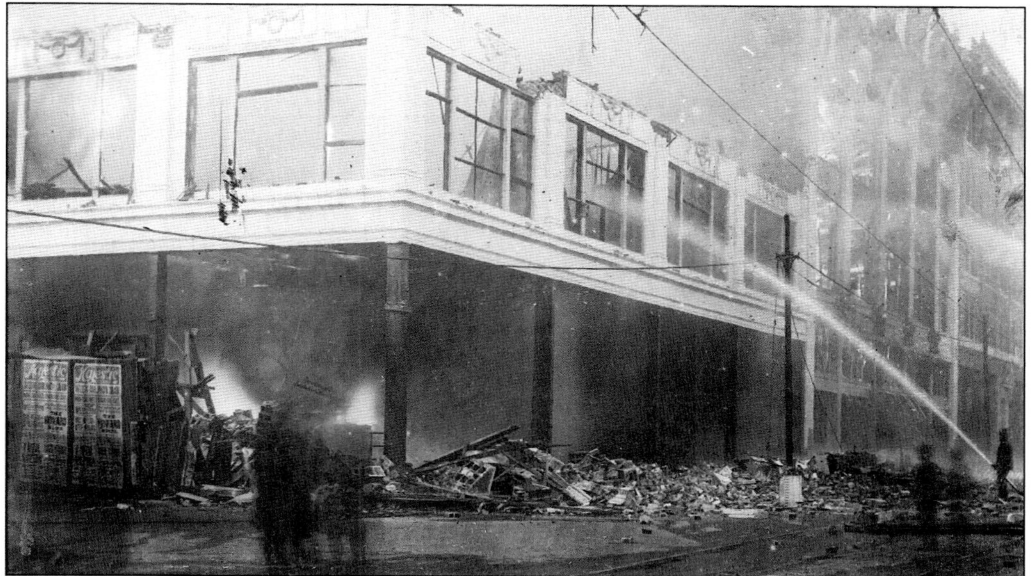

On November 13, 1911, some months after the great fire, Jones Furniture relocated to the 600 block of Main Street and was restocked with new inventory. After only a month in the new location, the fire demon struck again. This second major fire in less than a year led to threats of cancellation of fire insurance for many businesses on Main Street. Meanwhile, Jones again relocated, this time to the old Kress building in the 500 block of Main Street, and was restocked once more. This 1911 card is part of the collection of Jim Pfeifer of Little Rock.

The Worst Fire in Little Rock's History

In the late hours of the evening of January 2, 1911, the winter's first snowstorm was settling in over Little Rock. Two teenage boys were cleaning up the Hollenberg Music Store on the fifth floor of a building owned by Governor George Donaghey in the 700 block of Main Street. Reports noted that one of the young men threw a lighted cigarette into a box of oily rags, which ignited a fire. The boys later said they poured a bucket of water over the rags and left, assuming the fire was doused. Five hours later, with the freezing dawn, flames burst through the upper windows of the building, and the worst fire in Little Rock's history was unleashed.

The fire raged for five hours, throwing embers for three blocks as the city's fire department tried to extinguish it with inadequate water pressure and equipment not suited for safely reaching the top of the five-story building. As the fire spread beyond the Hollenberg Music Store, the Jackson-Hanley Hardware Company was engulfed. Finally the roaring flames reached the huge Jones Furniture Store, which had advertised plans for the largest sale ever held in Little Rock only two days before.

Almost the entire block of Main between Sixth and Seventh Streets was lost. Crowds filled the surrounding downtown streets in the subfreezing weather to watch the pyrotechnic display; soon the flames reached the Martin Arms Company, which housed ammunition and fireworks. Reports in the *Arkansas Gazette* reported that "the din resembled the rattling of field guns," and that the crowds had to dodge a barrage of fireballs unleashed when a large supply of roman candles was ignited. The newspaper headlines proclaimed a $1 million loss, with the greatest proportion of that loss being borne by Gov. George Donaghey and the Jones Furniture Company.

As with most early-20th-century events, the photographers turned out—and the best record of the fire was saved on the postcards their work would produce.

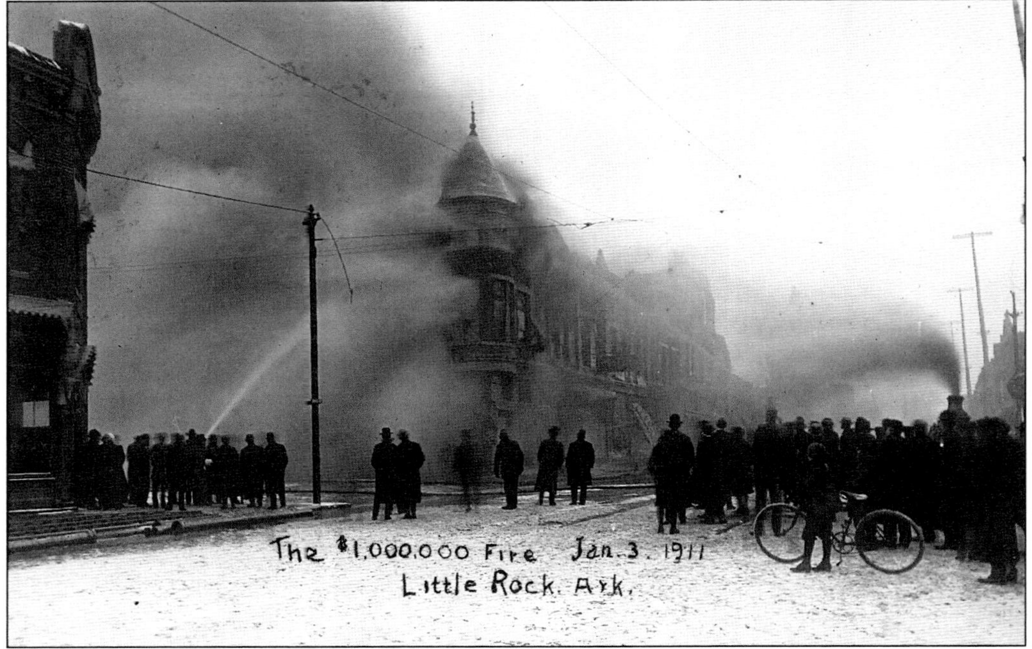

With the early morning light, firefighters began to halt the spread of the flames, which at one point threatened much of the downtown area. To the right is seen a plume of smoke from one of the city's steam-powered pumper trucks, which proved inadequate to handle the blaze.

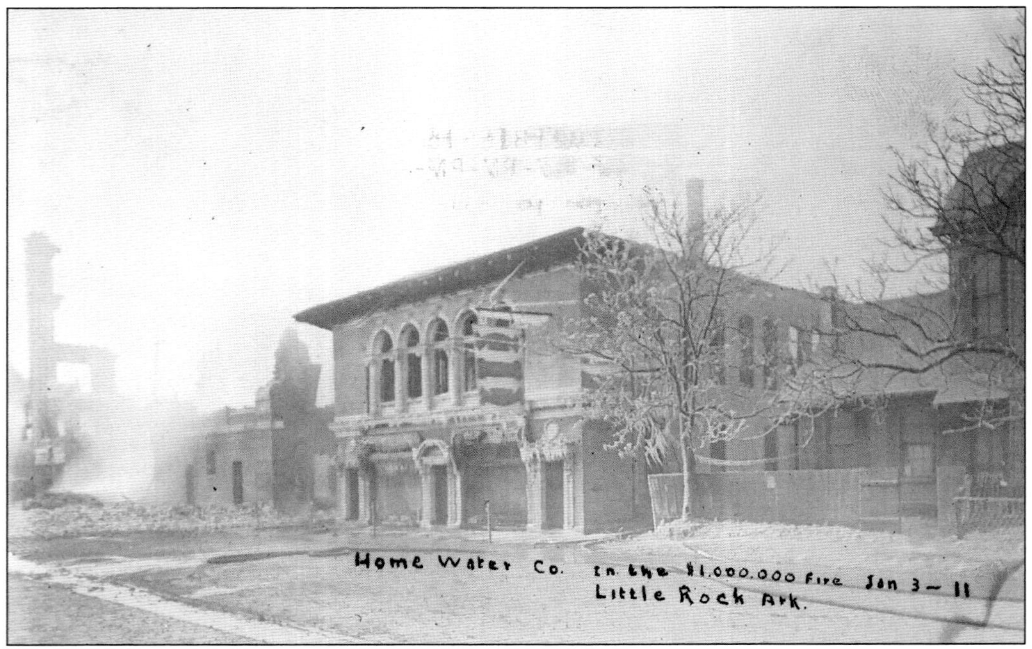

This arch-windowed building, which housed the Home Water Company and the YWCA, was located behind the Main Street building where the fire began. By morning, the leaping flames had reduced the building to no more than a burned-out shell.

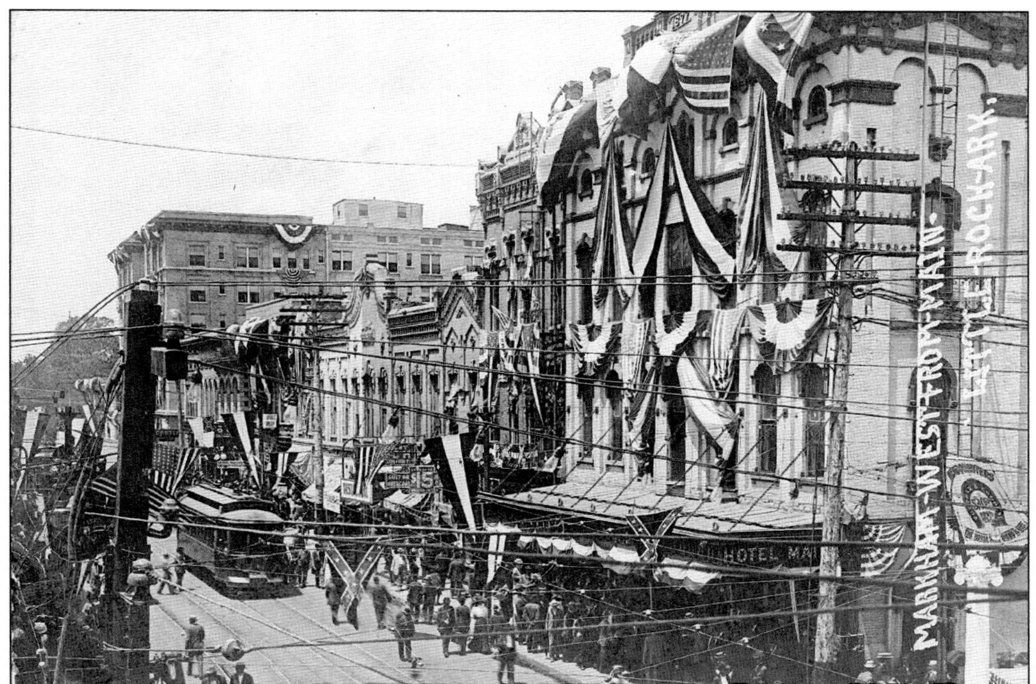

The headquarters for the UCV reunion was the Hotel Marion seen in the distance; the Hotel Main is in the foreground. Markham Street was decorated with Confederate flags and banners reflective of the festive, welcoming mood of the city and its business community, which hoped to profit from the throngs invading Little Rock. One department store, M.M. Cohn's, advertised, "We have in stock for immediate delivery Confederate gray uniforms for veterans and sons of veterans—prices $9, $12, and $15."

The South Rises Again: The United Confederate Veterans Reunion of 1911

The year 1911 marked the 50th anniversary of the firing on Fort Sumter, which ignited the American Civil War. Arkansas became one of 11 states to secede from the Union. Fifty years later, the city of Little Rock successfully bid to host the annual reunion of the United Confederate Veterans. The result was a record number of visitors flooding the city, a record that was not broken until election night 1992, some 80 years later, when Arkansas Gov. Bill Clinton was elected president.

The population of Little Rock was 45,000 in 1911, but grew to 150,000 during the three days of the reunion, according to newspaper accounts. The meeting brought 11,000 former gray soldiers to town, along with thousands of other visitors. The May event was truly one of the most remarkable in the city's history. Thankfully, photographers were present to produce a series of postcard views, which represent the best surviving record of this gathering of the rapidly thinning gray line of the Confederacy.

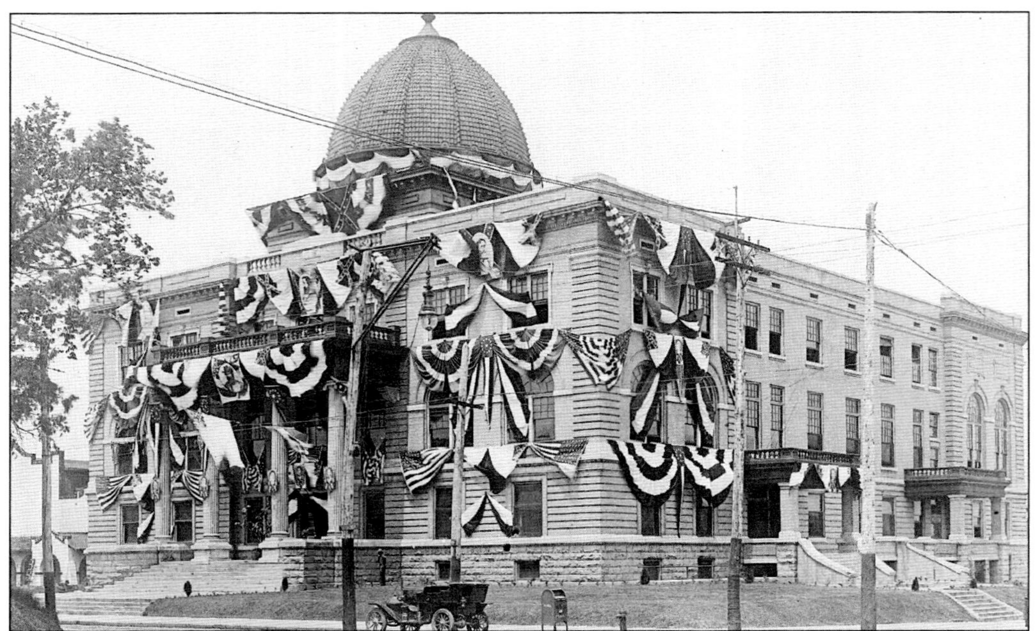

Little Rock City Hall was decked out for the reunion. The welcome of city fathers carried over into the press, as shown herein the reflective musings of the *Arkansas Gazette*:

> Most of the men who camped with Lee and Forrest and fought with them in the dark days of civil strife have already camped on the other side, and the few who remain are but awaiting the bugle signal to come up higher. Comrades of the past, men who fought battles of the world, will clasp hands and march together in Little Rock for the last time. It is unlike any other reunion ever entertained by Little Rock, because of the fact that many of those who come here will join the great reunion above before the muster roll is called for another reunion here.

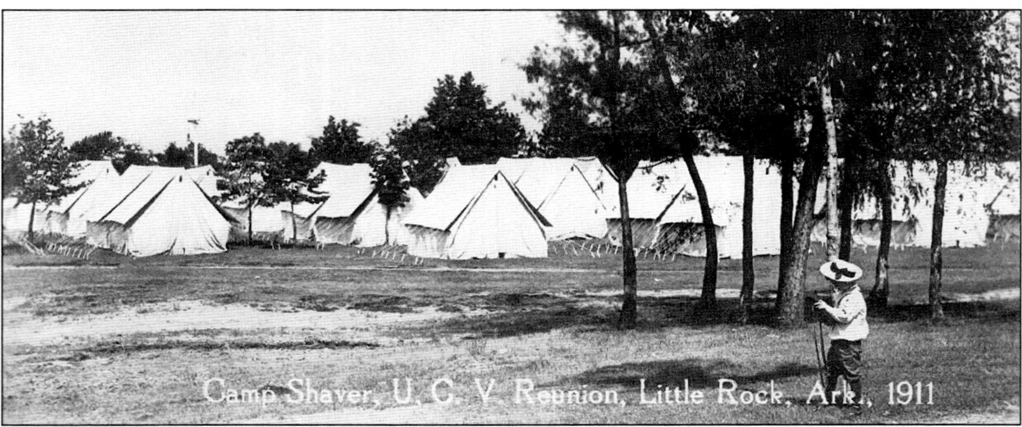

The number of veteran soldiers who flocked to Little Rock exceeded expectations by several thousand, straining the city's pledge to feed and house the veterans free of charge. With the help of the army post at nearby Fort Roots, 1,100 tents were set up in City Park to house the veterans in an encampment christened "Camp Shaver." The camp was named for "Fighting Bob" Shaver, a former Confederate general who lived in Mena. Shaver commanded the 27th Arkansas Regiment, and at the 1862 Battle of Shiloh reportedly had four horses shot from under him. Wounded in the hand, he wore a white glove for the rest of his life.

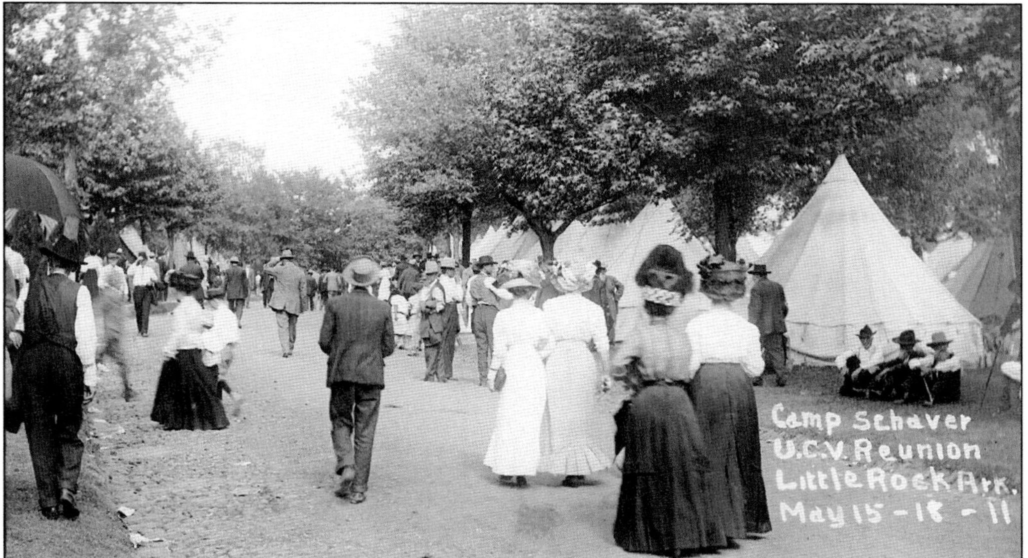

At certain times the public was admitted to Camp Shaver to visit with the veteran soldiers and to listen to the tales of battles won and lost half a century before. In the camp, the city not only housed the old rebels, but also fed their great appetites. Newspaper accounts itemized the food provided free of charge at the camp: over three days the men were fed 54,000 meals, from provisions that included "16,000 loaves of bread, 8,000 pounds of steak, 3,000 pounds of roast, 110 cases of eggs, and 1,700 pounds of coffee." One veteran quipped, "had General Lee's troops been so well fed, the South would have won the war."

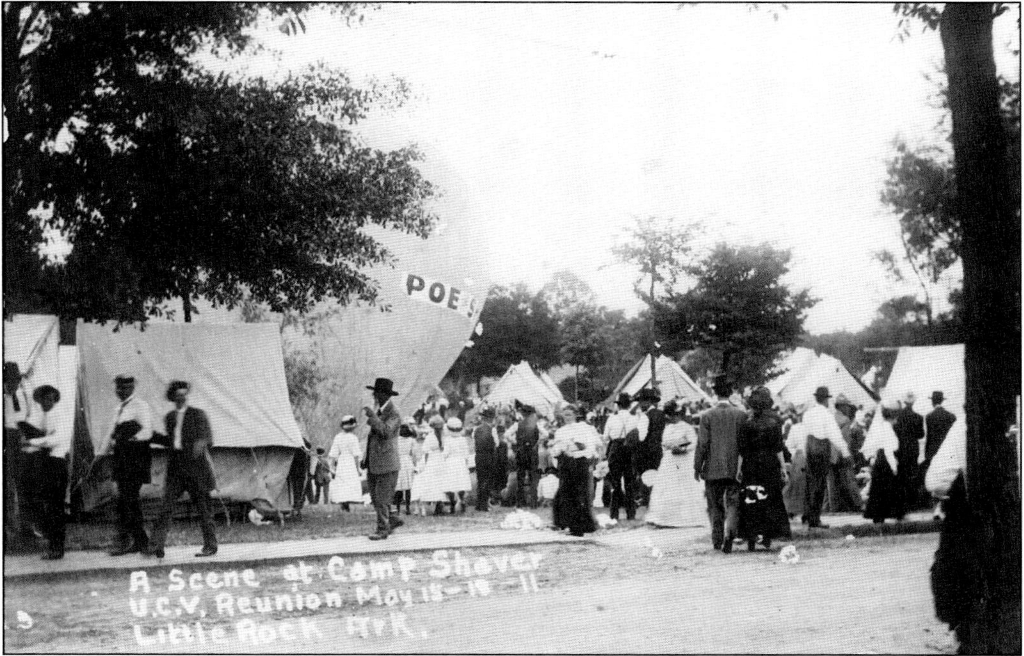

The city worked to provide entertainment for the veterans, which included free ascension rides in this tethered balloon anchored among the tents of Camp Shaver. Unfortunately, the balloon, which had been shipped in from Arizona, would not rise because it was filled with defective gas.

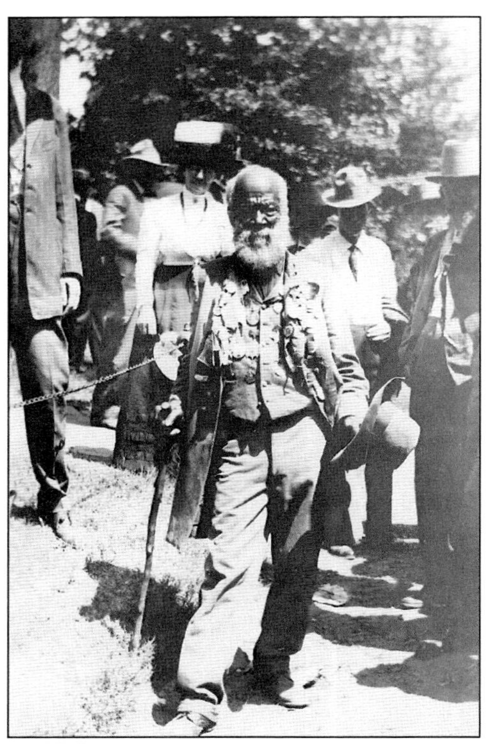

In the history of the UCV reunion at Little Rock is the story of another reunion held simultaneously, a meeting of the "Negro body servants" who cared for the Confederate officers and did chores around the camps during the war. One of these elderly black men posed for this postcard photo, decked out in his medals. The leader of the small group, in a speech in front of City Hall, was quoted in the *Arkansas Gazette* as saying: "We are gathered here today to give thanks to the good people of the City or their kind treatment toward the Negro veterans. . . We have met with many reunions but we would like to say the Lord lives in Little Rock. If I were permitted to do so I would change the name of Little Rock to 'Little Rock Paradise,' or I would call it the 'Paradisiacal City.' " (*c.* 1911.)

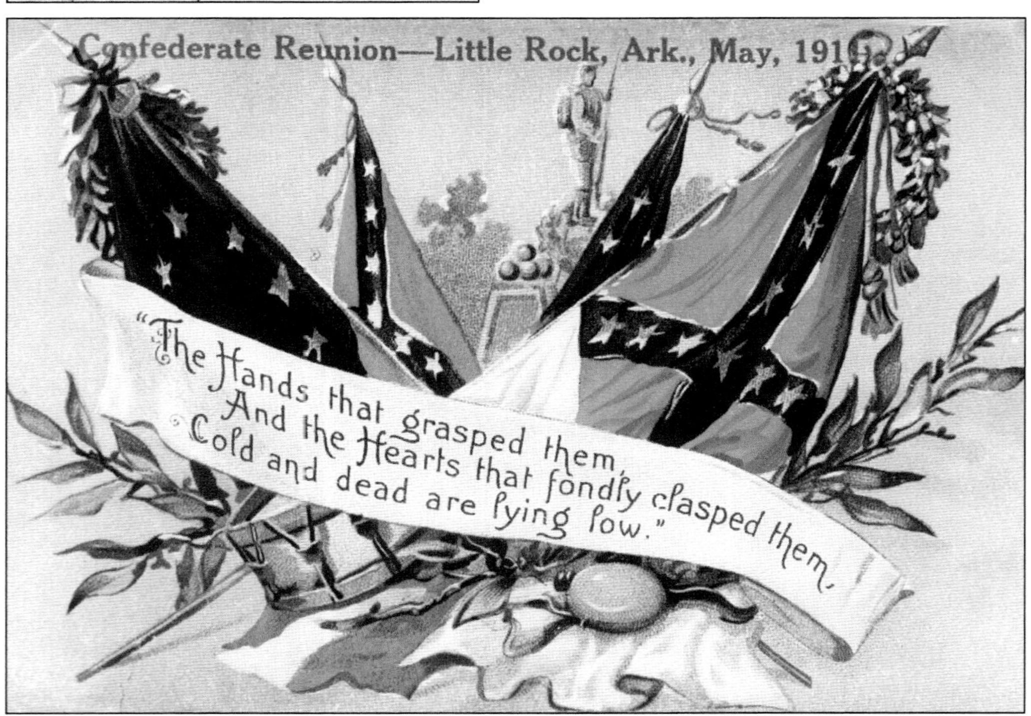

Among the most telling postcard images of the passions evoked by memories of the old rebel soldiers might have been on this card, "The Hands that grasped them, And the Hearts that fondly clasped them, Cold and dead are lying low." This *c.* 1911 card is one of a series of similar cards produced as souvenirs of the reunion.

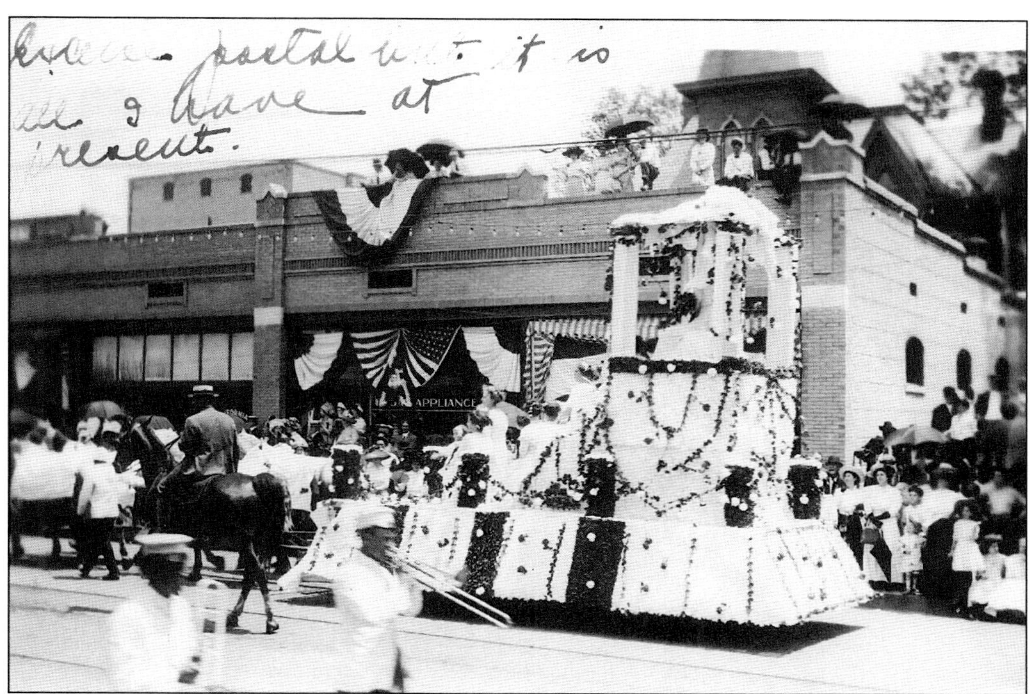

During a two-hour parade, the veterans' reunion held its grand finale. The UCV Queen of the Ball is seen here in her horse-drawn float, passing through South Main Street. The float had to stop for a moment when a buggy bearing young women was brought to a halt by its balky horse. When the horse failed to move, cries of "build a fire under him" rang out. A powerful twist of the beast's ear by a burly policeman got the parade moving again.

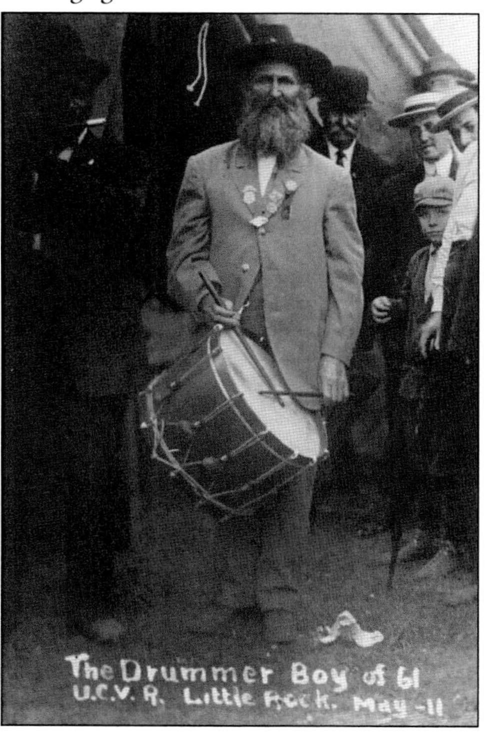

To the surprise of some, there were no fatalities among the thousands of marching veterans in the parade, but there were some close calls. The man featured on this "The Drummer Boy of 61" postcard had a grueling experience. While playing his drum in the march up Main Street, he collapsed in the heat. Ladies rushed out to fan him with their handkerchiefs after he fell into the arms of a policeman, crying out, "Just fan me a little and help me along, and I will finish this march or die in the attempt." The former soldier was taken to a nearby hotel for treatment, where he refused to give his name. This photo, part of the collection of Tom Mertens, became a very popular postcard.

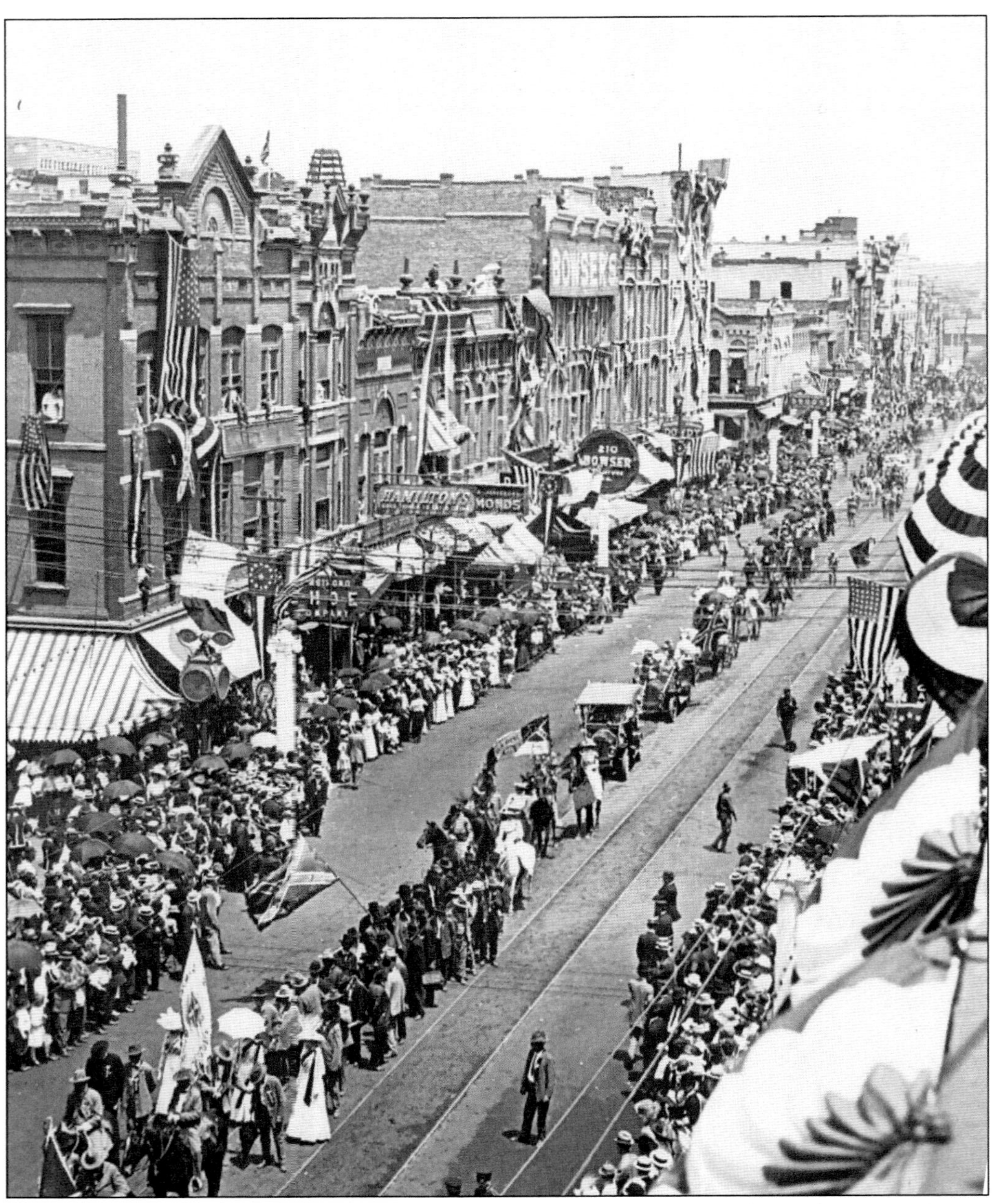

The UCV closing parade began at the Old State House on Markham and passed up Main Street, along a 20-block route lined with 150,000 spectators. Rebel yells and the strains of "Dixie" played by 400 marching musicians carried over the crowd as the soldiers, many in their 80s, walked in the heat bearing shot-riddled flags and tattered uniforms. This view was taken from the roof of one of the taller buildings on Main Street, looking north toward the river.

Two

1920 to 1939

Decades of Growth and Depression

At the opening of what American history refers to as the Roaring Twenties, the greatest downtown building boom in Little Rock's history began. The huge reserves of lumber, steel, and bricks that had been stockpiled for the demands of WW I, along with generous financing from expanding lending institutions, made possible the construction of many landmarks. Many of them are still standing today, though often in altered condition.

By 1920, Little Rock's population had swelled from 38,000 to 65,000. The city's residents and visitors still sent postcards documenting their activities and environment. Although not as great in number as in the preceding decade, the postcards captured most of the new buildings of the era, and now preserve the images of bustling activity along Main Street, which remains the crossroads of the state.

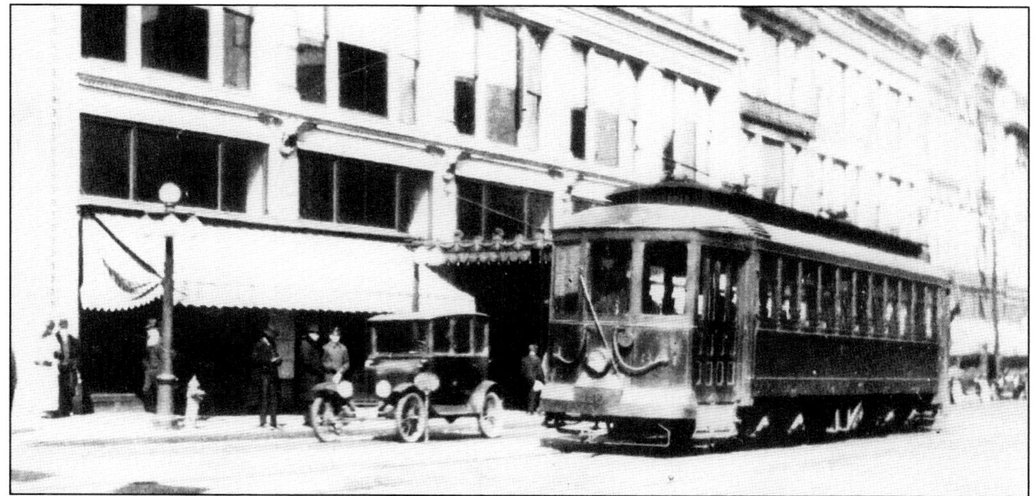

This *c.* 1920 view of Main Street captured a Model T and a streetcar along the north end of the street. Perhaps the streetcar conductor standing in the front of his car looked down at the growing number of automobiles and paused to wonder about the future of his chosen employment.

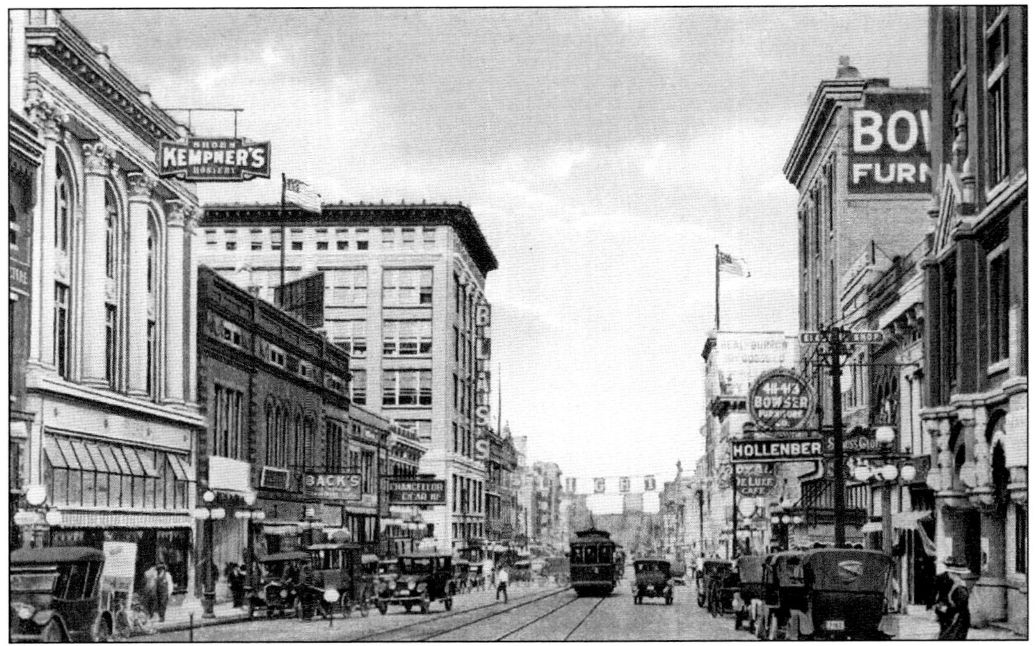

Looking north from Fifth Street down Main are seen such notable businesses as Kempner's (left), Blass Department Store (center), and Bowser's Furniture (right). The Hollenberg Music Store, relocated after the fire of 1911, stands beside the DeLuxe Cafe. (*c.* 1920).

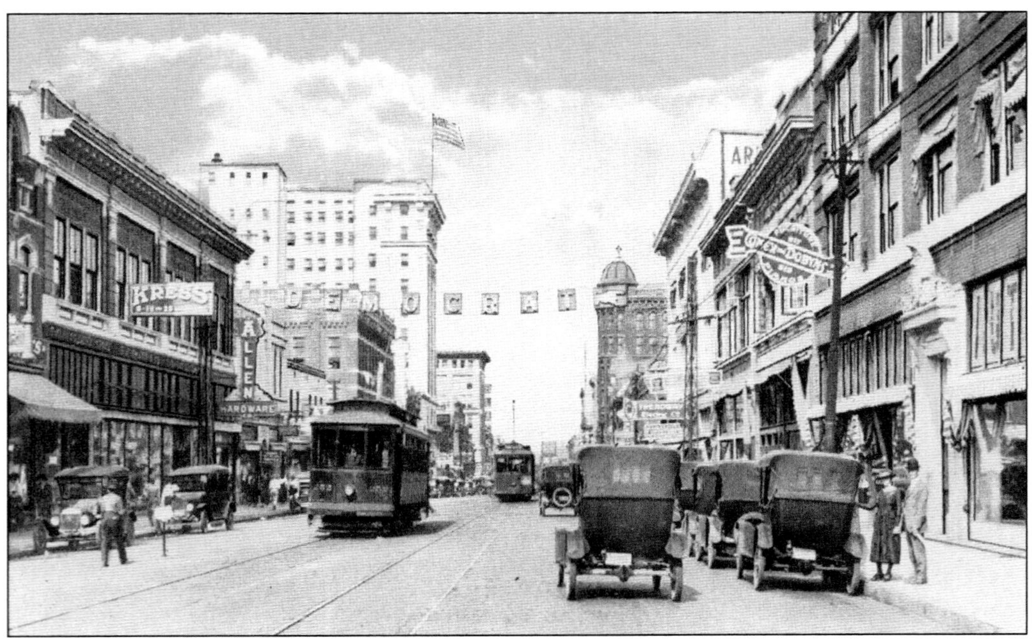

Canvas-topped automobiles were becoming increasingly visible on Main Street, along with the streetcars seen in this 1921 view from Seventh Street. Stores pictured on this postcard include Kress 5-10-25 Cent Store (left) and Allen's Hardware Company (right). The Boyle Building (formerly State National Bank), which is topped with an American flag, can be seen in the distance.

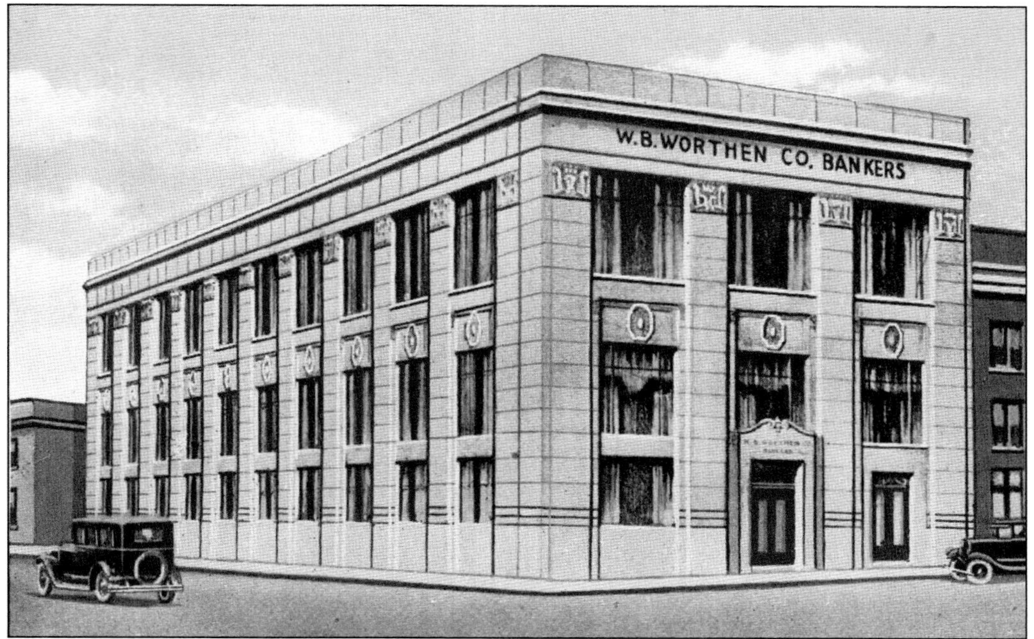

W.B. Worthen founded his first bank in 1877. By the late 1920s, booming growth led the bank to pay $175,000 for a lot at Fourth and Main Streets, on which this Carthage marble construction was erected only two months before the stock market crashed in October 1929. The bank recovered from the financial depression to become one of the state's leading financial institutions. Today it has been absorbed into Bank of America and no longer bears Mr. Worthen's name. The building shown in this 1929 photo is presently home to the television station KATV.

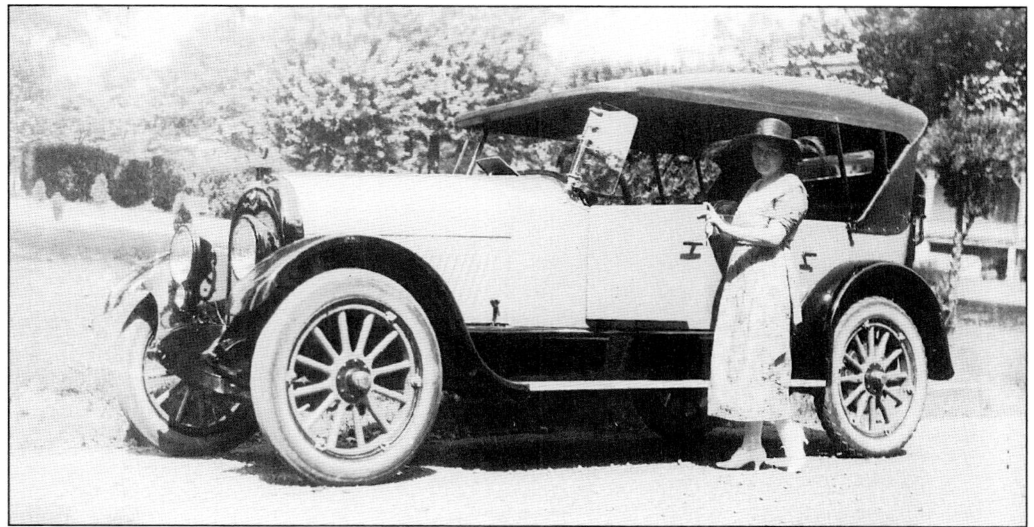

In 1919, three businessmen, led by Mr. William Drake, set up shop on East Seventeenth Street to manufacture the automobile they named "the Climber," one of which is shown in this *c.* 1922 photo. The company advertised its cars in the *Arkansas Gazette* as having "essential goodness and permanent value," with prices ranging between $1,200 and $2,400. The Climber Motor Corporation built and sold around 200 vehicles before going bankrupt in 1924. Banks refused to finance the rather expensive vehicles.

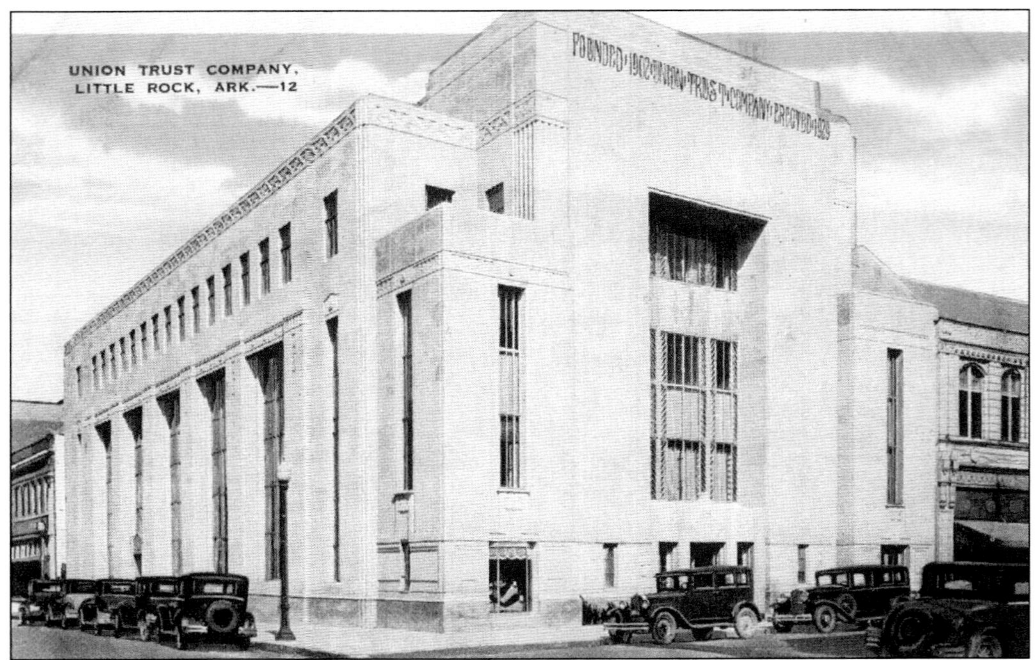

The Union Trust Company building was erected in 1929, in a distinguished Art Deco architectural style. In later years the business became Union National Bank, which moved from this building to a new high-rise structure in 1969. Sadly, this very serviceable and architecturally significant building was torn down in 1978 to make way for a parking lot.(*c.* 1930.)

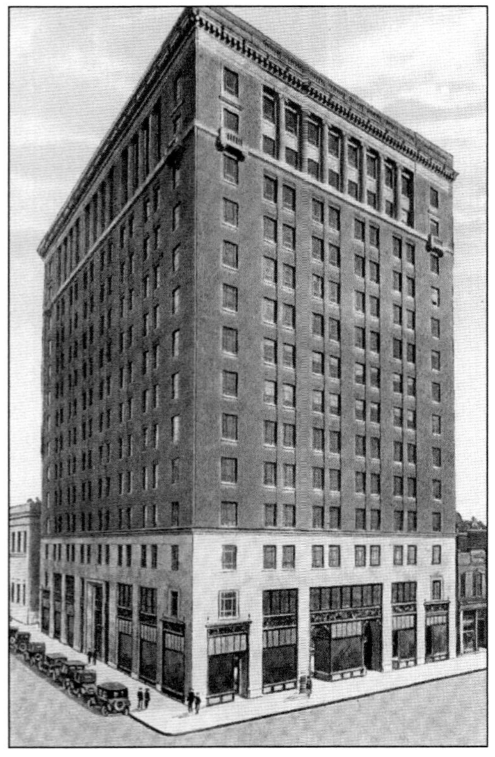

In 1926, former Gov. George Donaghey had erected at Seventh and Main Streets what was then the tallest building in Arkansas. The 14-story Donaghey Building was touted as having been constructed after the great skyscrapers of Chicago and New York, with fireproof design and high speed elevators. For years the building housed many of the city's physicians, lawyers, and insurance companies. Today the building is almost completely occupied by the Arkansas Department of Human Services.

"Believe me, the Southern girls are really something to write home about" was the message conveyed to Michigan on the back of this 1933 card of the Hotel Ben McGehee, which was located at the corner of Markham and Main Streets. Erected in the 1920s one-half block from the upscale Hotel Marion, the Ben McGehee was used by traveling salesmen and those on a more restricted budget. It was renamed the Grady Manning Hotel in later years and torn down in 1980, along with the Hotel Marion, to make way for construction of a new convention center.

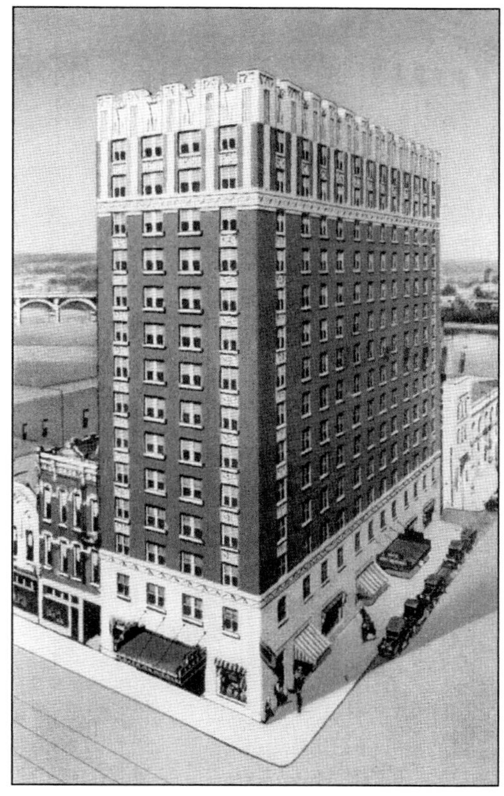

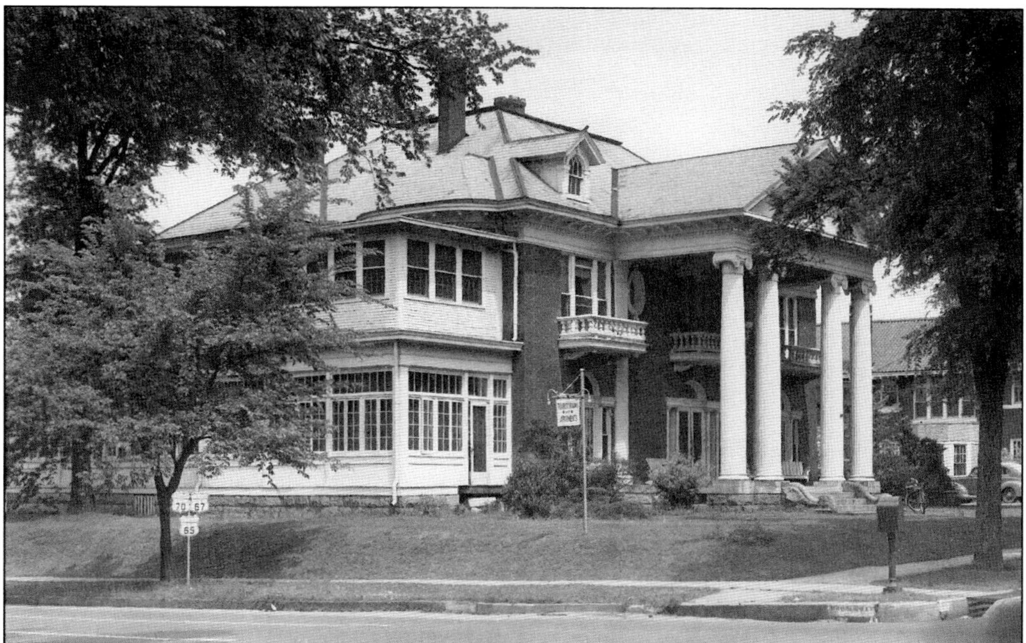

Garm's Tourist Home, located at Eighteenth and Broadway, was converted from a stately home which hosted tourists at rates starting at $2 per day. This prime location at the bypass of Highways 67 and 70 drew many travelers who sent home postcards such as this. The building in this *c.* 1935 picture was demolished in the 1960s.

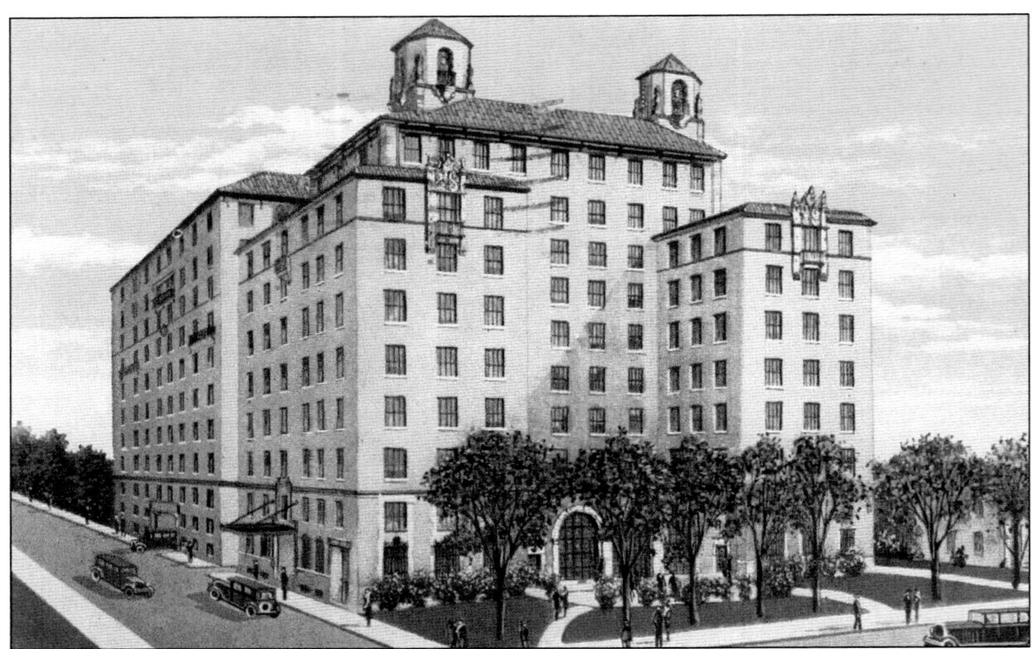

"Little Rock is only a small place," a guest of the Albert Pike Hotel wrote on this 1930 postcard. The hotel was completed in 1929, just before the crash of the stock market. Among the stockholders in the million-dollar hotel building was former Gov. George Donaghey. The hotel was converted in the 1970s to serve as a retirement home operated by the Second Baptist Church.

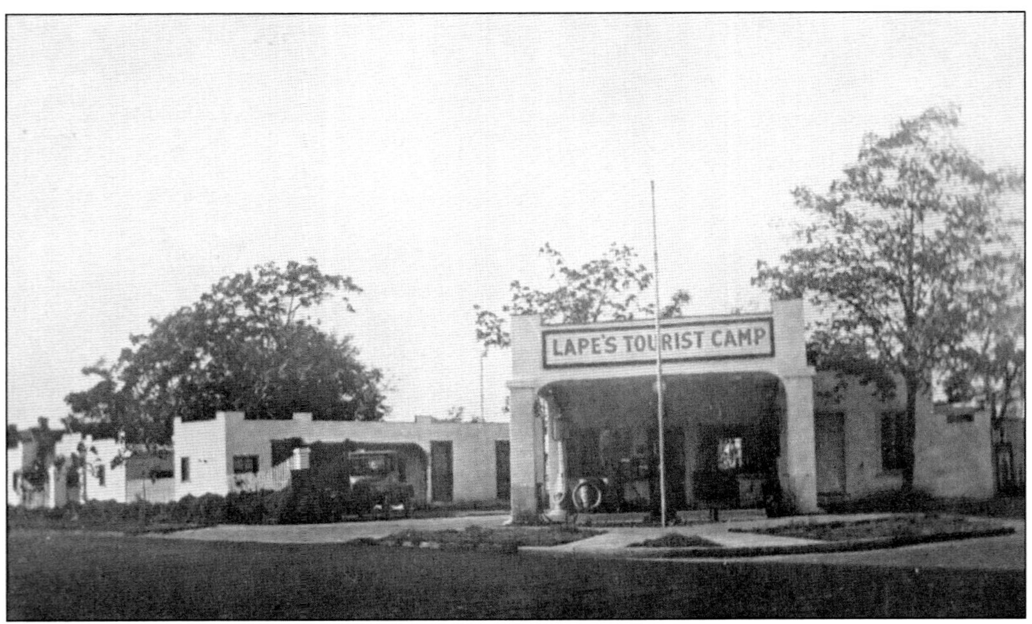

The era of the "tourist court" had arrived, just in time to accommodate the motoring public. Lape's Tourist Camp, located at Fourteenth and Ringo Streets, provided gasoline and auto repairs for its guests. Today only a portion of the foundation marks the site of the business. (*c.* 1935.)

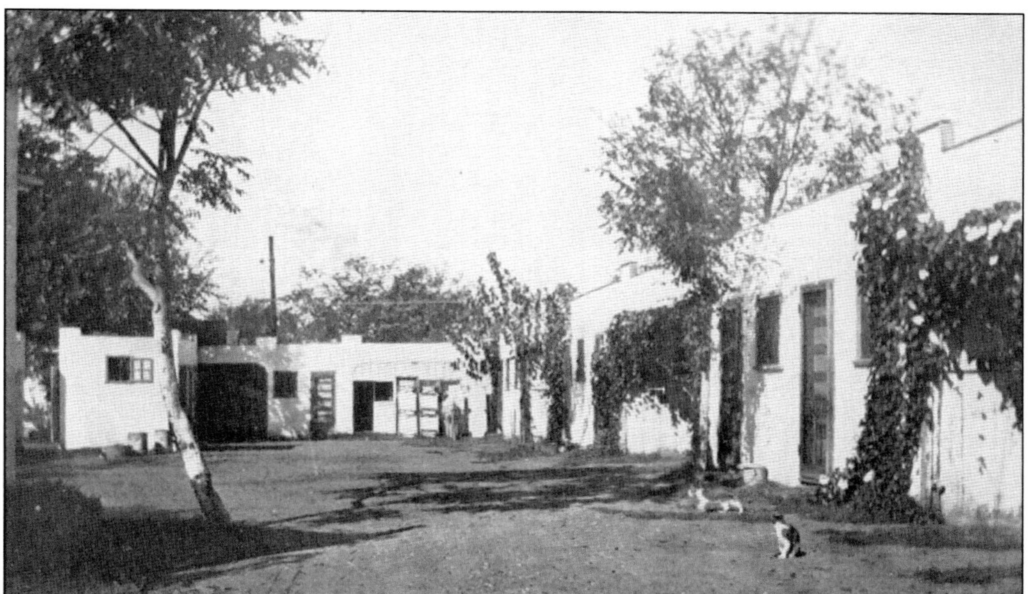

After registering at Lape's, the motorist pulled his or her automobile into this courtyard to park in the garage provided with each room. Guests checking in the day this *c.* 1935 photo was made appear to have taken interest in the two tabby cats.

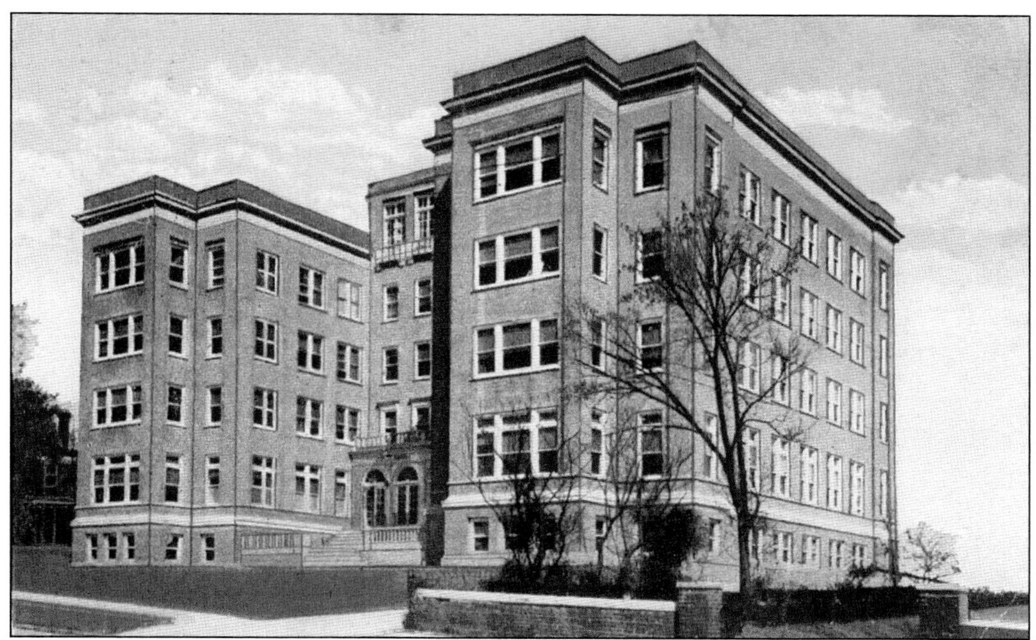

"This place is wonderful. . . . don't worry about me—I'll be all right" were the words from a patient at the Missouri Pacific Hospital, on a 1932 postcard sent to her parents in Louisiana. The hospital was built in the early 1930s on Lincoln Avenue, which is now known as Cantrell Road.

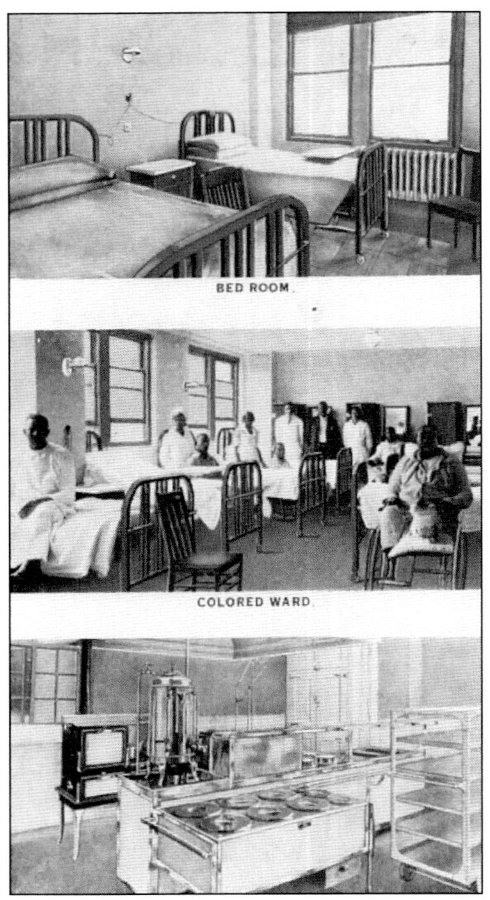

Facilities at the Missouri Pacific Hospital were functional, if not opulent, for the employees of the railroad. Pictured in the 1935 postcard folder is a patient room, the "colored ward," and the kitchen. Black employees were critical to the operations of the railroad, hence a dedicated section of the hospital in segregated America. The man in a wheelchair (left) lost both legs, a hazard of railroad employment. The hospital later admitted non-railroad employees as patients and served as a drug and alcohol treatment facility. The building was razed in the 1980s, and the impressive river-front site became part of the property adjoining the headquarters of the Dillard's Department Store Company.

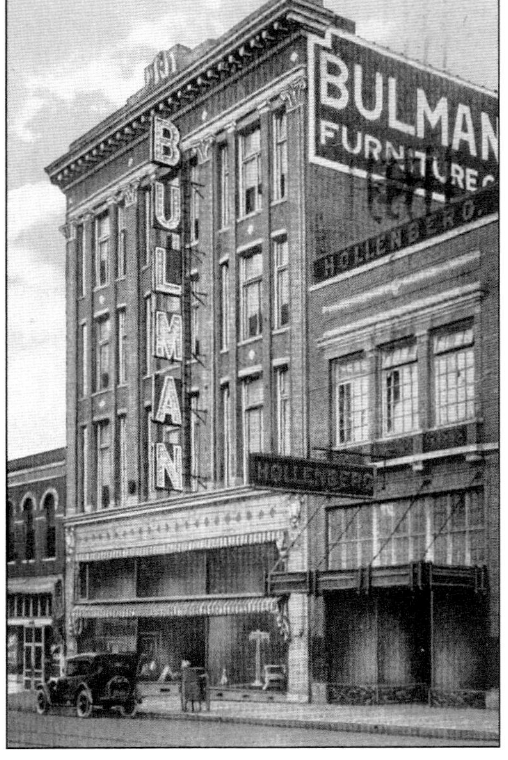

Bulman's Furniture occupied the tall building at 411 Main Street beside Hollenberg's Music Store (right). The back of this 1925 card proclaims, "Your credit is good at BULMAN'S. . . We sell everything for the Home, from the Cheapest that's good to the best that's made."

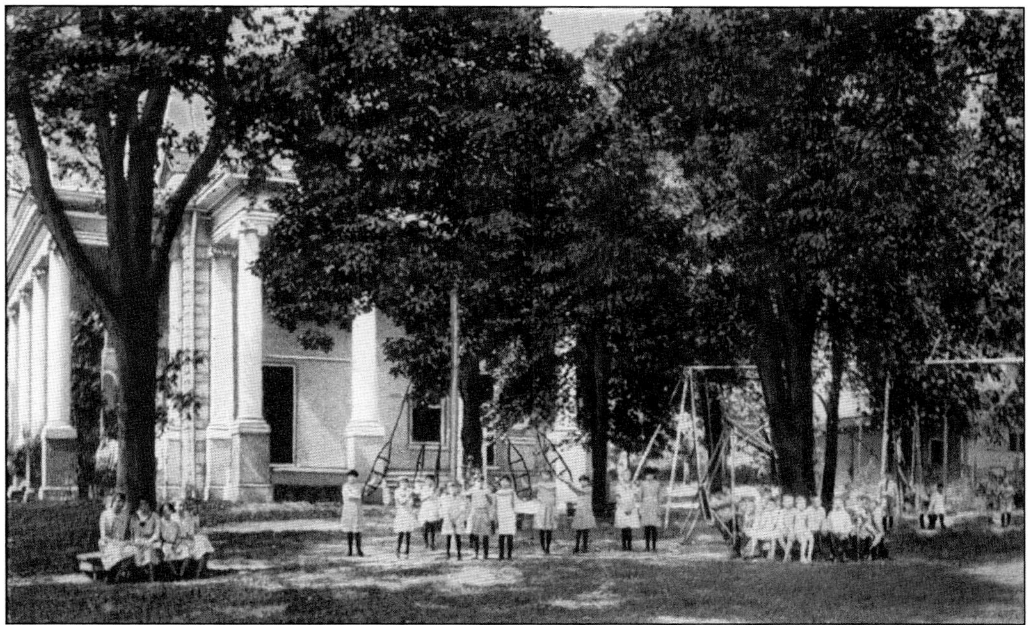

Led by Little Rock businessman Horace Pugh, a group of concerned citizens founded the Arkansas Children's Home in 1912. In an effort to provide much needed medical care to youngsters, Superintendent Orlando P. Christian, a retired Methodist minister, added a hospital in 1926. The orphanage closed in 1954, but the Arkansas Children's Hospital has grown to become one of America's leading pediatric medical centers. (*c.* 1925.)

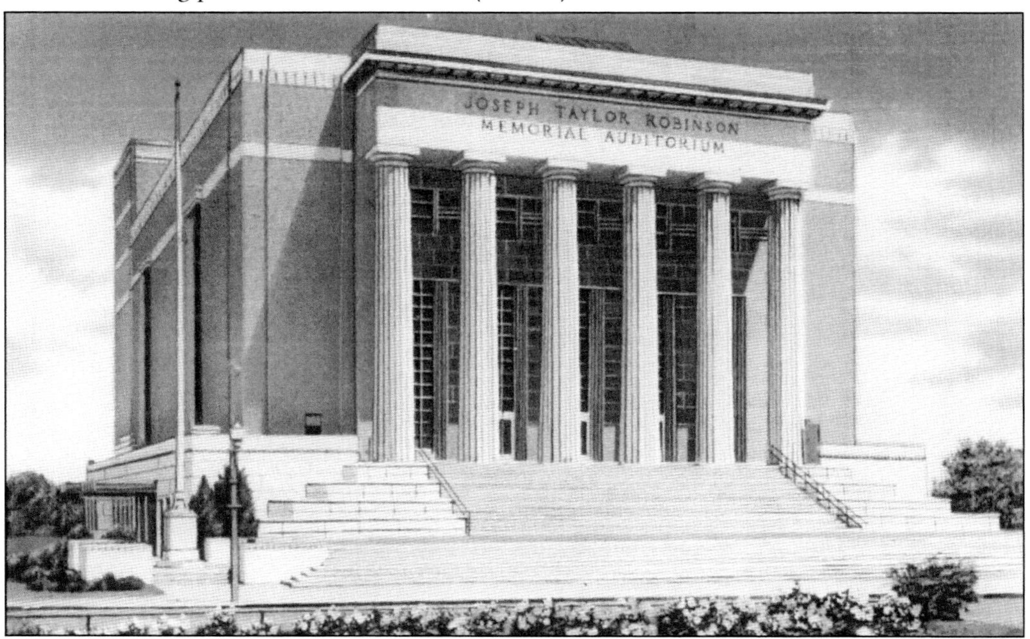

Among the greatest 1930s-era construction projects in Arkansas was the Joe T. Robinson Auditorium, named for the man who served as a congressman, governor, and U.S. senator before his death in 1937. Today the building at the corner of Broadway and Markham Streets is joined on the right by the Doubletree Hotel and convention center, where it hosts the Arkansas Symphony, Ballet Arkansas, and most major touring musical productions. (*c.* 1939.)

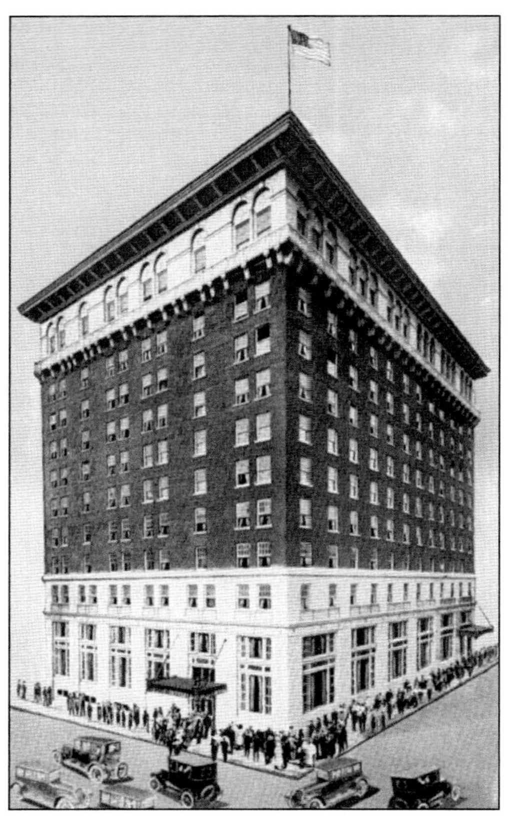

The 11-story Lafayette Hotel opened at Sixth and Louisiana Streets in 1925, placing it five blocks from the main hotel district along Markham Street. The Lafayette boasted 300 fireproof rooms, with baths and circulating ice water in all rooms; rates started at $2.50 per night. The Great Depression led to the hotel's closure in 1933, but it reopened in 1941. The popularity of more convenient motels led to the Lafayette's final closure in 1973, but the hotel gained a new life in the 1980s with its conversion to an office building. It is now largely occupied by various agencies of state government.

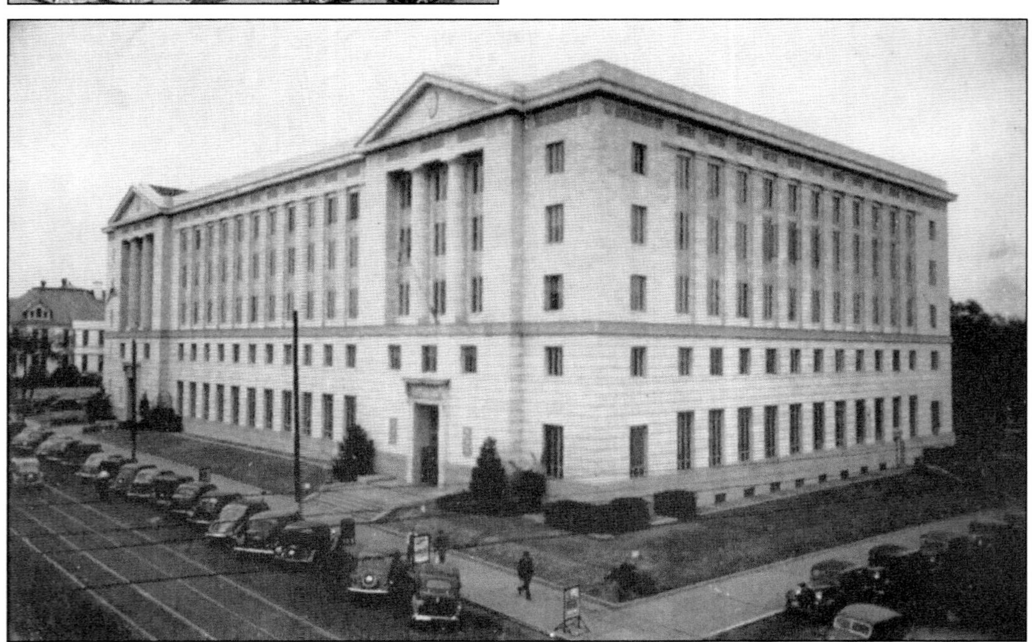

In the depths of the Depression, this impressive new post office was completed at Capitol Avenue and Gaines Streets in 1932. The Peabody School (far left) was torn down in the 1950s to make way for a new federal building, when the government outgrew the building seen in this 1930s view. Today the building is used entirely for federal courts.

Three

1940 to 1960

Recovery, War, and Social Change

By 1941, Little Rock and Arkansas were recovering from the Great Depression. The event brought population growth and major construction almost to a dead halt in Arkansas. With a population of just over 80,000, Little Rock was by far the largest city in the state. The coming of WW II would forever change the city and the state, as industries geared up and new people poured in to help with the war effort. Pulaski County played a key role in this effort, particularly with the revitalized army post of Camp Robinson. The 1950s brought social turmoil and change, as politicians played both sides of the race issue and Central High School put Little Rock on the map of the world. While the postcard volume and quality of earlier decades was diminished, there were still enough produced to document a number of the changes that swept over the community during this period.

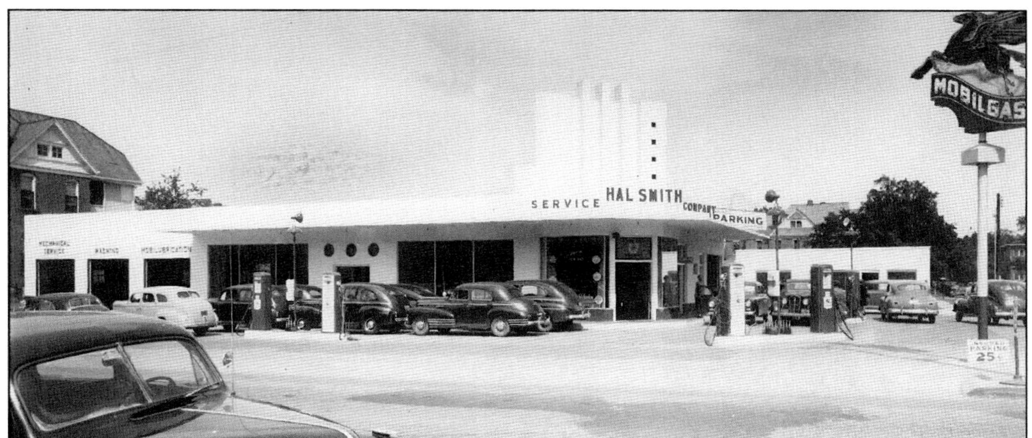

Hal Smith's Service Company at Capitol and Scott Streets operated a repair center and parking garage, selling Mobil gasoline under the trademark red-winged horse. According to the sign, parking cost 25¢. Today a parking lot marks the site. (*c.* 1950.)

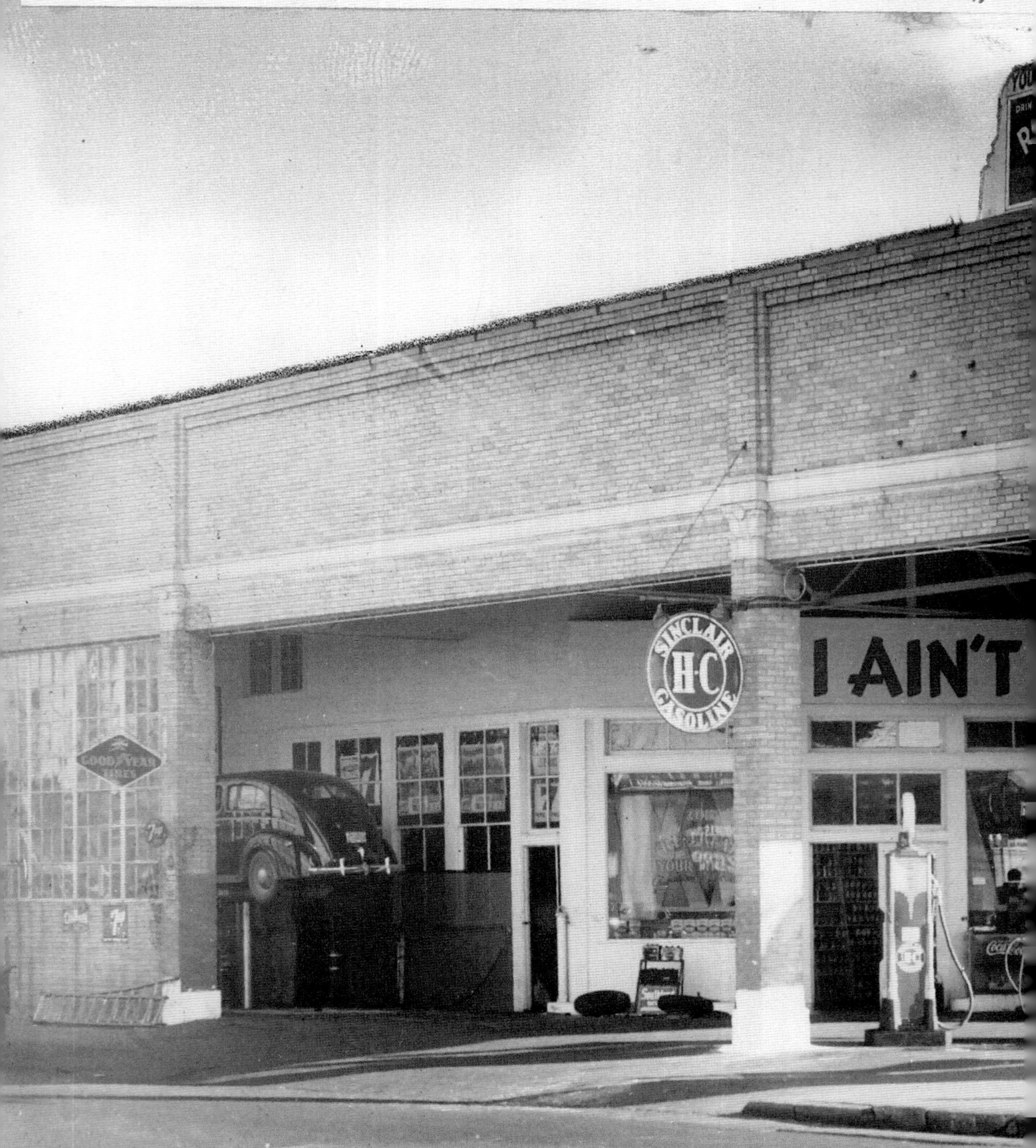

"I AIN'T MAD AT NOBODY," proclaimed the sign over the door to Young's Tire and Service Company at 801 Broadway in this *c.* 1941 card. The sign was directed toward those who purchased

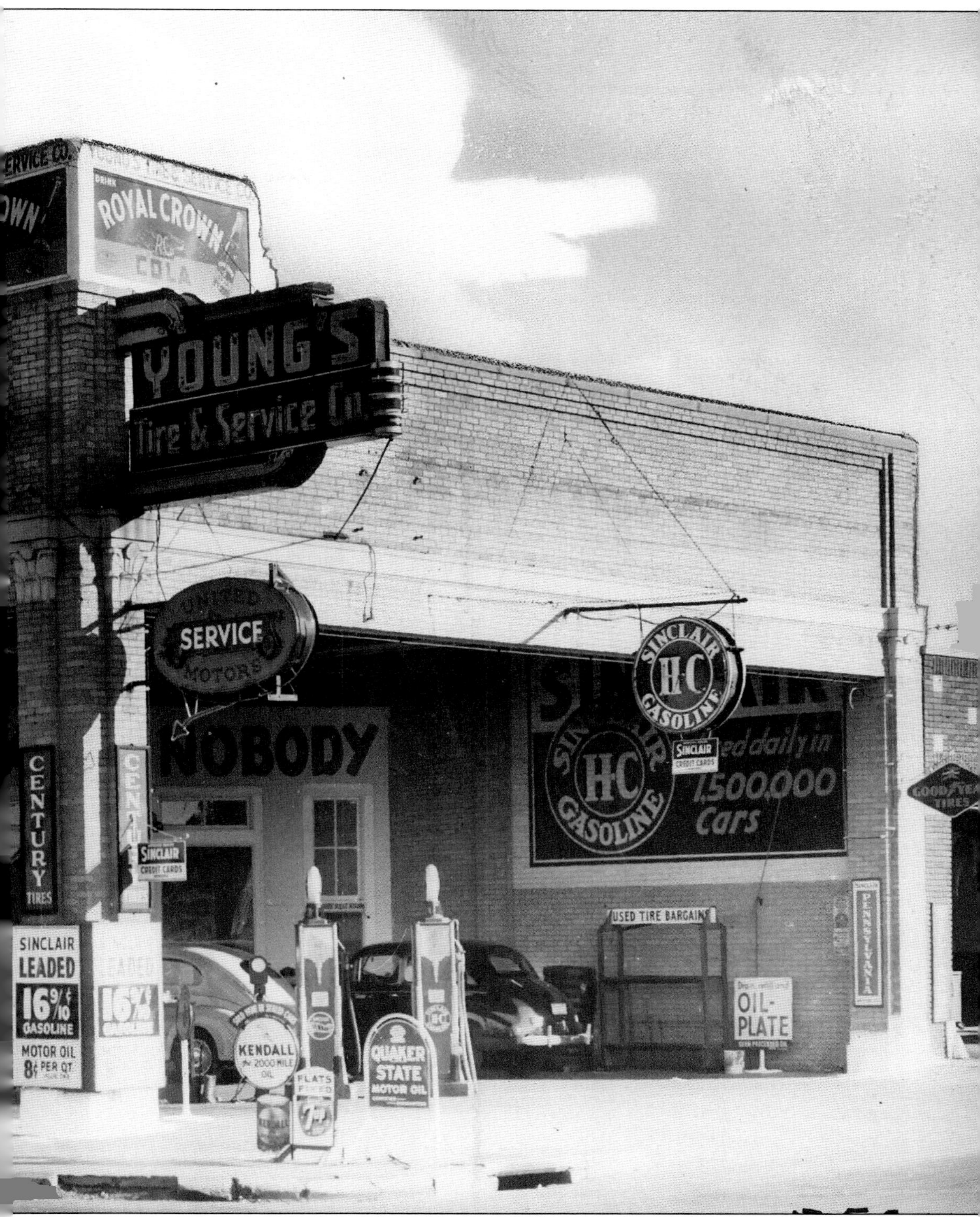

gasoline on credit during the Depression and never paid off their accounts. Now that times were good again, Young wanted paying customers and was willing to forgive past unpaid debts.

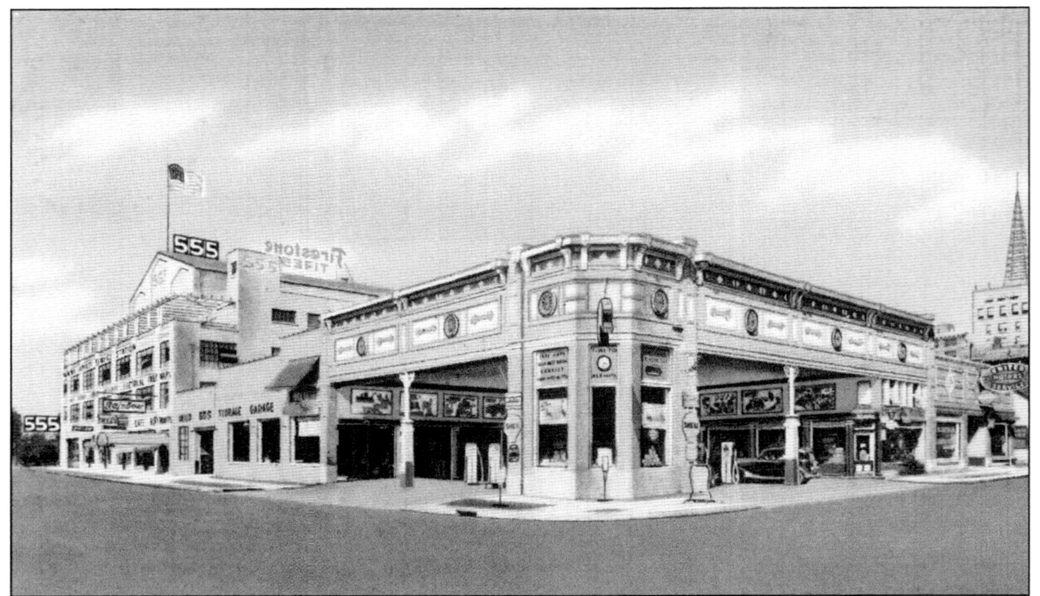

The 555, Inc. Auto Center, at the intersection of four major highways, billed itself as "The World's Largest Service Station." Since it took up an entire block at Third and Broadway Streets, the claim may have been factual. The building stood diagonally opposite from the Robinson Auditorium. In this *c.* 1945 view, the flagpole and the prominent "Firestone Tires" sign marked the location of a popular dance club on the top floor of the building.

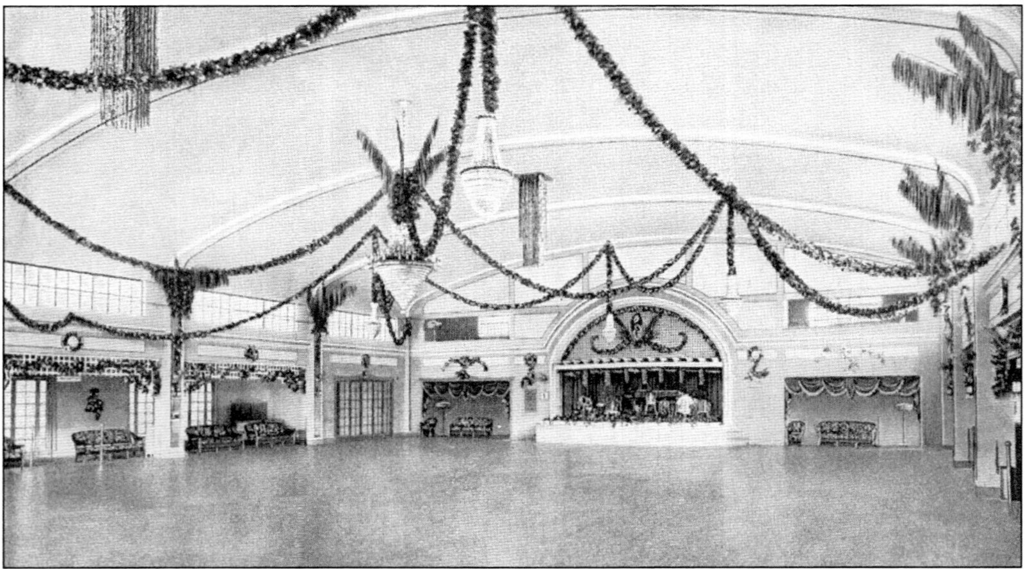

The Rainbow Garden, on the top floor of the 555 Building, was billed as "The South's Most Beautiful Ballroom." It was all the more remarkable because it was located on top of an auto service station. Later known as the "Nut Club," the nightclub in the mid-1940s promised the largest dance floor and the best music in the city, along with beer and good food. Patrons were drawn by special events such as Friday dance contests, Saturday "Whoopee Nite," and Tuesday bargain night (women got in free, while men paid 40¢ to see the floor show). Private booths were available, and music was often provided by Frankie Littlefield and his ten-piece band. The entire building was razed around 1960 to allow for construction of an insurance office. (*c.* 1940.)

The M.M. Cohn Co., which had been a Main Street fixture for 50 years, proudly opened this brand new five-story department store in order to compete more effectively with the Blass Department Store one block away. It was the last of the large stores to be built on Main Street. Today Cohn's and all the major retailers have left the downtown area for distant shopping centers. (*c.* 1948.)

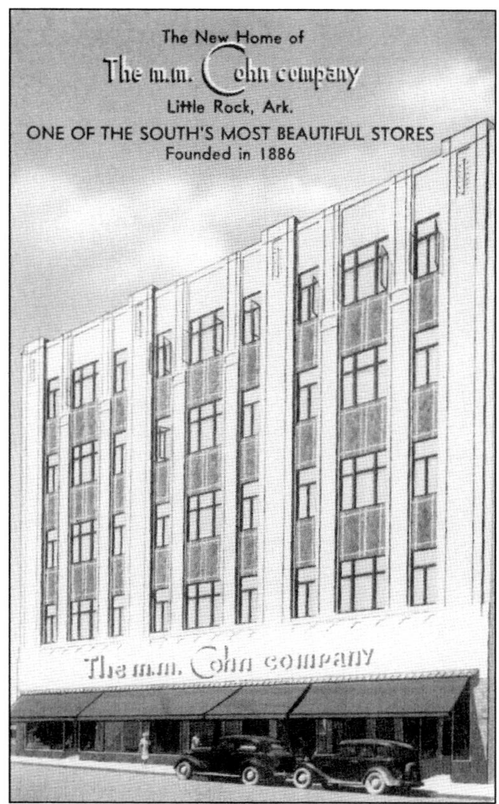

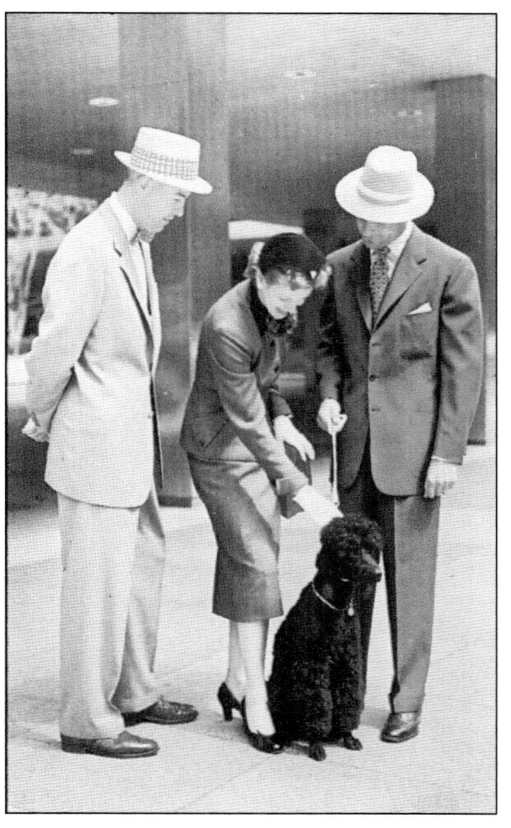

Pfeifer's Department Store sent this 1953 card to those on its customer list, advertising the sale of Palm Beach suits; slacks were $10.95, and a two-pants suit sold for $40.90. Over the years, postcard advertising has given way to newspaper and television promotion.

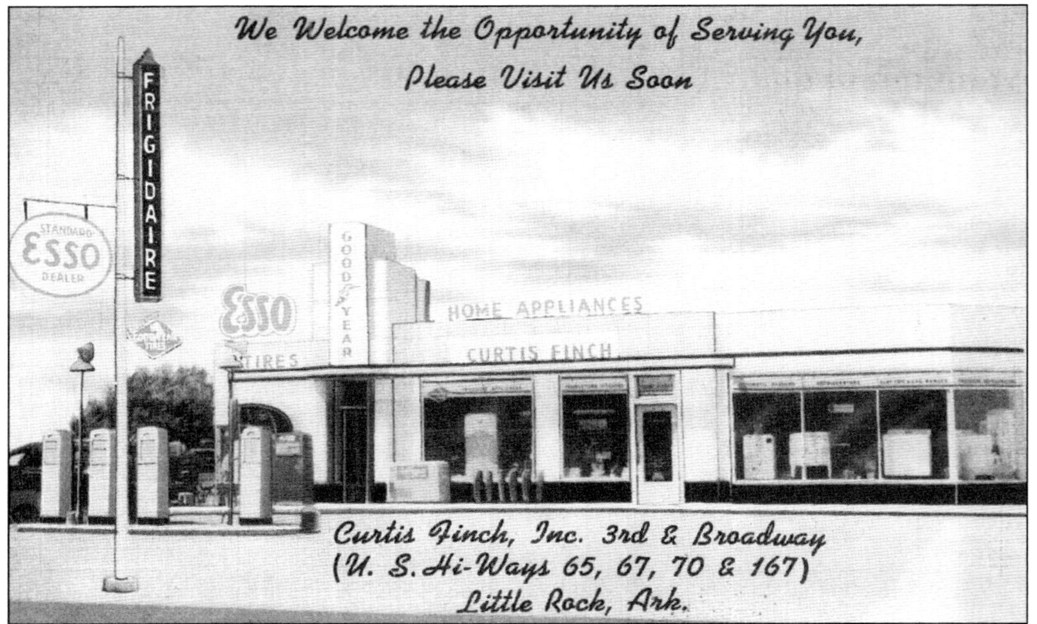

"Every customer must be satisfied" was the motto of Curtis Finch, whose diverse business attracted many customers. On the back of this 1949 card, 600-by-16 four-ply tires were advertised for $8.88, with 156 tires to sell at that price. In an era before the rise of chain stores and shopping malls, businesses like this sold a wide array of products, from auto service to appliances and radios. The business at Third and Broadway Streets later relocated, and this building has been removed.

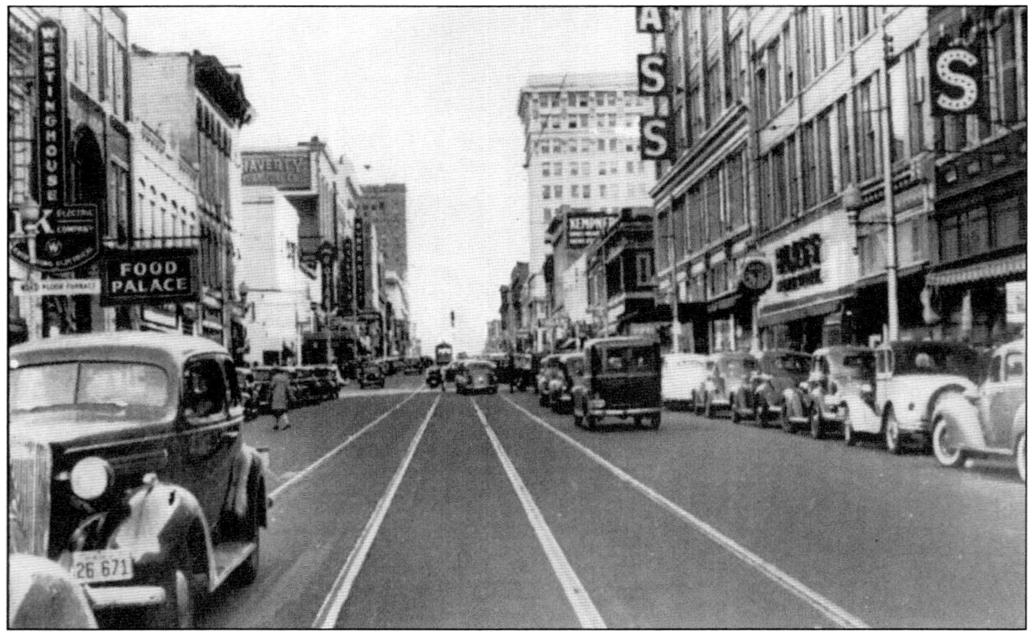

Little Rock's Main Street remained the retail center of the county in the 1940s—the first suburban shopping center was still more than a decade away. In this *c.* 1941 view, a single streetcar is seen in the distance. Its days were numbered; in 1947, a fleet of buses replaced all of the streetcars.

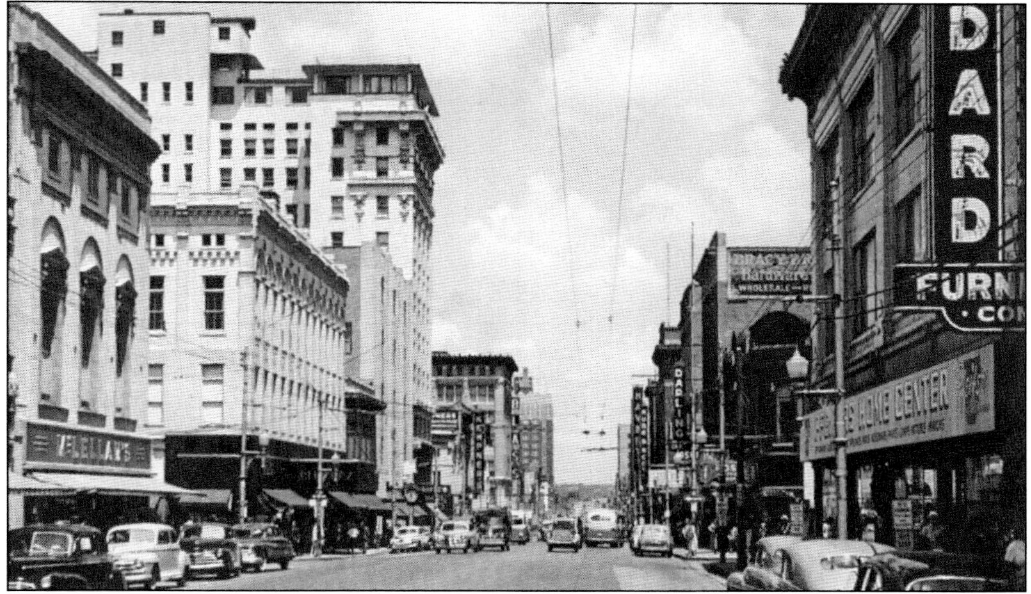

The intersection of Sixth and Main Streets is seen in 1950s photo from the post-streetcar era, with a bus visible in the distant right. On the left is McClellan's "five and dime"—a site which is today a parking lot. Across the street on the right is Pfiefer's Home Center and Standard Furniture. Pfiefer's was long ago absorbed into Dillard's Department Stores, and its building is the present home of the Arkansas Repertory Theater.

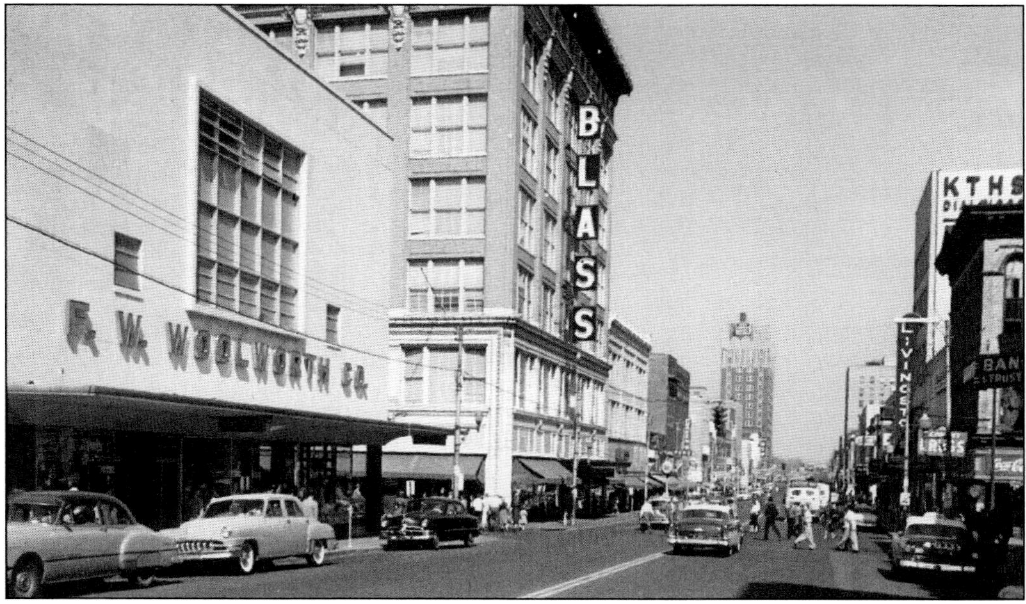

At the time this *c.* 1957 postcard was made, streetcars had been out of service for a decade and the first suburban shopping center, the Village Shopping Center, had just opened at Asher Avenue and Hayes Street (today University Avenue). The exodus of residents and shoppers to the distant parts of west Little Rock began as a trickle, but became a flood over the next few years. F.W. Woolworth (left), closed in the 1970s, and Blass Department Store, still standing in its proud 1919 building, soon followed. In the distance is the Grady Manning Hotel, now gone and replaced by the convention center.

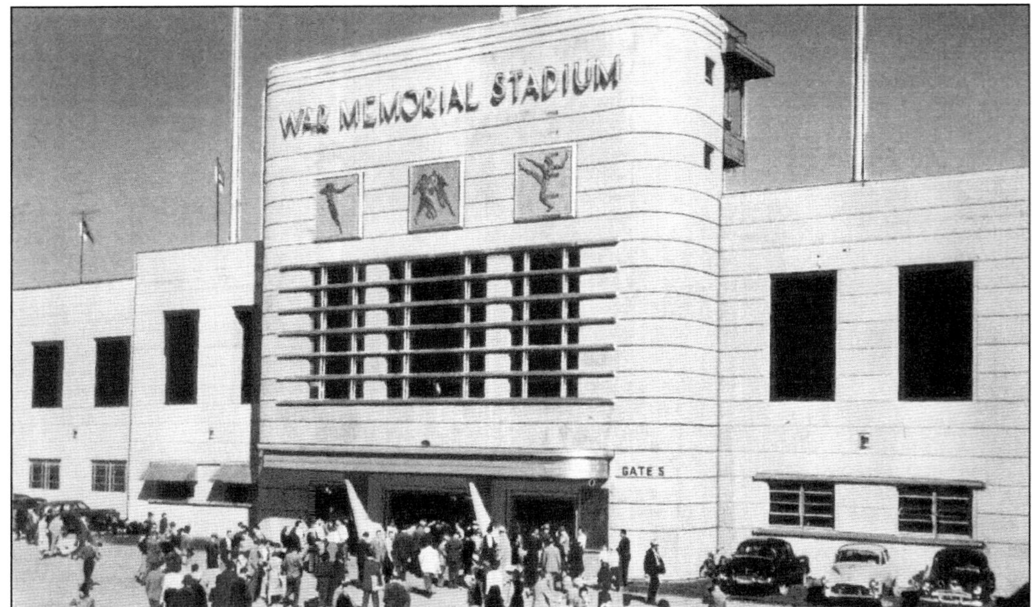

In the late 1940s, War Memorial Stadium was erected on the developing western edge of the city. In decades to follow, the stadium (with seating for more than 40,000 fans) hosted many football games played by the University of Arkansas Razorbacks. The first stadium sell-out came in 1954, when the Razorbacks thrilled their fans by defeating Ole Miss 6-0 with a spectacular 66-yard touchdown pass. (*c.* 1950.)

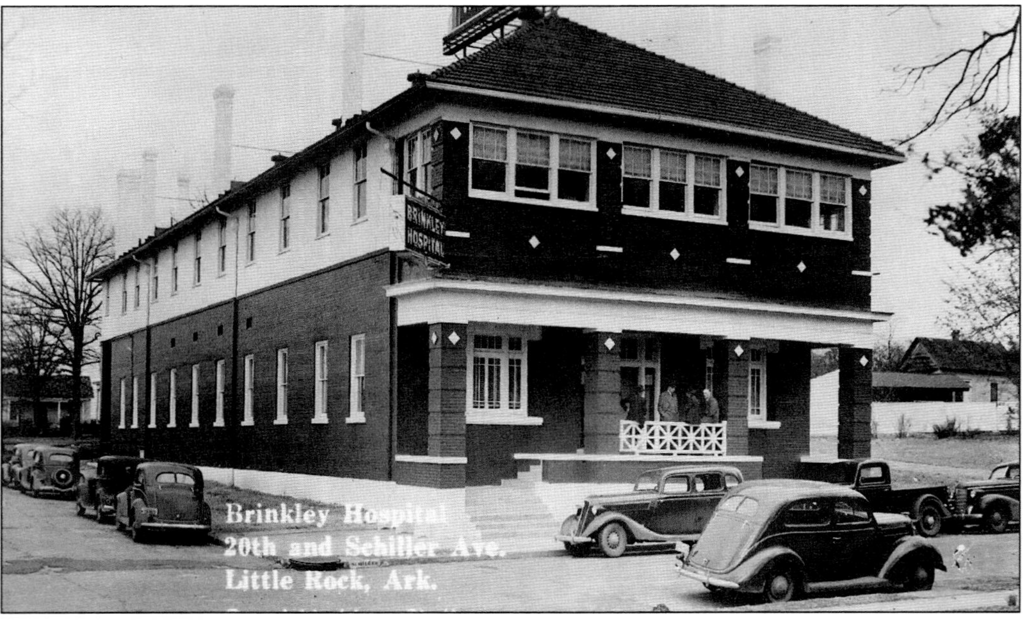

Dr. John Brinkley operated his hospital at Twentieth and Schiller Streets and promoted his sometimes unorthodox healing methods nationwide by radio. Among his procedures was one reported to cure impotence through a transplant of goat testicles. In local usage, it was said that if someone was in a hurry they might be moving "like a goat past Brinkley hospital." After more than a decade of controversy and investigation, the federal government put Dr. Brinkley out of business. (*c.* 1945.)

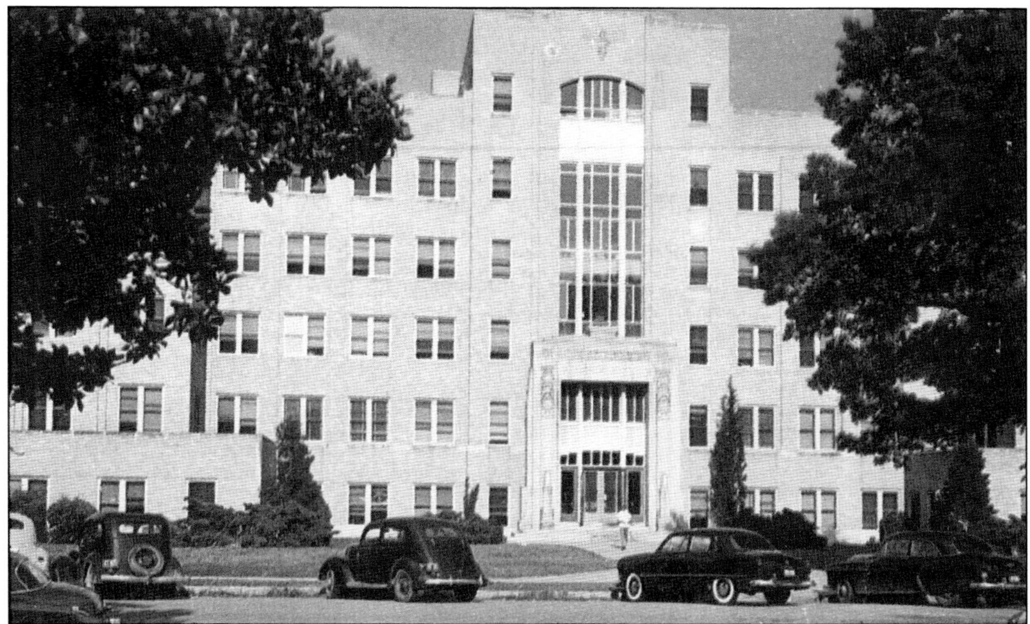

The School of Medicine of the University of Arkansas was located in east Little Rock in this building near MacArthur Park. Originally founded in the 1870s, the medical school and hospital continued to expand and moved to a modern campus on West Markham Street in the late 1950s. Today the hospital is known worldwide for its specialized treatments for cancer. (*c.* 1950.)

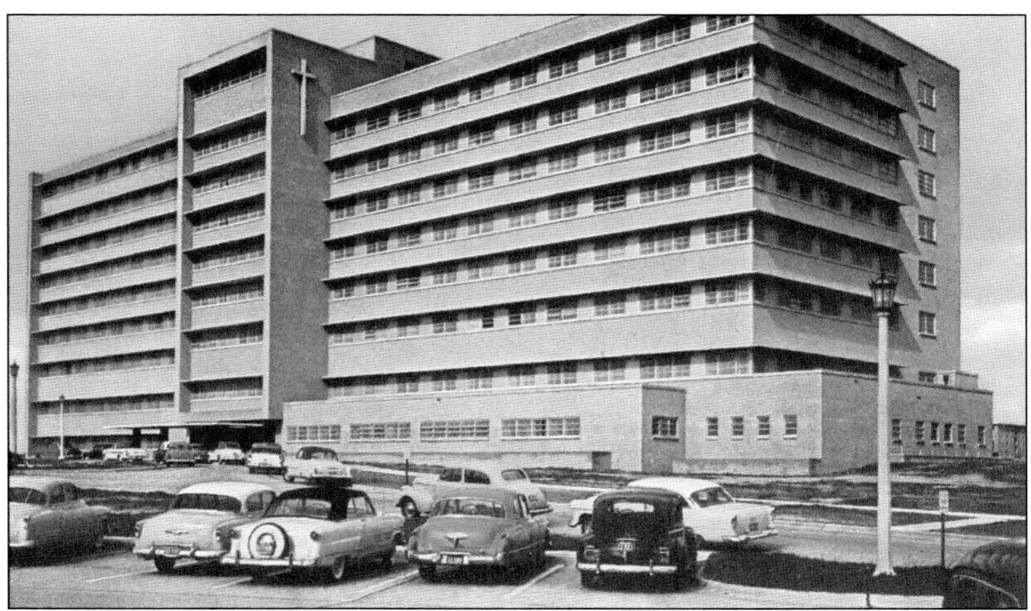

In 1954, St. Vincent Infirmary relocated from its High Street location to this modern nine-story hospital building at Markham and Hayes Streets (later University Avenue). The hospital continued to expand; with the acquisition of adjacent Columbia Doctors Hospital in 1997, St. Vincent's was poised to become the largest hospital system in the state. This represents significant progress, considering the facility started with six nuns coming to Little Rock in 1888. (*c.* 1955.)

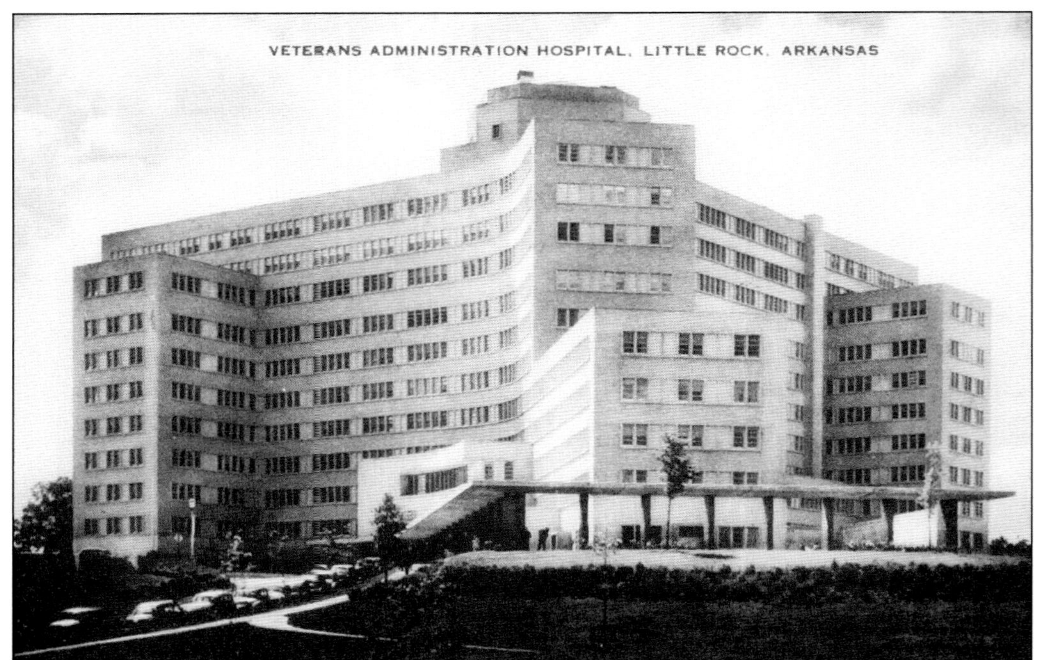

The demand for medical care for the soldiers of WW II led to the construction of the towering Veterans Administration Hospital on Roosevelt Road. The massive facility was closed in the early 1980s when the new McClellan VA Hospital opened adjacent to the University of Arkansas Medical Sciences Campus on West Markham Street. Today this structure stands vacant, plagued with residual asbestos. (*c.* 1950.)

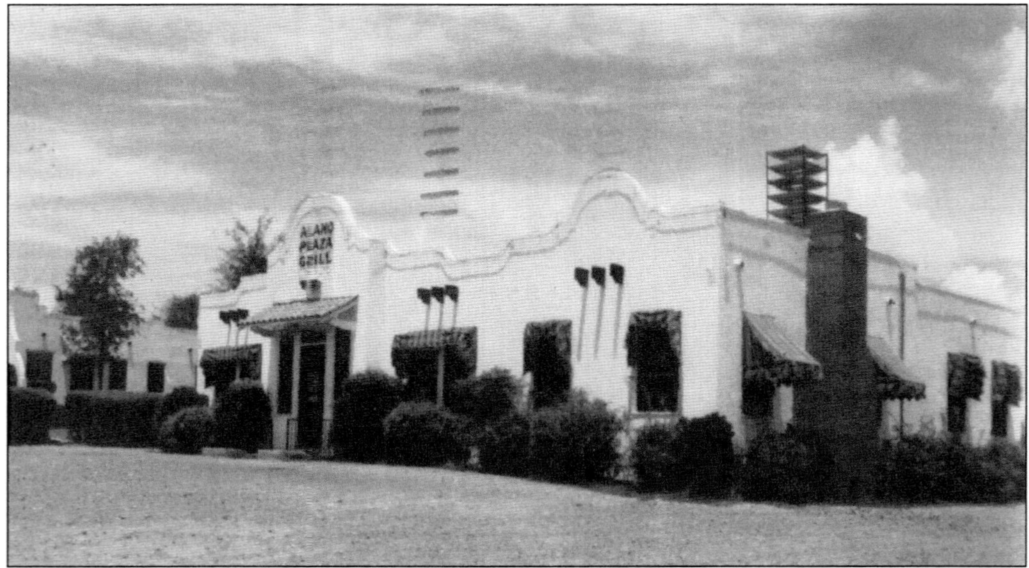

Beginning in the late 1930s, Roosevelt Road, a mecca for lodging and dining, was billed the "Broadway of America." It carried the route for Highways 67 and 70, and helped expand tourist courts and some of the city's finest restaurants. The Alamo Plaza Grill and Court was a Roosevelt Road landmark for more than 30 years before its demolition. The Alamo Court motel chain was seen in a number of locations across the southwest, all with the unique architecture inspired by the San Antonio landmark. (*c.* 1949.)

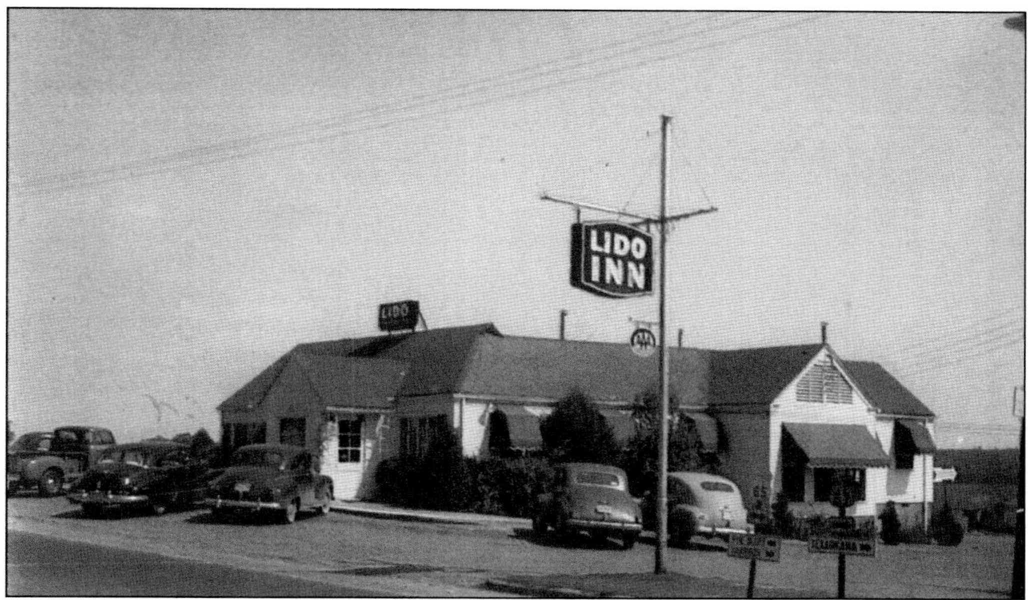

The Lido Inn was located at the corner of Main Street and Roosevelt Road. The ad on the back of this 1950s card describes the restaurant as "One of Little Rock's smartest eating places." No trace remains of the building today. With the coming of the interstate and the western expansion of the city, the Lido and other businesses faded away along Roosevelt Road.

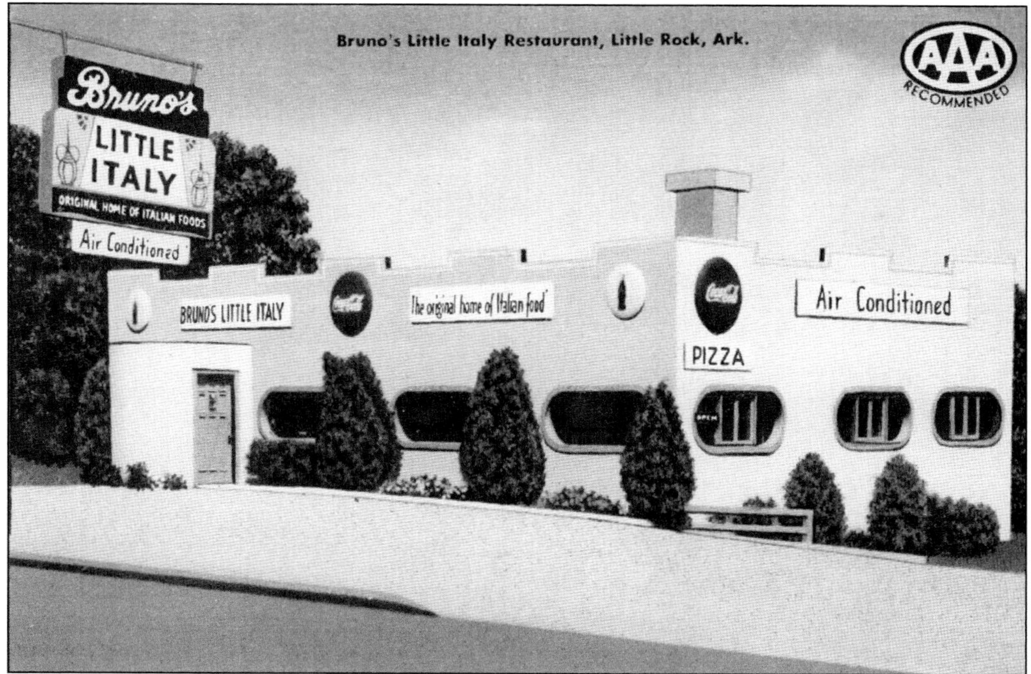

Bruno's Little Italy Restaurant, located at 3400 Roosevelt Road, was perhaps the state's most popular Italian eatery. The restaurant relocated to west Little Rock in the 1970s. (*c.* 1945.)

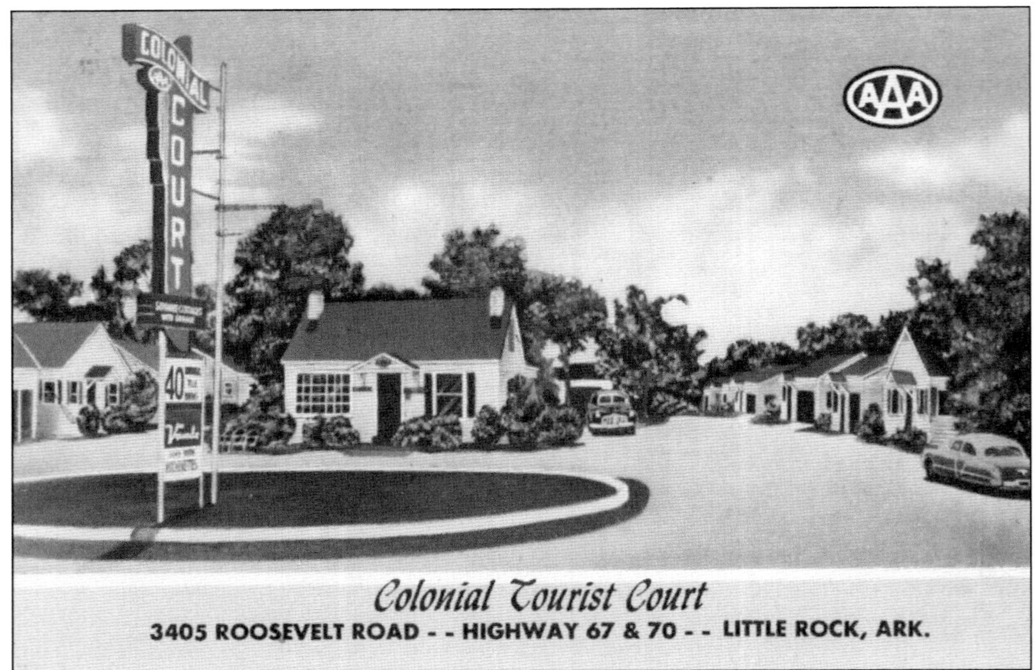

"We are in our cabins for the night. It is terrible hot. They told us at a filling station it was 110 degrees. Our cabins are cool—everything is dry." Among the numerous tourist courts and motel that sprang up along Roosevelt Road was the Colonial Tourist Court. The Colonial (now gone) advertised 40 cottages, Beauty Rest innerspring mattresses, and air-conditioning. The latter was perhaps the main feature that drew in the traveler who sent this 1954 card on such a hot day.

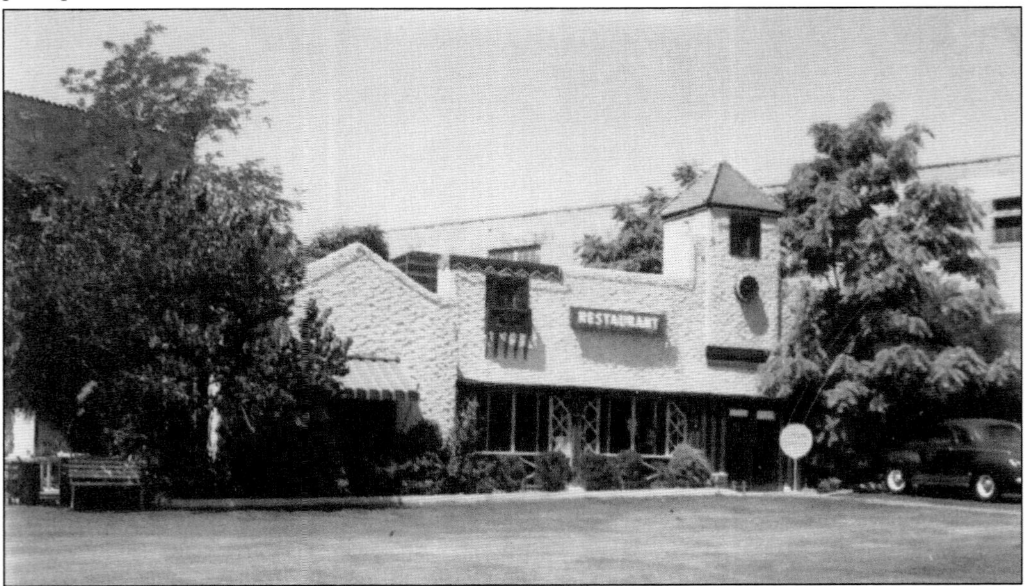

Today the intersection of Fifth (now Capitol) and Broadway Streets lies in the shadows of the state's tallest buildings, but during the 1920s craze for drive-in curb service dining, the major draw to the intersection was Old King Cole. The restaurant was famed for such dishes as eggplant casserole and hot fudge sundaes. The business, which advertised curb service at all hours, has been gone for several decades. (*c.* 1950.)

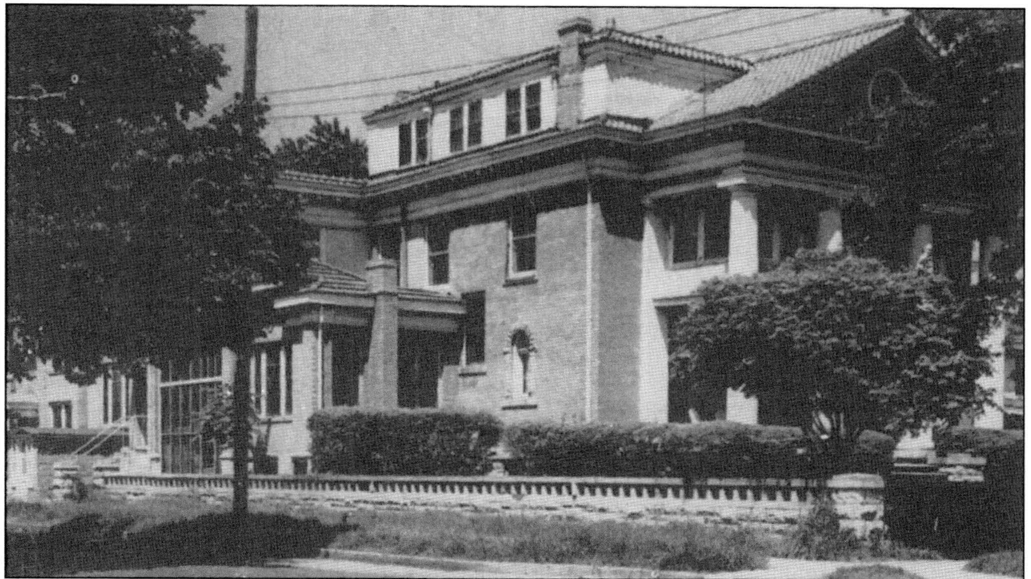

Hotel Charmaine, adapted from a grand home, was billed on the back of this 1950s card as "Arkansas's finest colored hotel, rates $2 up to $5 per day." In that still-segregated era, blacks worked in the finer hotels in the city, but as paying guests, they came to lodgings like the Charmaine at Fourteenth and Izard Streets. This card is part of a collection belonging to Jim Pfeifer of Little Rock.

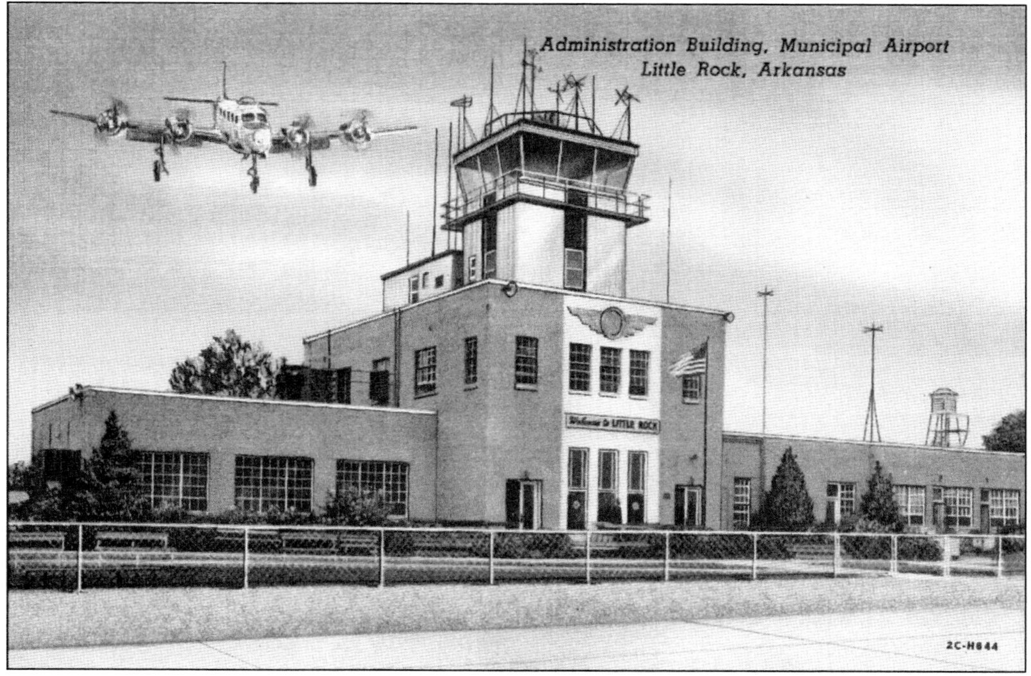

Little Rock's airport began in an Army airfield in eastern Little Rock in 1917. Transferred to the City in the 1920s, the airport was later named Adam's Field, in honor of George Adams, who died in an accident on the field in 1937. The terminal shown in this 1950s photo served until 1972, when a new one was opened nearby.

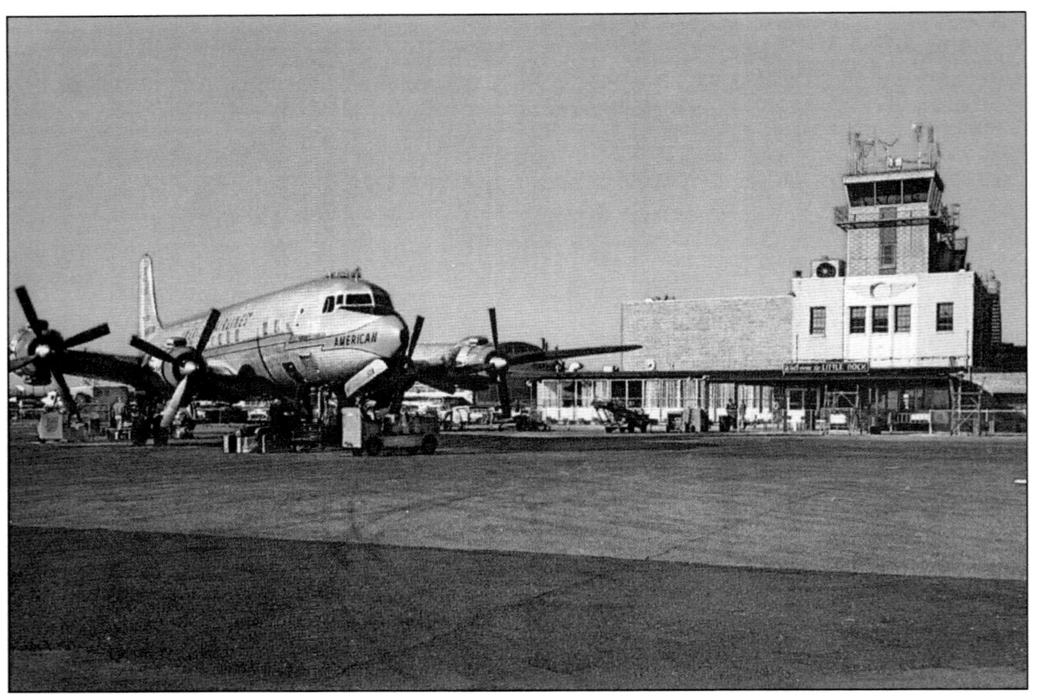

American Airlines began flying into Little Rock in the 1940s, giving the city a major boost. Today the expanded facility known as Little Rock National Airport is served by almost all the nation's major airlines. (*c.* 1950.)

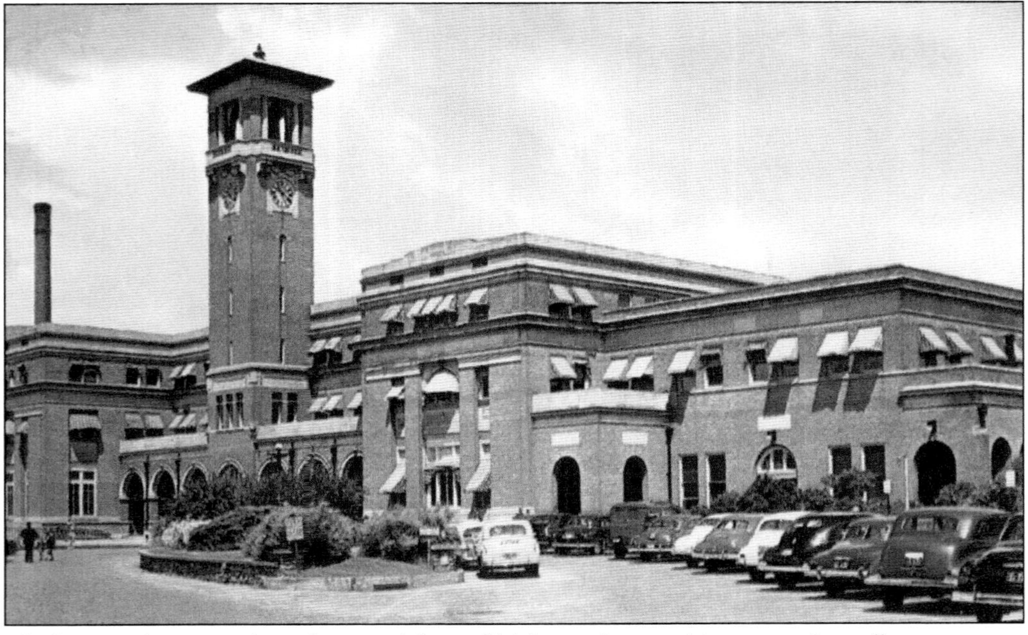

The burgeoning expansion of automobiles and highways began taking a growing toll on passenger rail travel, but the 30-year-old Union Station was still busy when this photo was made in the 1950s. Passenger rail service ended in the 1960s and was revived on a limited basis with the creation of Amtrak. Portions of the depot presently house a restaurant, an antique market, and the Children's Museum of Arkansas.

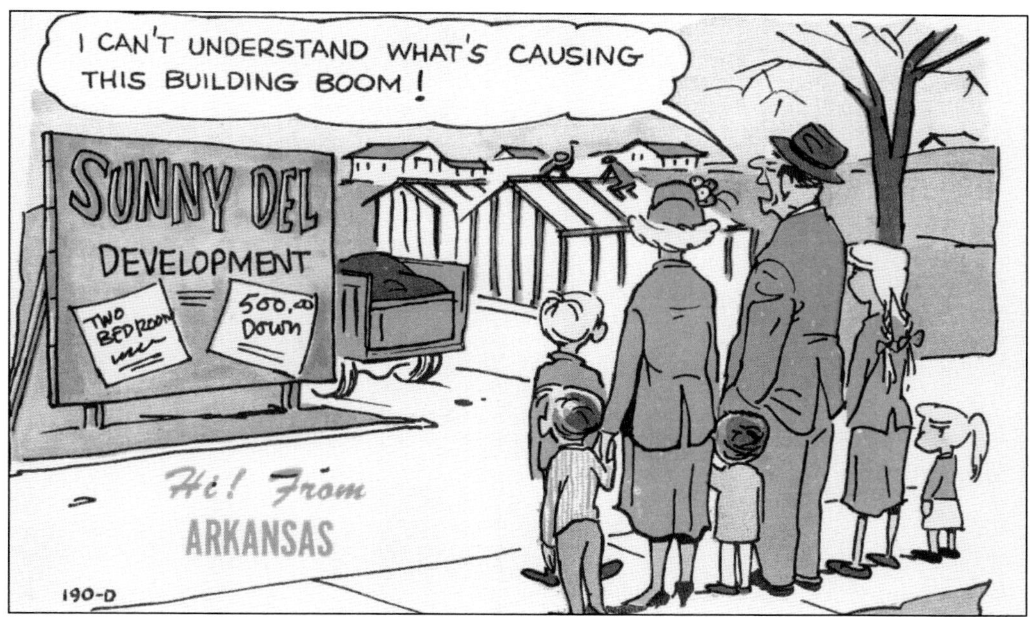

Soldiers returned home to Arkansas after winning a war, the baby boom was on, and greater Little Rock shared in the economic benefits as housing developments went up rapidly. This humorous 1950s card illustrates a nationwide phenomenon, the impact of which would be felt for decades to come.

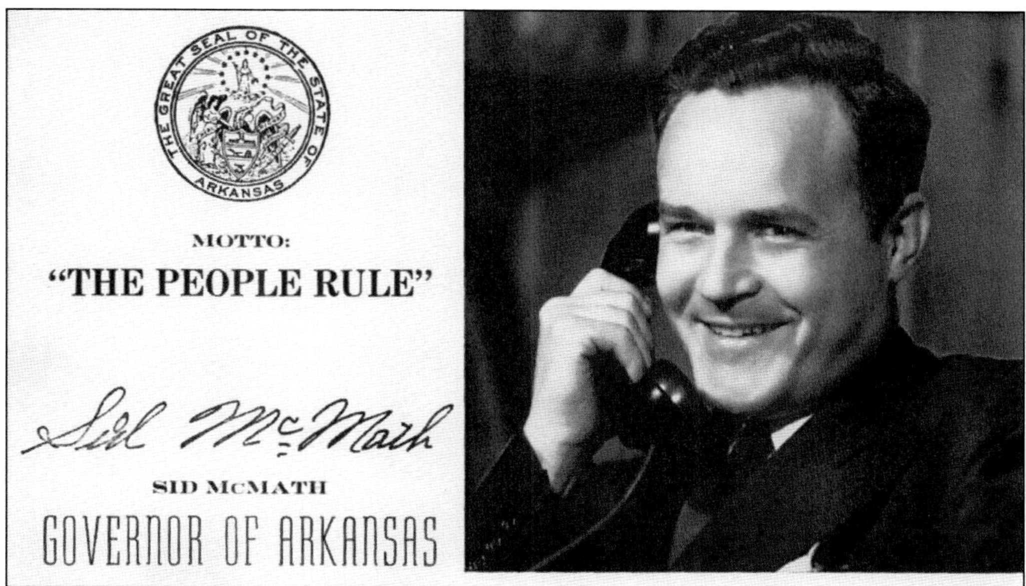

World War II veteran Sid McMath moved into the Governor's Mansion in Little Rock after running in 1948 as a reformer. McMath made an appearance on the national radio program hosted by Arthur Godfrey and talked about improving Arkansas's roads and its image. Ironically, it was a highway funding controversy which led to McMath's defeat at the hands of Francis Cherry in 1952. McMath remained a Little Rock civic leader and a highly regarded attorney for decades after he left the governor's office. Among his many accomplishments was the 1967 establishment of an award-winning Marine Junior ROTC program at Little Rock's Catholic High School for Boys. It was only the third such program in the nation. (*c.* 1950.)

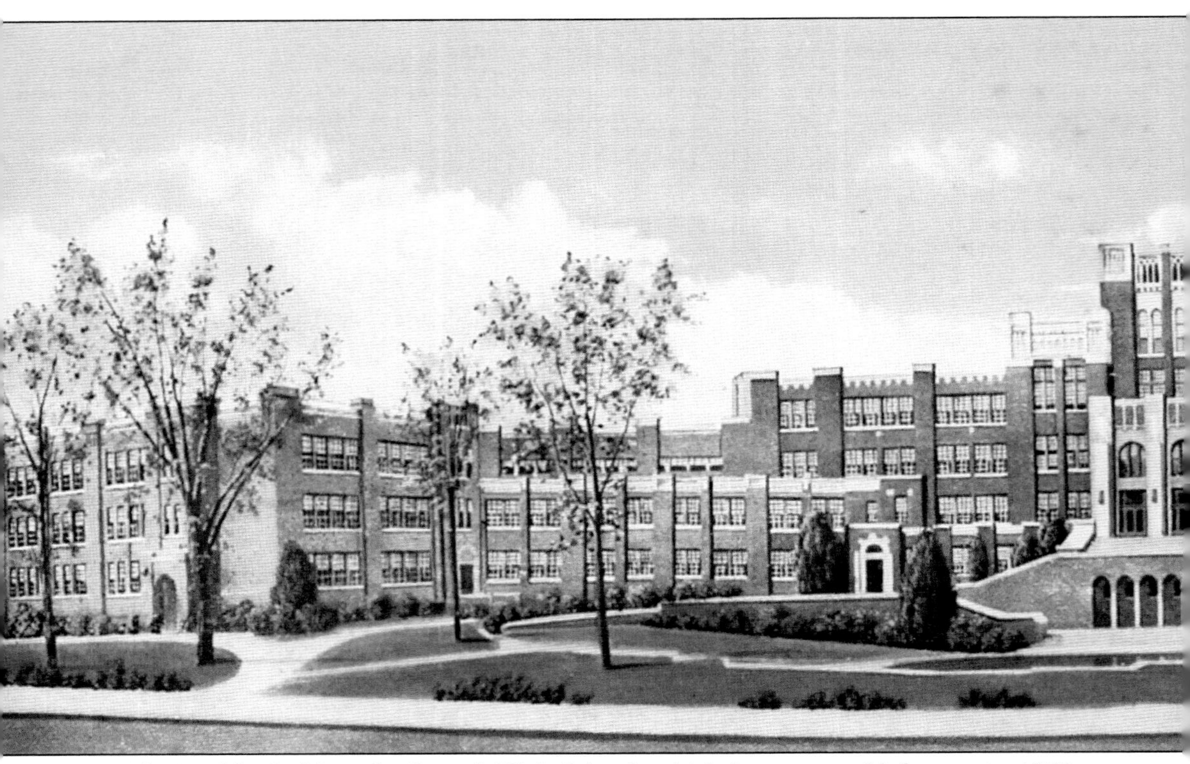

Little Rock's Gothic-style Central High School, which became world famous in 1957, was designed by a committee of five local architects and opened in 1927. The school was hailed in the *Arkansas Gazette* as "The Most Beautiful School Building in America" and "the pride of the

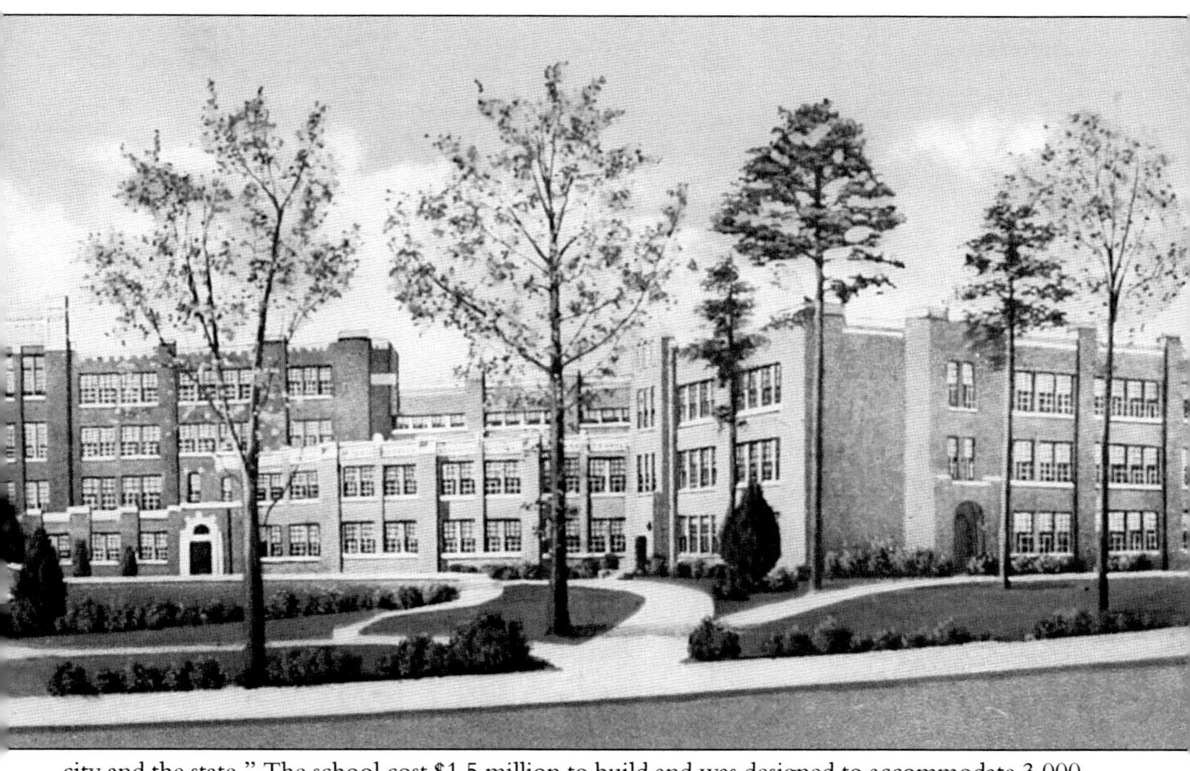

city and the state." The school cost $1.5 million to build and was designed to accommodate 3,000 students at its location on Fourteenth and Park Streets.

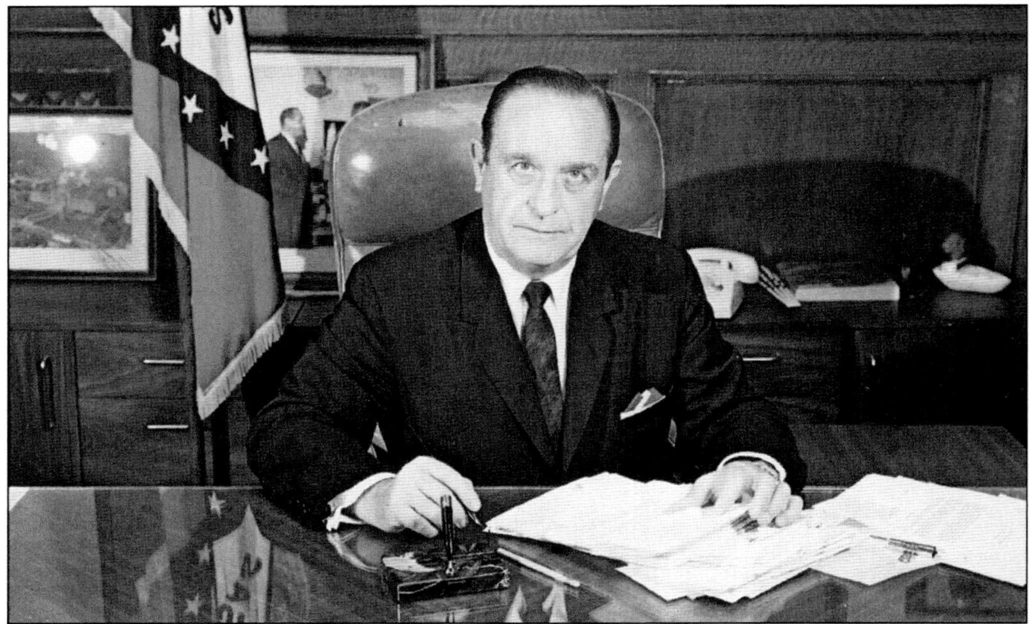

To the surprise of many, Orval E. Faubus, a teacher from the Ozark Mountains and small-town newspaper publisher, defeated Governor Francis Cherry in the 1954 election. Faubus was elected six times and served for 12 years. He is best remembered for bringing Little Rock to the attention of the world during the crisis at Central High School in 1957. (*c.* 1960.)

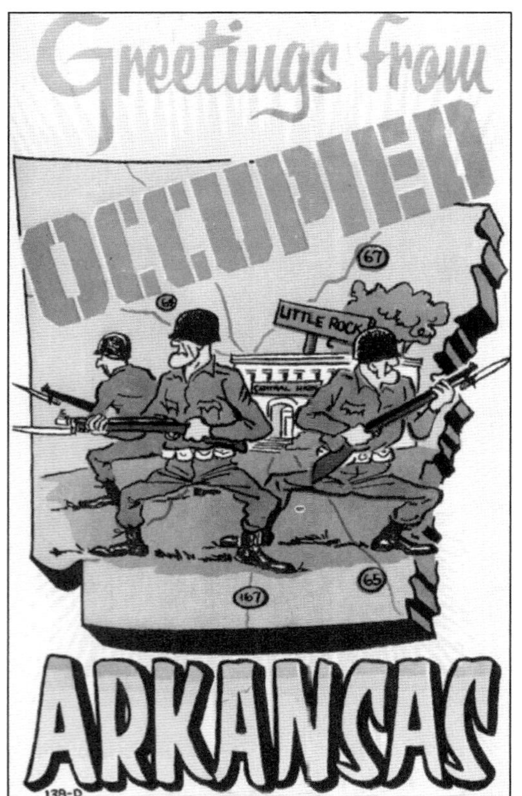

In September 1957, Gov. Orval Faubus mobilized the Arkansas National Guard to prevent nine black students from integrating Little Rock's Central High School. After court hearings and front-page confrontations, President Eisenhower federalized the National Guard and finally sent 1,200 battle-equipped troops to enforce the desegregation rulings. This rare "occupied Arkansas" postcard was printed during this tumultuous time in Little Rock's history.

Four

Argenta and North Little Rock
The Capital City's Across-the-Bridge Neighbor

Little Rock's neighbor to the north, according to some accounts, traces its beginning to 1812, with the tiny settlement of Crystal Hill (which was actually larger than Little Rock for several years). Crystal Hill was considered as a site for the Territorial Capitol, but Little Rock won out and became the dominant community. In 1846, a U.S. Army officer named DeCantillon staked out a town site on the north bank of the Arkansas River, west of what is now Main Street in North Little Rock, and named it "DeCantillon." The venture, however, attracted neither investments nor residents and soon faded.

Following the Civil War, a train depot and rail yard developed on the north shore, but most of present-day North Little Rock remained the very large farm of Col. Robert Newton. The Newton farm was broken up by 1870, and local developers platted a town site with the name "Argenta," so-called because of the alleged silver deposits nearby. The ore turned out to be mostly lead. The unincorporated community of Argenta grew in population, but lost a battle in 1890 when its 2,600 residents were involuntarily incorporated into neighboring Little Rock as the Eighth Ward of the capital city.

According to the "Little Rock Handbook" by Jim Bell, the new ward was ill-treated by Little Rock. The residents of the Eighth Ward began to rebel after the opening of the Free Bridge, which linked their community with the rest of Little Rock in 1897. It became glaringly clear that the Eighth Ward had none of the newly paved streets, concrete sidewalks, or electric streetlights that were seen on the south side of the river. A clever political plan was developed to help the area break away from Little Rock.

W.C. Faucette, a state legislator from the ward, crafted a piece of legislation called the Hoxie-Walnut Ridge Bill, named for two adjacent small communities in northeast Arkansas. The bill permitted citizens of a satellite community to vote on which adjacent incorporated area they wished to be annexed to. In 1901, the angry Eighth Ward element pretended to form a new school district just outside of the ward boundaries, but instead quickly incorporated the area into a town called North Little Rock. The new city then proceeded in 1903 to call an annexation election, using the Hoxie-Walnut Ridge law.

Try as they might, the leaders of Little Rock could not block the election. North Little Rock succeeded in wrenching away the capital city's Eighth Ward. To lessen the odds of again being seized by Little Rock, and to give themselves a distinct identity, North Little Rock changed its name to Argenta in 1907. Postcards from that city carried that name for the next decade. In 1919, by then confident of its ability to maintain independence, the city renamed itself North Little Rock, and the name Argenta is unfamiliar to the memories of most of its citizens.

North Little Rock made its major contribution to greater Little Rock as the site of sprawling military bases. With the coming of WW I, local civic leaders donated thousands of acres of land to the federal government for the purposes of building Camp Pike. The military base was developed for the training of thousands of soldiers to fight the Germans in France. During WW II the base was renamed Camp Robinson.

Today North Little Rock and Little Rock peacefully work together as partners in the state's major metropolitan area. Many citizens employed in Little Rock choose to reside in the less urban atmosphere of the north shore. Though very few postcards were published of North Little Rock during the middle years of the century, many were made of the city's military installations, and a few cards can be found of other sites in Little Rock's neighbor to the north.

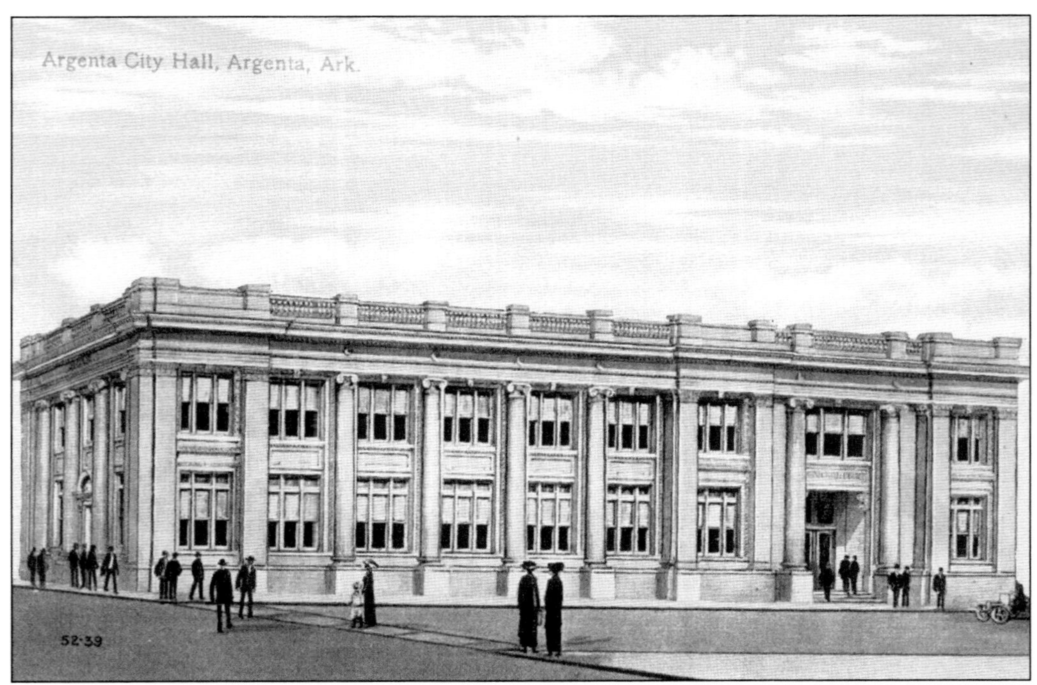

The dream of W.C. Faucette, the man who pried Argenta away from Little Rock, became reality when the new city hall building was erected in 1914. The white Florentine marble building, on the corner of Broadway and Main Streets, was filled with decorative touches beneath a stained-glass skylight. The entire structure was built upon bales of cotton—a common practice at the time due to the area's swampy ground. The building is now on the National Register of Historic Places and continues to serve North Little Rock. (*c.* 1915)

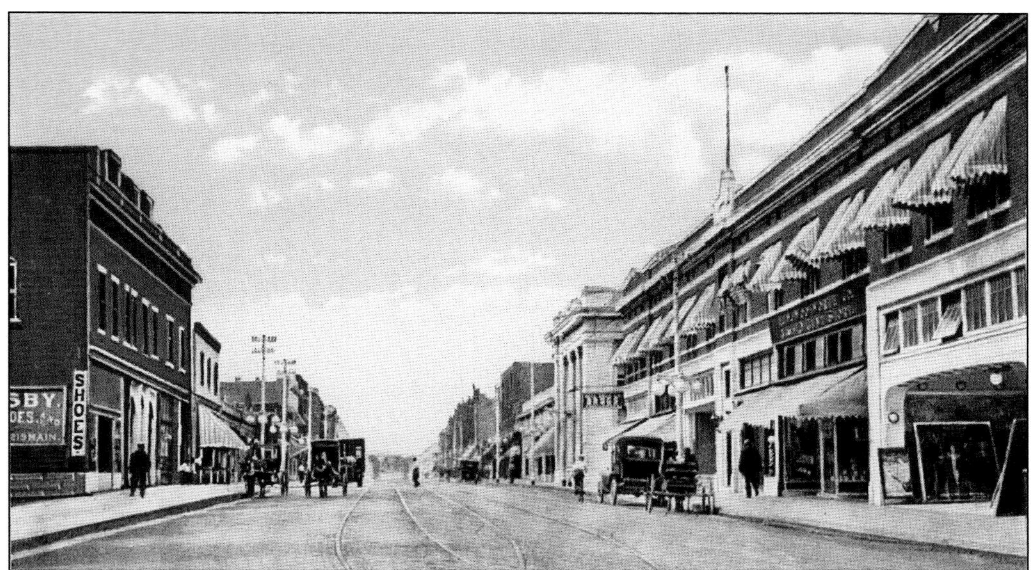

In this view are the Matthews building (right) and the wide entrance to the Princess Theater (foreground), beckoning residents to its ten-cent movies. Beside the Princess, sporting canvas awnings, is Gus Moser's Cafe. Charles Schneider, a local tailor, ran his apparel and shoe shop across the street. Farther down the block were two of the six drugstores that served the small community.

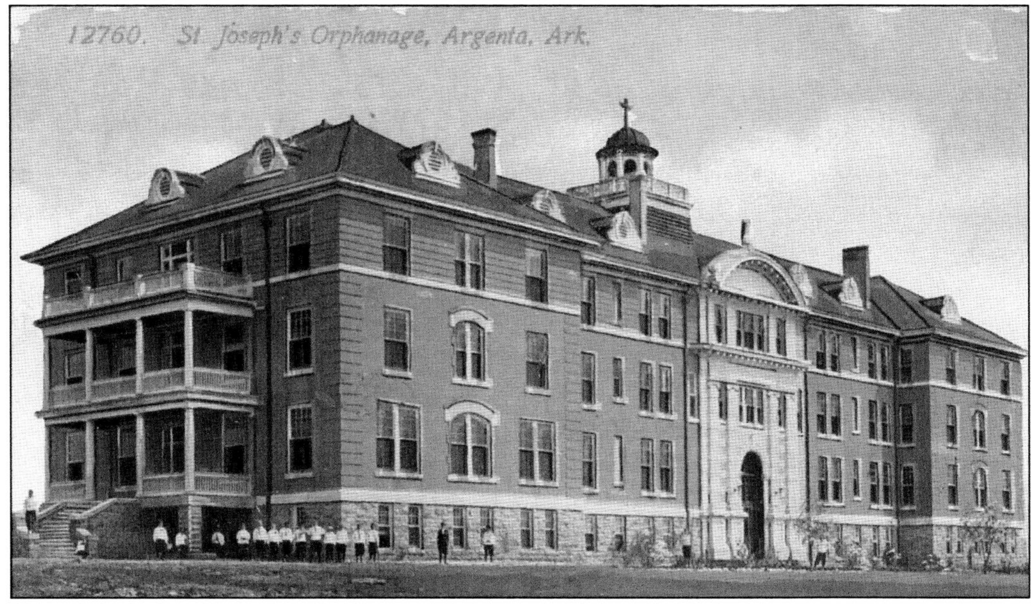

Catholic Bishop John Morris led his Arkansas flock into the new century, determined to improve the lot of those most in need. One goal he set was to build an orphanage, which he did with the support of Christians from a number of denominations. The Little Rock Board of Trade also gave him a helping hand in his admirable efforts. St. Joseph's Orphanage, built high on a knoll outside North Little Rock, was operated for many years by Benedictine sisters, who cared for thousands of children before the orphanage closed in 1978. The building still stands on well-kept grounds, with its red-tile roof visible for miles, awaiting a future commission. (*c.* 1910.)

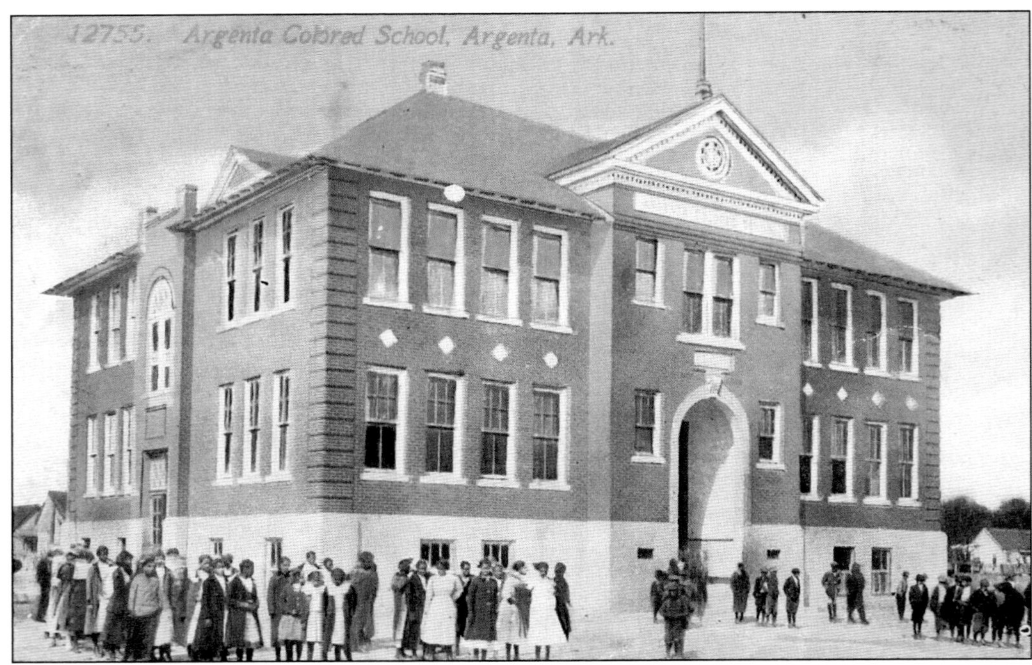

Built in 1909, the Argenta Colored School was renamed "Hickory Street High School" within two years of completion. By 1917, all 12 grades for black children were housed here. In 1928, the school became Scipio A. Jones High School, named for a prominent black leader of the city. The school closed in 1970 and burned down shortly thereafter. Only the school's gym still stands.

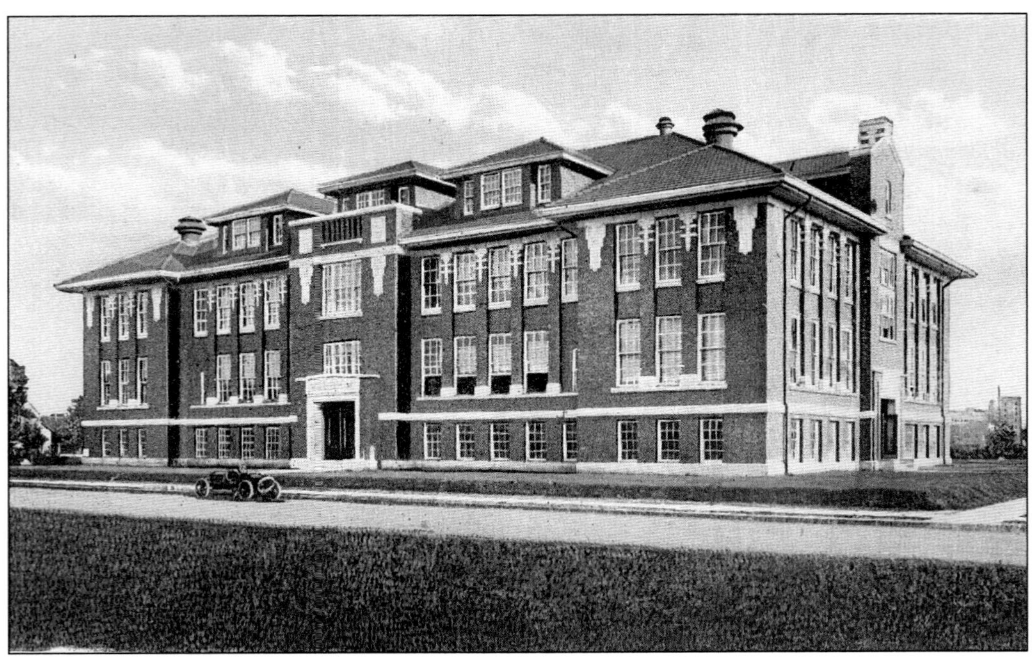

Argenta High School opened in 1912 with 16 classrooms, an auditorium, a recitation room, and a gymnasium. By 1917, there were 450 students enrolled in the school. It was replaced by a new school in 1929 and was demolished in 1976.

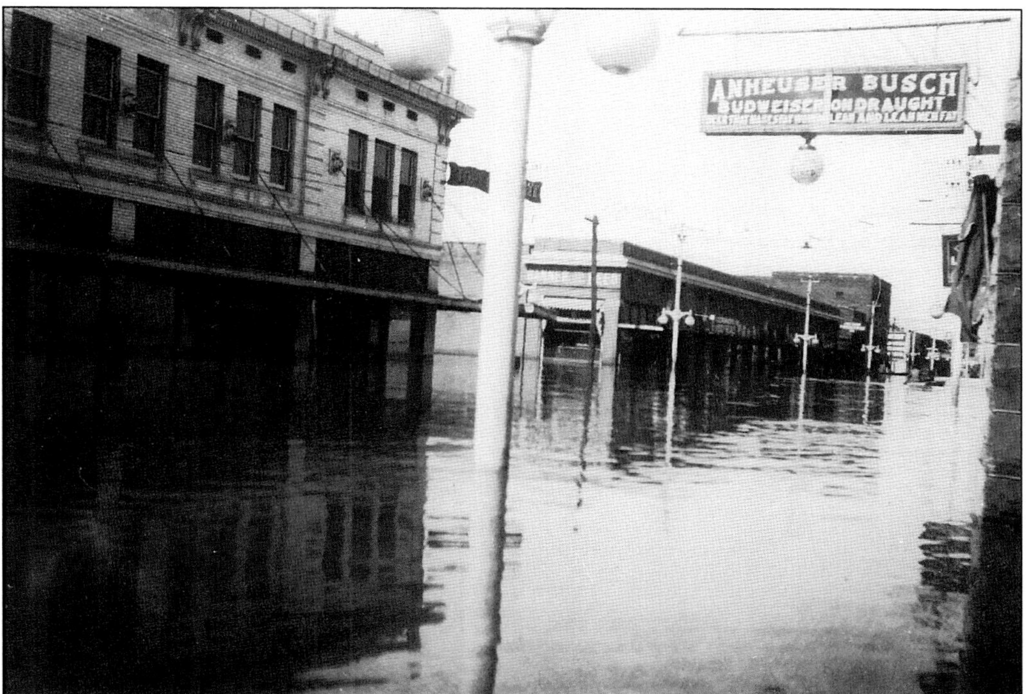

The Great Flood of 1927 swamped much of Arkansas, and in Pulaski County, North Little Rock suffered the most. Washington Avenue was completely covered by the waters of the Arkansas River. In this view, a beer sign is seen suspended over the floodwaters. It reads as follows: "Beer that makes fat women lean and lean men fat."

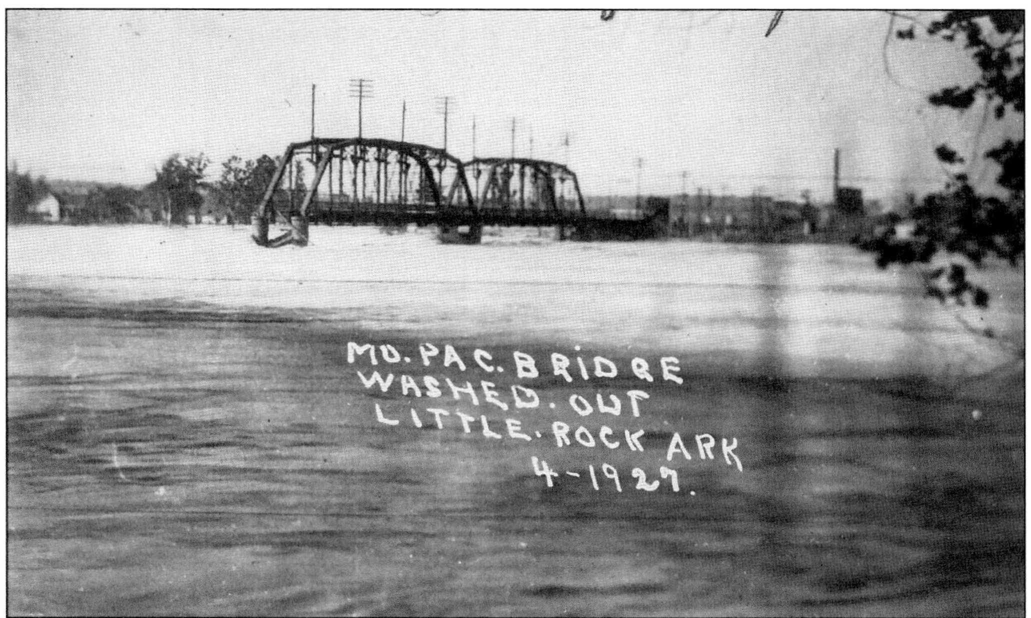

The Baring Cross railroad bridge had spanned the Arkansas River since 1873, but it could not withstand the flood of 1927. In a futile effort to stabilize the bridge, a trainload of coal was parked across the spans. Sadly, the raging river took both the bridge and the train. This postcard is part of the collection of Peg Smith of Little Rock.

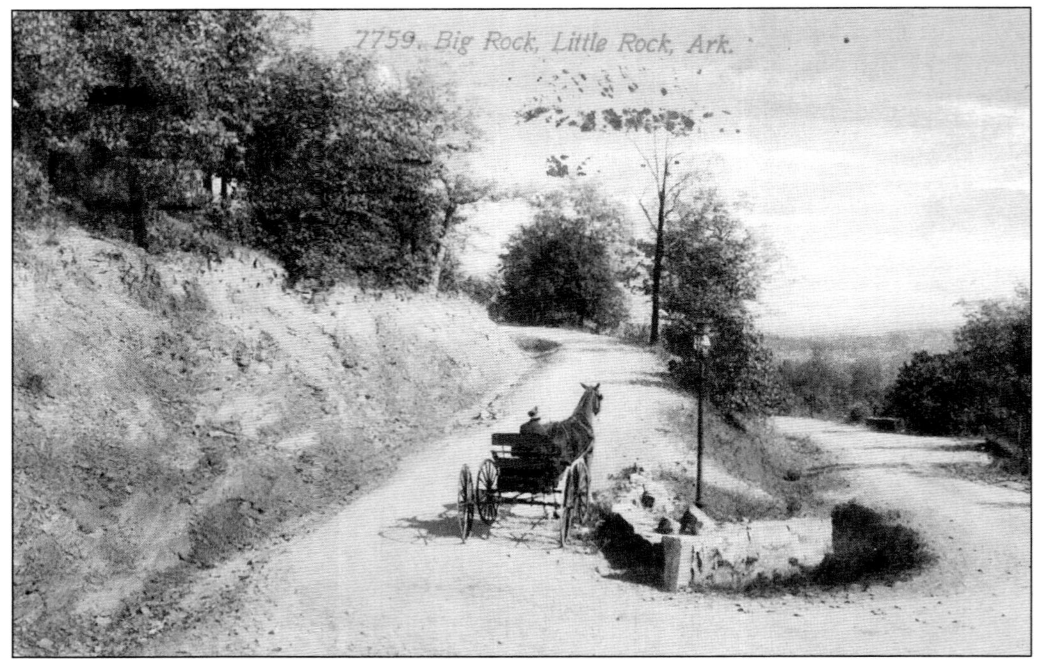

Big Rock (as opposed to Little Rock) was the name given to a prominent bluff overlooking the Arkansas River on the north shore. When the federal government was seeking a site for a major army post, local leaders secured several hundred acres of the scenic mountaintop. The site became home to Fort Logan H. Roots, which was named for the retired colonel who led the drive to secure the economically important post. The winding road seen in this 1910 view is now paved.

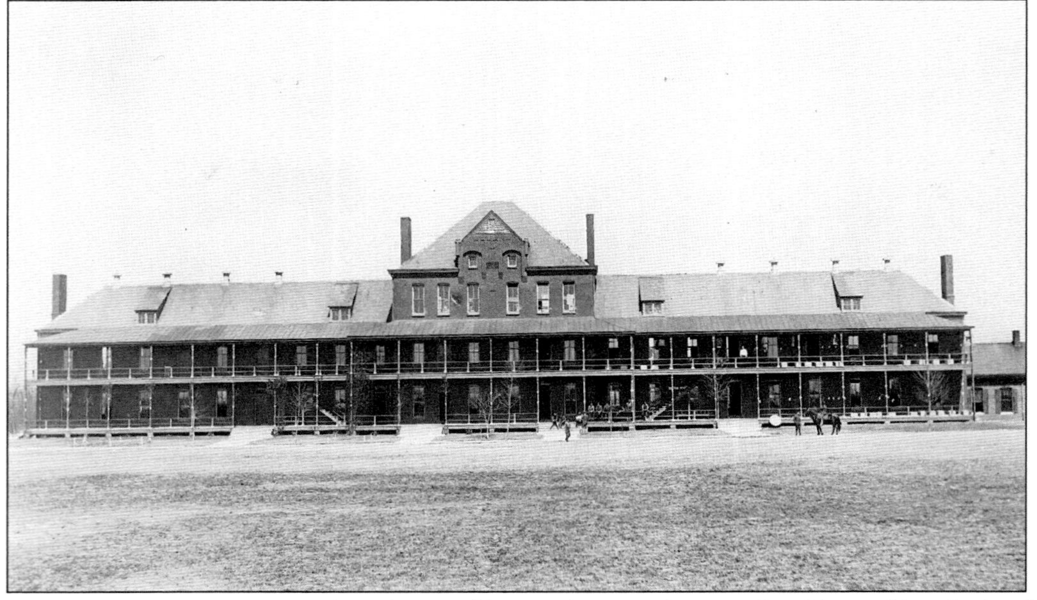

The sprawling Fort Roots, with its frontier-like parade grounds, trained and housed hundreds of soldiers who frequented the streets of Little Rock and Argenta. After contributing to the winning of WW I, the fort was decommissioned in 1921 and a VA hospital opened on the site. Many of the historic buildings remain on the campus of what is now a modern medical facility.

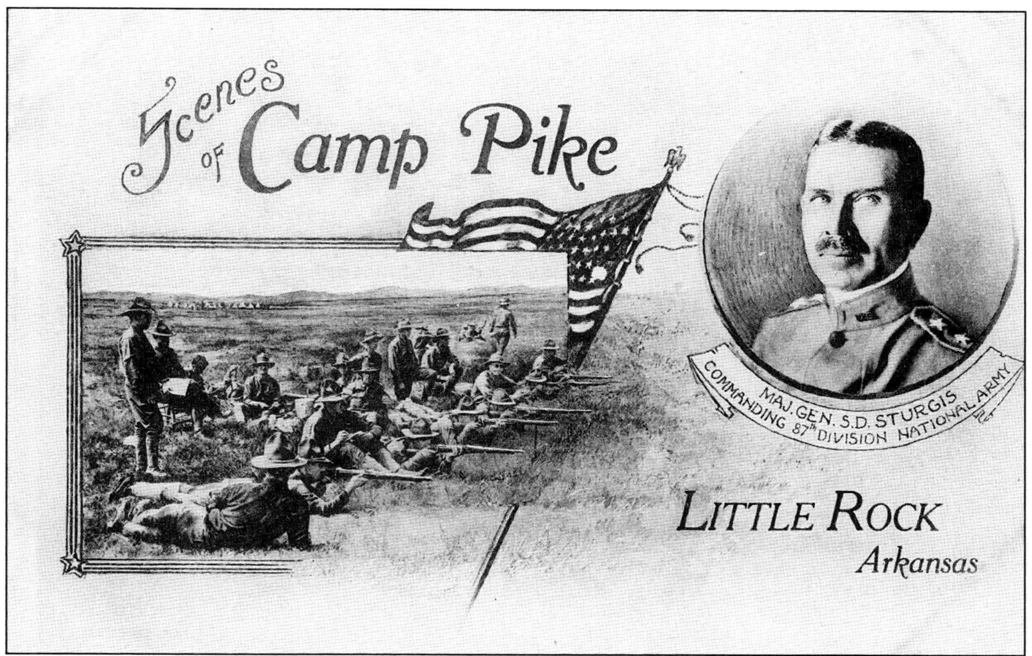

When the United States entered WW I, business leaders from both Little Rock and Argenta worked together to secure 13,000 acres of heavily wooded land to be deeded over to the federal government for the purpose of building an army training camp. Camp Pike was named for Zebulon Pike, a famed frontier explorer. Pictured on the cover of a 1917 book of souvenir postcards is Major General S.D. Sturgis, who was commander at Camp Pike at the time.

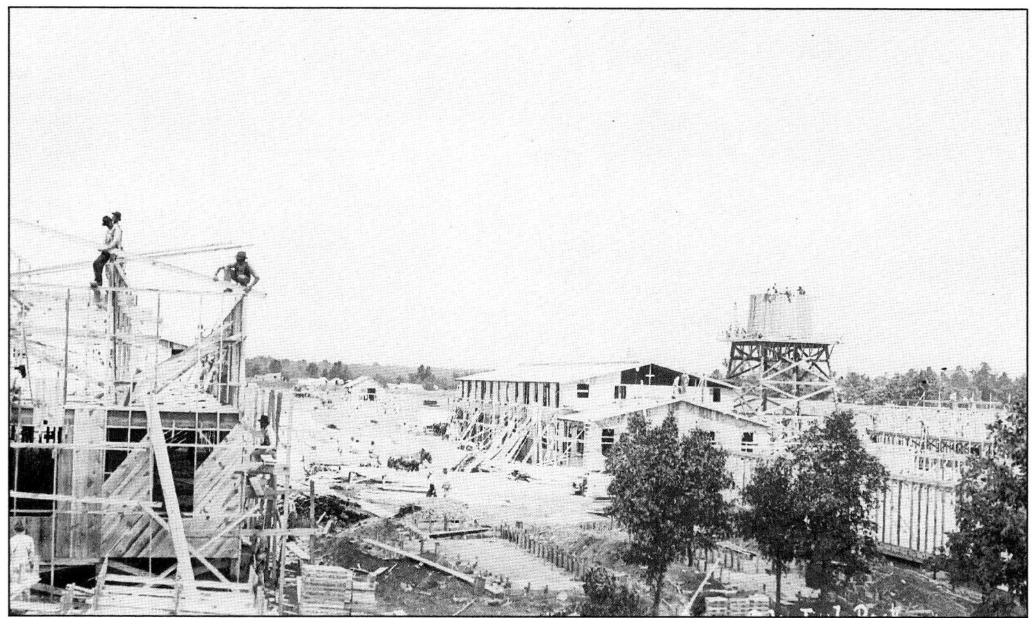

Camp Pike, under construction in this 1917 print, went up in record time and contained 2,000 buildings intended to house 65,000 troops. Ready access to Arkansas timber was vital to the quick construction of the camp, as it required 40 million feet of lumber. The $300,000 per week payroll at the camp was a great economic boost to Pulaski County.

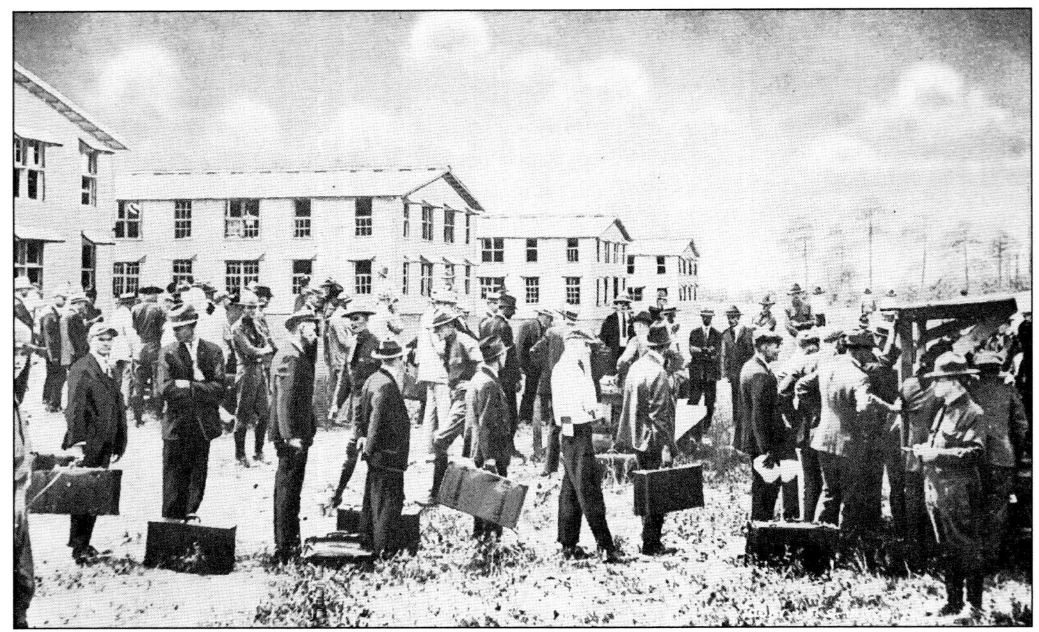

Recent draftees, still in civilian clothing, were photographed arriving at their barracks at Camp Pike in 1917. More than 70,000 Arkansans served in WW I and over 2,000 of them died, mostly of disease. Fewer than 500 were actually killed in combat.

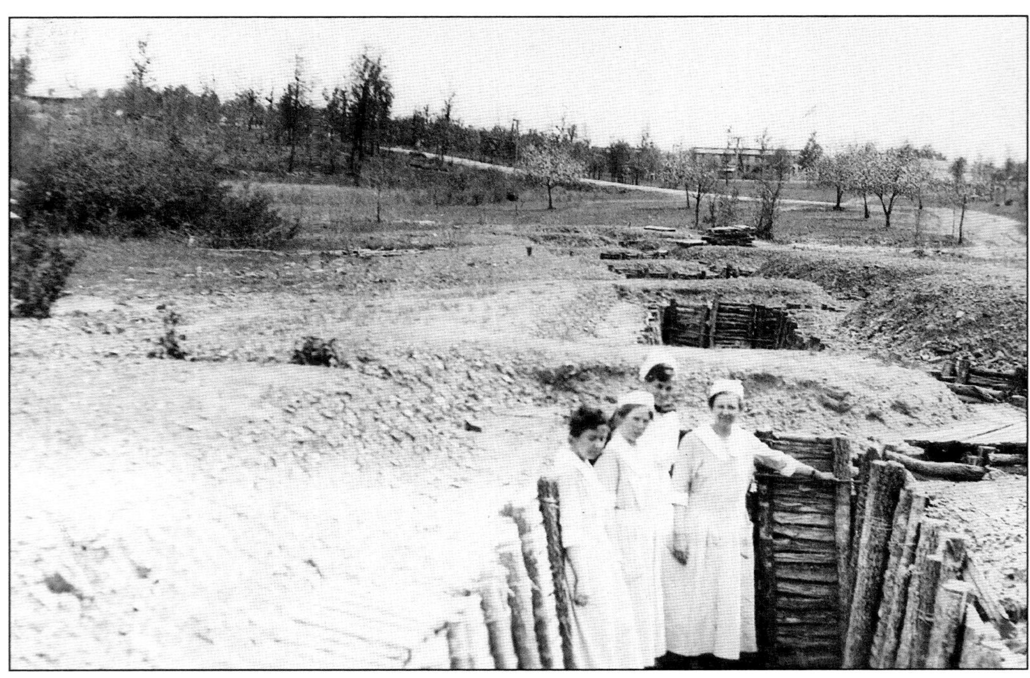

French Army officers came to Camp Pike to train American troops to fight the trench warfare they would face in Europe. In this 1917 card, camp nurses pose in one of the training trenches.

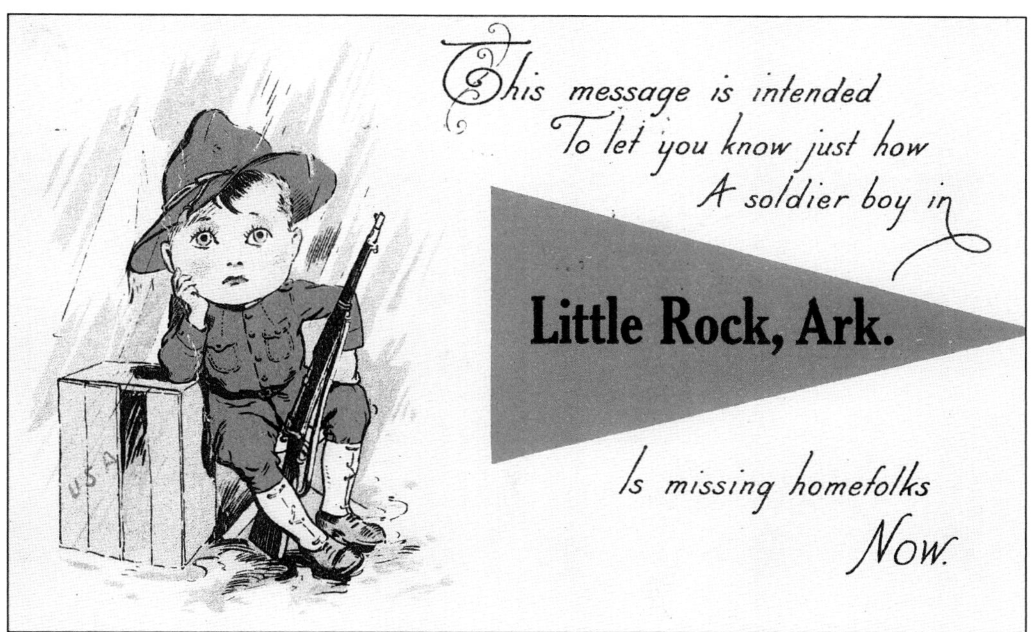

On this 1917 card penned by a homesick soldier were these words: "Am in Little Rock for this evening and thought about you, why no letter from you? Suppose you are home for Thanksgiving." Such comic cards, both from U.S.-based training camps and from cities in Europe, were printed in large quantities during the war.

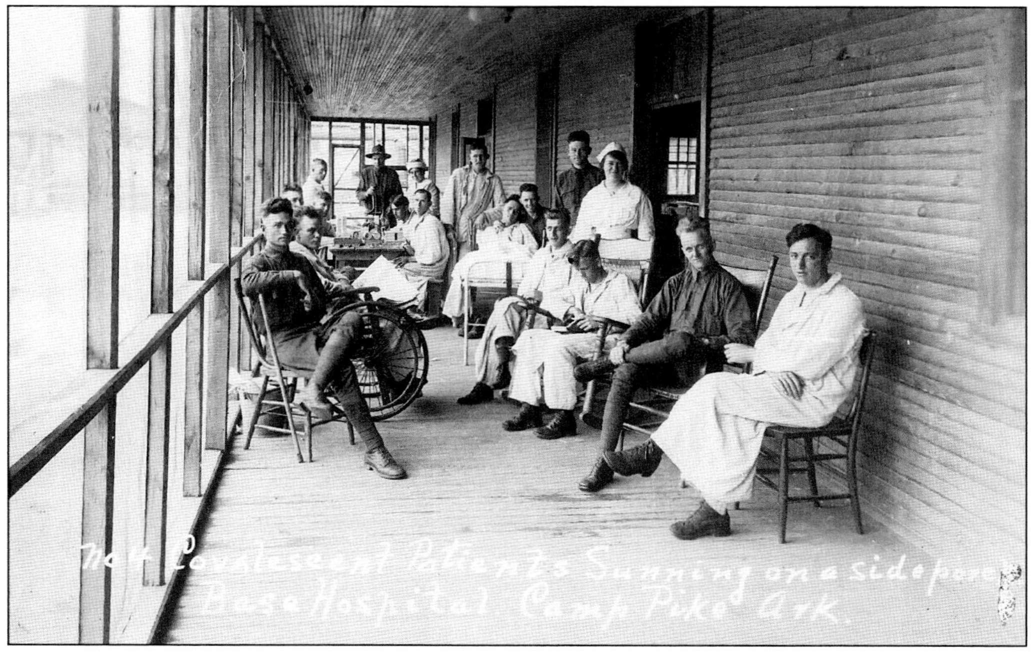

The base hospital at Camp Pike provided this long screened-in porch for its patients to benefit from the fresh air and sunshine in their recovery. Newspapers, books, and a woodworking project were among the diversions available to these men.

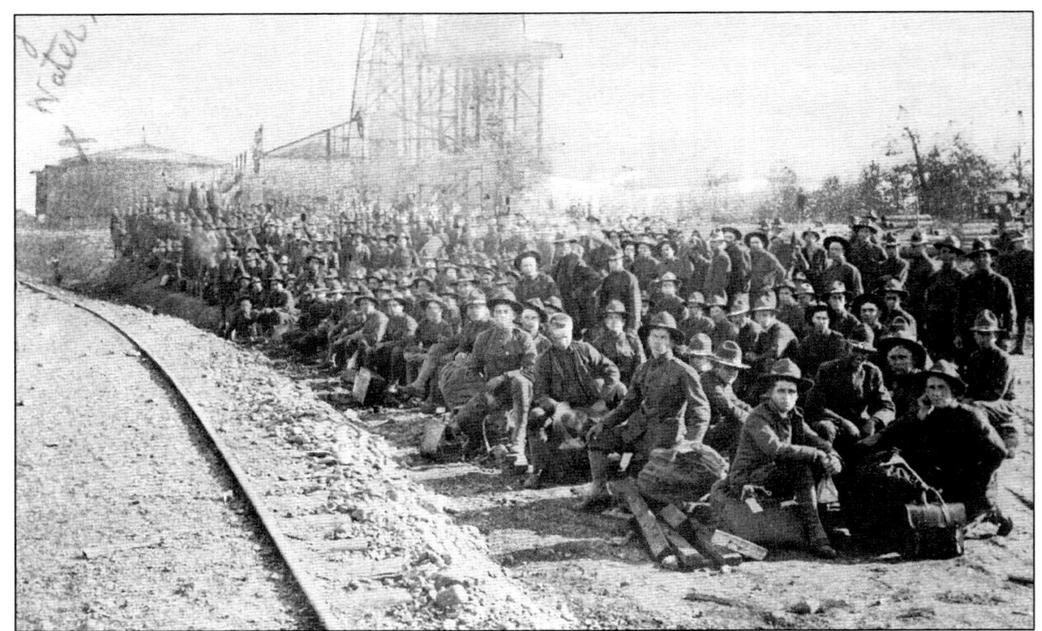

Having completed their training, these soldiers were awaiting a train that would take them to the East Coast, where they would have likely shipped off to the war raging in France. (*c.* 1918.)

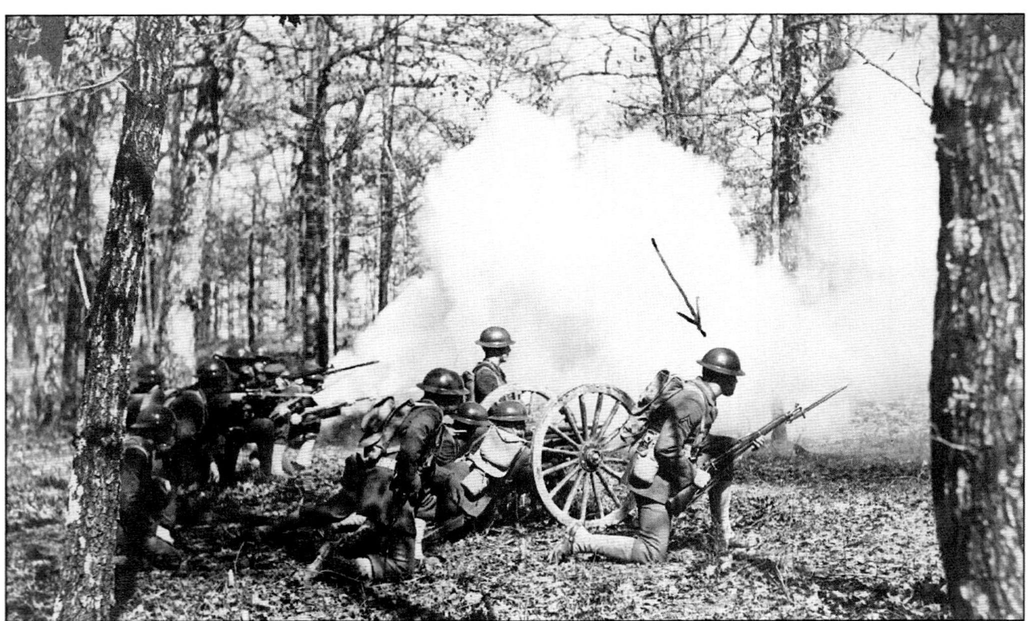

With the coming of WW II, Camp Pike was reactivated under the name of Camp Robinson, in honor of Arkansas statesman Joseph T. Robinson. In this 1941 card, the troops of the 35th Division stationed at Camp Robinson were training for battle, still wearing WW I-era equipment. These particular troops are an anti-tank gun crew. The arrow denotes the soldier who sent the postcard. On the reverse side, he makes mention of the smoke screen in front of the men.

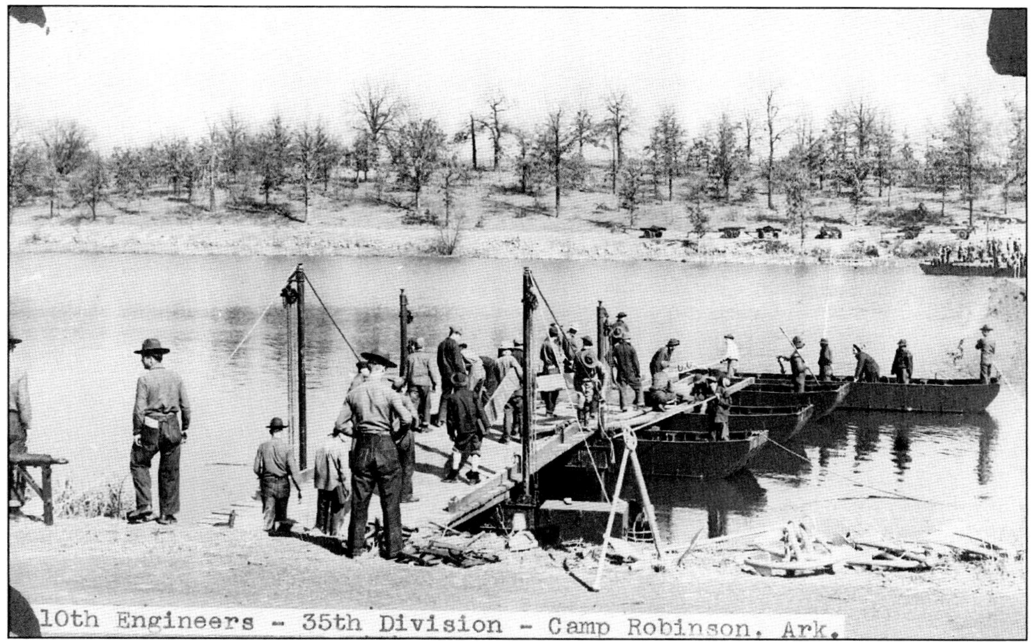

In this 1941 photo, the Tenth Engineers of the 35th Division at Camp Robinson were learning to construct a pontoon bridge, a skill which proved vital in moving troops and equipment on the battlefields of the world over the next four years. In the years after the war, Camp Robinson became a National Guard training center.

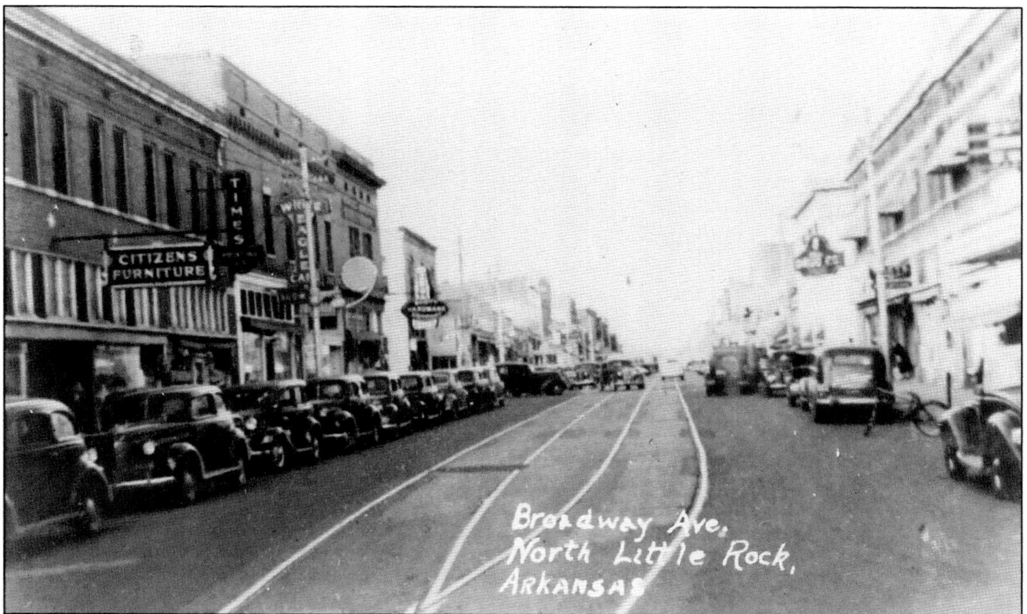

In the years after WW II, North Little Rock continued to grow. In this *c.* 1946 postcard, cars lined the city's Main Street business district ("Broadway," as printed on the card, is in error). Businesses seen in this view include Haverty's Furniture, Economy Drug, and the White Eagle Cafe. Note how the trolley tracks cross with a line that ran from the Main Street bridge to the North Little Rock city limits.

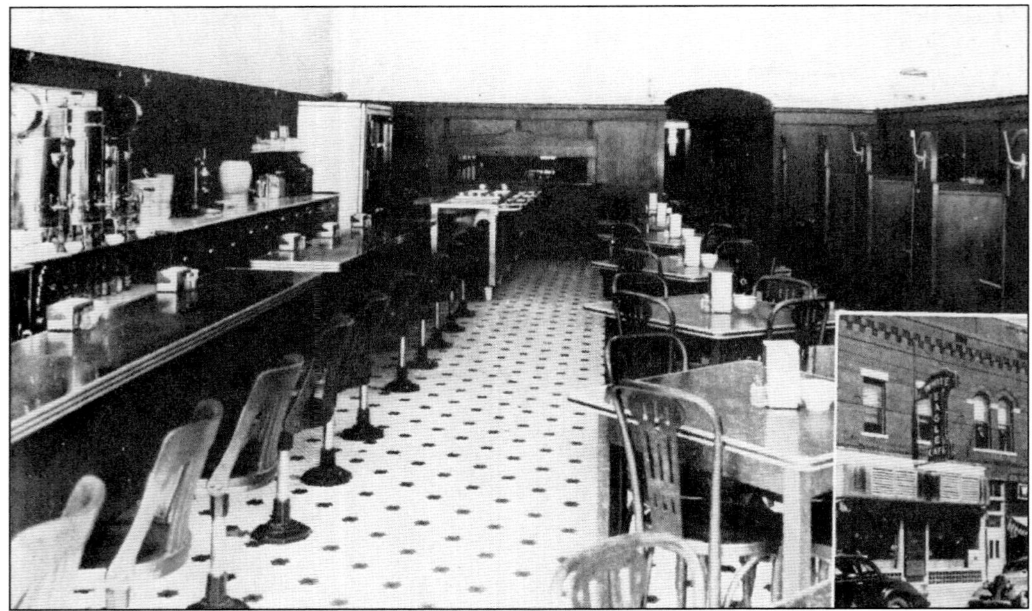

The famous White Eagle Cafe was started by Theo Stahkais, a local Greek businessman. The eatery was known for its plate lunches. It bragged on the back of this 1946 postcard, "We serve the best to the best." The restaurant closed a few years after WW II ended.

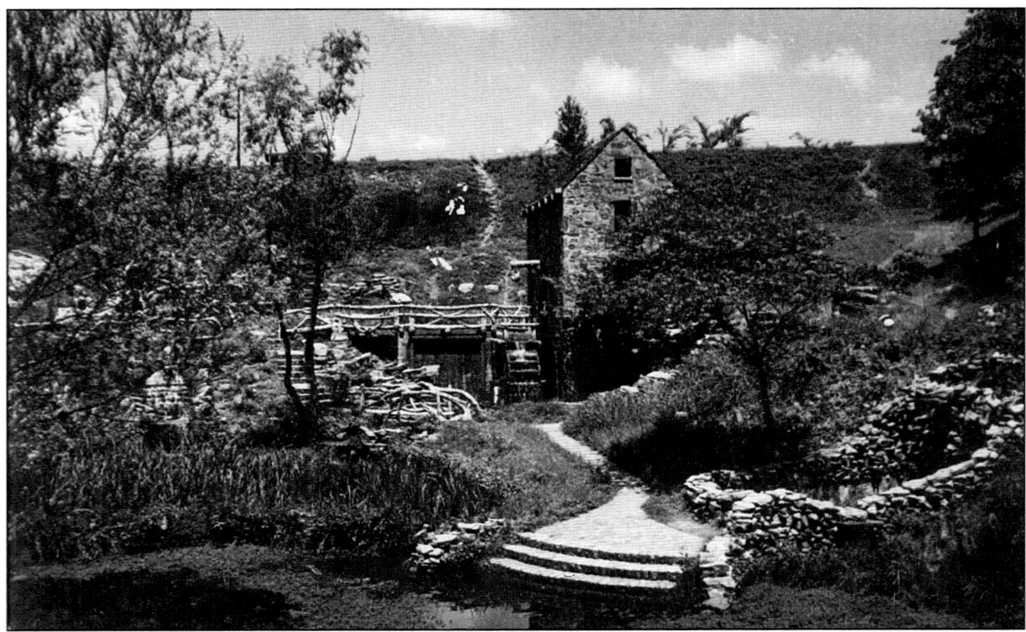

T.R. Pugh Park, known locally as "The Old Mill," was built as an attraction for the nearby Lakewood housing development designed by Justin Matthews. Erected in 1932, this replica of a vintage gristmill is surrounded by bridges and other decorative elements. Composed entirely of concrete, the mill was designed by Mexico City artist Dionicio Rodriguez. The mill is shown in the opening of the movie *Gone with the Wind.*

Index

Airport 110
Alamo Plaza Grill 106
Albert Pike Hotel 92
Ancient Order of United Workmen 64
Argenta City Hall 116
Argenta Colored School 118
Argenta High School 118
Arkansas Children's Hospital 95
Arkansas Gazette 65
Arkansas Insane Asylum 35
Arkansas Reform School 33
Baptist Hospital 73
Baring Cross Bridge 25
Bethel Church 25
Blass Department Store 103
Blind School 34
Boyle Building 88
Braddock's Park 55
Brinkley, John 103
Bruno's Little Italy 108
Bulman's Furniture 94
Camp Pike/Camp Robinson 121–25
Capitol Hill School 40
Capitol Theater 58
Central High School 112–13
Christ Episcopal Church 47
City Market and Arcade Building 67
Climber Motor Company 89
Colonial Tourist Court 108
Confederate Soldier's Home 35
Cotton Belt Railroad 27
Deaf School 33
Donaghey Building 90
Elks Lodge 77
Faubus, Orval 114
Faucette, W.C. 116
Finch, Curtis 102
First Baptist Church 43
First Christian Church 46
Flood of 1927 119
Fort Logan H. Roots 120
Fred Kramer Public School 38
Free Bridge 23
Gan's and Son 68
Garm's Tourist Home 91
Gus Blass Dry Goods 66
Hamilton's Drug Store 69
Haverty's Furniture 103
Hollenberg Music Store 79
Hornibrook, James H. 48
Hotel Ben McGehee 90
Hotel Charmaine 109
Hotel Marion 71, 72
Immanuel Baptist Church 44
Jones Furniture 78
Kempner Theater 59
Lafayette Hotel 96
Lape's Tourist Camp 92
Lido Inn 107
Little Rock Board of Trade 61
Little Rock City Hall 31
Little Rock City Park 56
Little Rock College 41
Little Rock High School 36, 37
Little Rock Public Library 30
M.M. Cohn 101

Majestic Theater 58
Main Street 19, 20, 21, 22, 87, 88, 102
Masonic Temple 75
McMath, Sid 111
Missouri Pacific Hospital 93
Missouri Pacific-Iron Mountain Railroad 24, 29
Mount St. Mary's 39
Old King Cole Restaurant 109
"Old Mill" 128
Old State House 14
Peabody School 39
Pfeifer's Department Store 101, 103
Philander-Smith College 42
Physicians and Surgeons Hospital 74
Pike, Albert 53
Pulaski County Courthouse 29, 30
Pulaski County Hospital 73
Robinson Auditorium 95
Rock Island Railroad 26
S.H. Kress and Co. 67, 88
Scottish Rite Consistory 76
Second Baptist Church 45
Snodgrass and Bracy's Rexall Drug 69
Southern Trust Co. 63, 64
St. Andrew's Cathedral 42
St. Edward's Catholic Church 48
St. Joseph's Orphanage 117
St. Vincent's Infirmary 72, 75
State Capitol Building 15, 16, 17, 18
State National Bank 62
State Prison 32
Temple B'nai Israel 47
Union Station 25,
Union Trust Co. 89
United Confederate Veterans 81–86
University of Arkansas for Medical Sciences 74
VA Hospital 174
W.W. Gibbs High School 40
War Memorial Stadium 104
Ward, Jimmy 60
White Eagle Cafe 126
Young Men's Christian Association 57
Young Women's Christian Association 57
Young's Tire and Service Co. 98–99